THE MARRIAGE OF JOSEPHINE

THE MARRIAGE OF
JOSEPHINE

by

MARJORIE CORYN

*"Never has love more pure,
more true, more exclusive,
possessed the heart of a
man."*

STENDHAL

D. APPLETON-CENTURY COMPANY

New York   London

PRINTED IN THE UNITED STATES OF AMERICA

CONTENTS

PART   PAGE

I.   1794 3

II.   1795 81

III.   1796 139

IV.   1796-1797 187

V.   1798-1799 249

PART I
1794

"I do more than deny the existence of the thing called love. I believe it to be positively injurious to society and to the personal happiness of men."

LIEUTENANT BONAPARTE

"Farewell, my friend. Console your-self with our children; be their comforter, and strive to prolong my life in their hearts."

ALEXANDER DE BEAUHARNAIS TO
HIS WIFE JOSEPHINE, JULY 22, 1794

CHAPTER

❧ I ❧

FROM THE HIGH-PLACED WINDOW OF THE LITTLE ROOM, A FLAT RAY of sunlight thrust obliquely through the dust-thickened air, bright and pale and hard as the blade of a steel knife. Between its walls, heat and the odor of stagnation lay as close-packed as stale water in a disused well. Into its imprisoned silence the small, hard tapping of the drum fell rattling, like dried peas into a wooden box.

The gray-haired woman on the straw pallet beneath the window turned a page of her book. The flaxen-haired girl on the pallet to the left thrust her needle in and out of her work. The young woman with auburn curls on the third pallet sat rigid, staring at the last card she had laid out on the stone floor before her. Her eyes had the round fixed intensity of a watching animal, but she saw nothing. All her senses were run together, like beads of quicksilver, and lay heavy and cold inside her, quivering under the vibrating rattle of the drum. A harsh, dry rattle, like the knocking of a bony fist against a door.

Knocking at the door. After it had knocked, it would come in. And she couldn't hide or escape from it, any more than she could from the fetid air that penetrated every pore of her skin. She could only crouch down inside herself, a small, hard lump of fear, and wait for it.

The harsh, dry rattle of the drumming ceased. With its cessation, the lump of fear that was herself swelled and swelled, until it filled the whole space of time in which she was caught—a space so enormous that she was lost in it, yet so narrow that she would never be able to squeeze through it.

In the straining silence that the drumming left behind, she

3

could hear the slight rustle of a turning page, the tiny pricking of a needle, and the small clickings of her own teeth, jerked at by the twitching muscles of her face.

Then it was there. The voice, that was *its* voice, the voice of Death. Though actually it sounded like the droning of a cheap actor, dull and monotonous with the over-repetition of an indifferent part.

"Jean-Louis Forrestier, cabinet-maker," it said. "Pierre. Bruneau, laborer. Henri de Champcenetz, ci-devant Chevalier. Paul Masson, wig-maker. Louis-Armand de Rohan, ci-devant Prince de Montbazon, and Françoise his wife. Claudine Perrault, actress—"

Françoise de Rohan, Princess de Montbazon, unhurriedly turned a page of her book, though her eyes did not shift to the new line of print. Delphine de Custine thrust her needle in and out, in and out, though her hand had jerked the thread loose from its eye. Josephine, Viscountess de Beauharnais, stared sightless at her cards.

The stale, indifferent voice droned on.

"Louis-Henri Gouy d'Arcy, ci-devant Marquis. Marie la Cagneuse, mendicant. Charles de Montfort, ci-devant Abbé. General Alexander de Beauharnais, ci-devant Viscount."

The drum tapped again, once, with the dull finality of a closing door. It was gone.

The Princess de Montbazon turned another page of her book, Delphine de Custine sewed on with her threadless needle. Josephine, Viscountess de Beauharnais, drew the tainted air of the little room deep into her lungs. It was foul with prison stench, but the infection of death had gone out of it. She had escaped again through the small, timeless eternity, the little space between life and death. For the moment, nothing else mattered.

Delphine de Custine said, "Fifty-four, this morning."

The Princess spoke without looking up from her book. "No, my dear," she said gently, "you are mistaken. 'And his wife.' That makes fifty-five."

Delphine made no reply, her threadless needle pricking in and out, in and out, unceasing. Françoise de Rohan, Princess de Montbazon, closed her book and laid it aside. She looked down at her hand, and with her forefinger lightly touched the wedding-ring that fifty years had grooved into her very flesh. She smiled a little. Then, from the end of her pallet-bed, she took up the small bundle that was all she had of possessions, and opened it.

4

Delphine went on with her sewing that had neither beginning nor end.

Josephine de Beauharnais looked at the last card she had turned up—the Ace of Spades. A sharp little giggle rose in her throat. Even Death could make social blunders, then. He had left his card at the wrong door. He was gone, and he couldn't come back again. Not at least until tomorrow morning. And tomorrow morning was unimaginably far away, a thing still hidden behind time's horizon. Then her throat contracted again. Death had made no mistake. He was here, in this room—in the white-haired woman seated on her pallet beneath the window. The white-haired woman was already dead and she, Josephine, was shut in with her. She was shut in with a corpse that breathed and spoke—a horror unspeakable!

Madame de Rohan pulled off her stockings of coarse white cotton, and sat ready to replace them with a pair of rose-pink ones of fine silk, taken from her bundle. She sat there on her straw pallet-bed, her head bent beneath the downward thrust of the thin, flat shaft of sunlight that was like the broad blade of a descending knife. Her bare feet were set down before her on the naked stones of the floor, clear white next their sordid gray, smoothly carved against their rough-hewn surface. Small feet, still high-arched and supple, despite the seventy years they had trodden, with fine-wrought, delicate bones. Madame de Rohan adjusted her stockings and put on a pair of little high-heeled slippers.

"Louis-Armand will be glad," she said. "You see, we—my husband and I—we have never been separated before. And at our age, it is difficult to form new habits. So he will be glad when we are together again."

She tied a clean muslin fichu about her shoulders. She ran a comb through the short waves of her shining white hair and patted it with her hands.

"It's a pity Henriette broke our mirror," she said.

Henriette. She who had had the fourth pallet-bed in the little room—how long ago? A long time. How could any one measure time by weeks or months when every day was a whole existence complete with its own birth and death?

Henriette, Duchess d'Aiguillon. She too had sat on her pallet-bed, holding up the mirror while she put rouge on her lips and cheeks. She had laid it on her lap while she combed her black curls up, away from the nape of her neck, so that the executioner might have no excuse to touch. Then, when the door opened, she had stood up, and the mirror had slid from her lap and smashed on the stone floor. She had touched the fragments with the toe of her shoe, and laughed.

"If I were superstitious, I would take that for an evil omen and refuse to go out today."

A little dust of the mirror still glittered within the cracks of the paving-stones. But the woman who had looked into it wasn't even dust. She was just gone. One needn't think about her any more. She wasn't frightening—not like a dead woman who put on rose-colored silk stockings, and smoothed her hair, and talked.... In that little room it was like being nailed down in a coffin with a dead body, and feeling it move against you, breathe on you....

A coffin. And she fastened up inside it so that she couldn't get out. Not to be able to get out—to get out! Josephine was at the door that was the wooden lid of the coffin, beating on it with her hands, screaming shrilly, flattening her body against it. With her small, red-brown head above the wide white flow of her dress, she was like a pale moth pinned to the dark wood, fighting against it with spasmodic flutterings and shuddering struggles. She screamed with the high, toneless shrilling of a small, terrified animal, and her own screams tore through her body like a wound, so that she screamed and screamed again with the pain of it, and with mounting terror because she could not stop.

Madame de Rohan gathered up the stockings and fichu she had discarded, folded them smoothly, and put them away in her bundle. Her clothing would go to the poor women of Paris; they must not be robbed of their meager heritage—and some of the turn-keys and jailers, she suspected, had an open eye and hand for small possessions left lying about after their original owners were gone.

Delphine de Custine frowned a little, set aside her work and, going to the frantic woman at the door, put her hand on her shoulder.

"Don't do that," she said, "don't. He is a soldier. He won't be afraid. And he wouldn't want you to be, for him."

Josephine hung limp and panting against the door, her screaming stifled by this new fear. Alexander! She had forgotten him. "General Alexander de Beauharnais, ci-devant Viscount," the voice had said. "And his wife—" She hadn't been his wife for

6

over ten years, but they wouldn't know—wouldn't care. She still had his name. And death had spoken it. She had Alexander's name—and Alexander. . . .

"I, too, loved Alexander," said Delphine.

Josephine turned her head over her shoulder, stiffly, like a wooden doll. She stared at the other woman. For a moment, curiosity shot through her fear, like a thin flame through smoke. Alexander and Delphine—in this place! Then the heavy pall fell again. She turned her face back to the door, staring at it as though she could pierce it with the very intensity of her gaze.

"Love?" she said. "What does it matter? I was his wife—can't you understand? They don't say, 'and his mistress,' they say 'and his wife.' His wife! And they'll kill me, too. They'll kill me! And I can't get out—I can't get out!"

Delphine made a sharp, hard little sound. She withdrew abruptly and stood back a pace, staring at the fear-convulsed back of the other woman.

She—the other woman—could hear the small scratchings of her own nails on the wood of the door, the thudding of her heart against it. It was not good. But yet she couldn't stop—she couldn't. . . .

Of a sudden there were sounds on the other side of the barrier, it vibrated from outside. Her body jerked stiff and erect, thrusting away from it. She had wanted desperately to get out, but not to "go out." Not that! Oh, not that! It wasn't her turn to go out. They hadn't called her name. Not yet—not yet! Not today. Not now! She recoiled step by step, back from the opening door, lest they should think it was she. . . .

"You will forgive me, Mesdames, if I go out before you, but I must not keep my husband waiting." Madame de Rohan passed between the wife and the lover of Alexander de Beauharnais, and went out.

The door closed behind her. Over her pallet-bed the thin, flat ray of sunlight thrust downwards to the stone-paved floor.

Delphine turned back to her pallet, carefully threaded her needle, and picked up her work.

Josephine clenched her chattering teeth, and for a little could not move because of the tautened shuddering of her muscles. She hated these people who went to the guillotine as though they were going to a ball at Versailles. And she—she who had never been permitted to share the pleasures of their life with them, why should she be forced now to share the horror of their death? It was unfair, unjust!

It was all unfair. She'd never done anything to harm Robespierre or his Revolution. She'd never even been interested. She'd just lived in the little house at Croissy or in the apartment in the rue Saint Dominique with Desirée de Hostein and tried, in spite of everything, to be happy.

And for a time she had been happy. There had been so many young men of the bright new society that didn't bother about patents of nobility so long as one was pretty and amusing; there had been so much money, and such delightful ways of spending it. She'd been happy, and she'd done no harm to anybody. But Robespierre had called it "having corrupt relations with public officials." And just for that—just for trying to be happy....

But today's lifetime was only just beginning. For today she was safe. She drew in a sobbing breath and lay down with her face to the wall, so that she needn't watch the girl who could sew calm-eyed at a garment that might well be her shroud, only they didn't let people have shrouds any more....

Oh, she, too, when she first came here three months ago had joined in their horrible play-acting. At first there'd been the satisfaction of social equality at last with Duchesses and Princesses, if only the equality of prison life. She, too, had been one of these great ladies, indifferent to so vulgar a thing as a Revolution. With them she'd bobbed and curtsied, rolled noble titles over her tongue, reclined with studied nonchalance on a straw pallet, swept with conscious dignity through filthy corridors. With them she'd cut her hair short, high up on the nape of her neck, so that—with a delicate shiver—the executioner might have no excuse to touch. She'd shivered, but at first she hadn't been afraid. Or only a pleasant fear, like ghost-stories in the dark. Such things didn't happen. Not to one's self. Not really. She'd even been able to look at the dark patches on the paving-stones of the courtyard where the priests had been massacred two years ago, in '92, and feel only the same little thrill of horror with which one looks at ancient instruments of torture, things out of history, unreal.

That was while there were still four of them in the cell together. Now they were only two, and she didn't want to be a great lady any more. She didn't want to uphold the honor of her name, only to be happy again. She didn't want to die with dignity. she wanted to live—to live! That was the only thing

8

worth having in the world now. Life. It didn't matter any more whether she was a great lady or not, so long as she was alive.

She stirred uneasily on her straw pallet. Only two of them left. The others had—gone. That was when the real terror began, making her beat on the door and scream until she couldn't scream any more from sheer exhaustion. Thinking where the Duchess d'Aiguillon had gone, and the Princess de Rohan. And of course, Alexander.

Alexander and Delphine. She turned her head and looked at Delphine—her needle ceaselessly pricking in and out, in and out, over her endless task that had no future. That was enough to make one scream again, in sheer desperation.

Delphine and Alexander. That was exasperating, too. It wasn't that she minded Delphine having Alexander, or a dozen other men either, for that matter. She wasn't selfishly jealous in that old-fashioned way. Besides, men in prison were scarcely worth the trouble, were they? No, it wasn't knowing that Delphine had had Alexander that was irritating, but not knowing *how* she'd had him. How? In a place like this, where Robespierre's Virtue was as much a law as Robespierre's Terror? Not knowing a thing like that gave one a sense of inferiority before other women that was even worse than social inferiority.

She sat up and saw her scattered cards on the floor before her. Her cards. There was a way of looking into a future that didn't depend on the beating of a drum, of imagining a life that wasn't just a past and a present. She looked at Delphine—Delphine trying to fasten the present and the future together with the fragile thread of her futile labors. Her cards were better than that, links in the strong chain of predestination that not even Robespierre could break. She gathered them up, and smiled at Delphine.

One ought perhaps to talk to her and try to be friendly again. After all, it would be childish, and unkind, to be on one's dignity with her just because she happened to have been the lover of a man who'd once been somebody else's husband, wouldn't it? Probably the poor girl hadn't had any choice. One couldn't imagine anybody deliberately choosing Alexander, could one? Besides, one couldn't find out anything by keeping silent.

"Madame," she said, "would you like me to tell your fortune for you?"

Delphine didn't even raise her eyes. "Thank you, Madame," she said shortly. "It has already been told."

Josephine shrugged. That, then, was that. Well, she herself

9

could be quite as indifferent as Delphine. Still, she would have liked to know. . . .

She shuffled her cards, cut, and began to lay them out.

From somewhere overhead a bell rang, twelve strokes. It was the bell that used to summon the sixty nuns of the Carmelite convent to their noon-day prayers, but now set in motion the seven hundred men and women crowded into the Revolutionary prison of the Carmes. The men would be going now from their side of the building, down the main corridor, to the refectory. In five minutes' time the women's doors would be unlocked, and they would go down the same corridor, but out of a different door, to the courtyard where for an hour they could breathe the free air, walk under the open sky, seek out their friends, talk, gossip, and whisper together. Then, at the end of the hour, the two sexes would change places, the women to the refectory, the men to the courtyard. But always by different doors, never two members of opposite sexes in the same room, courtyard, or corridor, together. Then how, in a place where one never spoke to a man, or touched one, or even saw one, was it possible? How?

The door was unlocked, kicked open. Delphine folded her work, rose, and left the cell. Let her go. She, Josephine, would follow in her own good time. She would finish her game first—it was coming out very well—then she too would go.

Out there in the courtyard she would find Desirée. There was a real friend, Desirée de Hostein. With her there was no need to mind your manners or your speech, or to pretend not to be afraid. A creole like herself, she could remember with her the old days in Martinique—and sigh to think how Martinique itself had felt like a prison then. Now it seemed like an earthly Paradise. A place where people didn't rush about or shout, or carry bloody heads through the streets on pikes. A place where no one tried to reform anybody else and where, since everybody had Negro slaves to do anything unpleasant that had to be done, there was no need at all to bother about Liberty, Equality, Fraternity. She and Desirée de Hostein had played together on the beach of Trois-Islets. They had played at the Revolution together; they had even been caught together. And in a few minutes she would go out to the courtyard and find Desirée, and they would embrace, exchange their little fragments of news, watch and discuss the other women prisoners—those who had come since yesterday and those who had gone since this morning. Doing that, they sometimes even managed to laugh a little together. Today there would

10

be something really worth giggling over. Alexander and Delphine —the precise, superior Alexander—the correct, aloof Delphine. It was almost too funny to be true. But it *was* true, though how—

There was the Queen of Hearts—herself, well placed beside the King of Hearts. That was a good omen—but who? She thought of all the men who used to come to Croissy. Though it wasn't likely to be any of them, now that Robespierre had finished killing his enemies and had started on his friends. Yet the cards didn't lie ... the Queen of Hearts—

"You will be more than Queen." That was what the old black slave-woman, Marion, had said. She had been her maid in Martinique some—well, a good many years ago. Josephine came home to Trois-Islets from the convent at Port-Royal, the day she was fourteen, an acknowledged woman grown. Old Marion had looked at the lines in her hand on that day and said, "You will be more than Queen."

That prophecy had haunted her dreams for months. Not that she had been a superstitious or ignorant girl. Oh, no. She didn't believe in spells or enchanted princesses. She knew all about the women who were more than Queen, the Montespans, the Pompadours, the du Barrys of this world. There hadn't seemed to be anything impossible about it. It had even seemed quite probable, when she had come to France three years later to marry Alexander. She had had the certainty of becoming at least Viscountess, and perhaps later, when a sufficient number of people had died, Marquise de Beauharnais. But even certainties, it seemed, weren't certainties in revolutions. A very great number of people had died, and what had it made of her? The Citizeness Beauharnais!

The Citizeness—but no, now she came to think of it, not even that. For an hour or more she'd been—the Widow Beauharnais. The Widow Beauharnais! It sounded somehow comic. She could almost hear Alexandar saying in his cold, disapproving voice, "My dear Josephine! Card-playing is scarcely a seemly occupation for a widow."

A giggle rose in her throat, and caught half-way. Alexander wouldn't be able to say that, because his head had been cut off. He hadn't got a head. He had no head. She couldn't sit there alone and think of Alexander without a head. She couldn't stay alone in a place where a man without a head might speak to her from a shadowy corner of the room. Alexander talking horribly through a bubbling hole in his neck, while his head—

"My dear Josephine—"

She clutched at her own neck with both hands and rushed out into the corridor.

Going from the atmosphere of the cell to that of the corridor was like going from an ill-kept privy into the cesspool that served it. That was because of the unspeakable buckets that stood in every corner, and that nobody bothered to empty until they were so full they slopped over on the floor when they were moved. Because, too, of the dried blood that hadn't been washed away since the September prison massacres. The air was so heavy with stench that it made the shadows seem like thick dark curtains that had to be pushed aside to get to the clear light and air of the courtyard outside. There were horrible, revolting shadows—but not so abominable as the shadow she had left behind her in the half-light of the cell. She picked up her skirts away from the foul slime of the floor, lowered her head against the nauseous shadows, and ran.

She ran, knowing that when she had run a certain number of steps, she could raise her head and see the white blaze of the courtyard before her. She closed her eyes and ran towards the sun-purified light, where there were no shadows. No shadows—there was a shadow in front of her that she couldn't brush aside, that would not let her pass. Solid, unmoving, barring her way, holding her, binding her helpless to it. The shadows of the walls had closed in about her—or that other, dreadful shadow had overtaken her, snatched at her, caught her, would not let her go.

She struck at it with all her strength, at this thing that was a shadow among shadows, yet was like a strong door closed against her, between her and the sunlight outside. She dared not open her eyes to see, for one couldn't look at a thing like that—a thing with only a dreadful, bubbling hole—

"What has your servant done that he deserves to be beaten?"

Her eyes jerked wide open and she looked, because it had become less horrible to see than not to see. But there was no horror. The man's head was there, dimly outlined in the shadows, high above her—higher than Alexander's would have been, even before—

A man. It was a man's living arms that held her, a man's hard body she was pressed against. She wasn't alone any more. There was something to lean against, to cling to. She dug her fingers into the stuff of his coat, she buried her face against it, while the rest of her went limp and flaccid, like wet seaweed rooted to a rock.

12

She felt the grip of his arms shift about her, she felt herself lifted, carried, realizing with a vague surprise the comfort of the simple physical strength of a man. She let herself sink into it, let it close over her, lift her from her feet, carry her away, content to lie slack and inert in the strength of the protecting male.

He carried her back through the evil-smelling corridor, down a narrower passage lined with cell-doors like her own. He kicked one open with his foot, carried her in, and set her down in a chair. A chair with cushioned arms and back; such a thing as she had almost forgotten existed. Yet it wasn't so great a luxury as his supporting strength and, feeling it withdrawing from her, she clutched at his sleeves, trying to return again to that brief security. He took her hands firmly between his own, knelt beside her, close against her knees, so that she could feel the comfort of his weight against her.

"What has frightened you, poor little woman?" His voice was half-laughing, half-caressing, as to a timid child. "A frightened woman! I'd forgotten that so charming a thing as that existed."

His words were meaningless, but his voice went through her warm and comforting, like honey-sweetened wine when one was frozen with the cold.

"Do you know, when I see how bravely our women of France go to their deaths, I, who am a soldier, feel I must tear my hair, weep, have hysterics, if only to adjust the natural balance of things. For when all our women-folk are heroes, what else is there for a poor soldier to do? Answer me that!"

He laughed a little and she smiled, as one did when men were amused, whether one knew what they were talking about or not. She could see him now, not just as something strong and protective to hide against, but as a person. A man. A handsome man too, and young, with hot brown eyes and hair the color of rust. A fine big man with heavy shoulders and powerful arms—even the heavy cloth of his uniform sharply molded by the hard muscles beneath. Not unpleasing—oh, not unpleasing at all, as young men went. And these days, even very young men sometimes had their importance. Though with this one it was impossible to tell, because the badges of his rank were gone from his uniform. In any case, she'd never been able to distinguish between the different colored epaulettes and the bits of embroidery that soldiers wore to tell each other apart.

"What has frightened you, little woman?"

She frowned a little. She wasn't a little woman, she was—

Memory of what she was, and of the threat that went with it, came back to her. Her fingers tightened on his hands, as though by their strength alone he could save her from it.

"Alexander—"

"Alexander?" he said. "Ah! General de Beauharnais. Then you are—?" She nodded, and he leaned closer to her.

"Then you mustn't torment yourself for him. Alexander de Beauharnais was a soldier. It's not so bad for a soldier, we're used to—unpleasant things. You mustn't weep for him. He wouldn't wish—"

A sharp spasm of irritation made her hands jerk in his.

"Don't!" she cried sharply. "Don't! You talk like Delphine! It isn't that. Don't you understand? Can't you see that I—I—"

She checked herself and bit her lip. She looked down at his hands that clasped hers in her lap. Big, square hands, still dark with the sun-stain that hadn't yet faded from them. But where his cuffs were pulled up a little, the skin of his wrists showed white as peeled almonds. Wide, flat wrists, with the thick, short, straight hairs that are supposed to denote great strength in a man.

"Don't I understand—what?" he said gently.

Her eyes still lowered, she went on haltingly.

"Oh, you—you mustn't make me say it. You shouldn't make me—tell you. But— You see, Alexander and I—we—we had never been separated before. And when—when one has lived with a man, and loved him, and shared everything with him, it's—it's difficult to make new habits. I thought—I thought I was still sharing with him, if only our loneliness. I—I shouldn't have been afraid when my turn came to—to go out too, if I thought it would be to go to him again—and I wouldn't have wanted to keep him waiting. Then, this morning, I—I found out—"

Her voice broke, her hands quivering in his.

"Yes," he prompted softly, "you found out—?"

Her mouth trembled, and she began to cry. Not the harsh, painful crying that made the nose run and the eyes blur, but a gentle, silent weeping, a slow welling up of tears until they overflowed and hung, clear and sparkling, from the tips of long, down-cast lashes.

"Delphine," she said, her voice choking on a sob.

He made no answer, but she felt the weight of his body a little heavier against her knees. She raised her eyes suddenly to his face. When one looked up like that after crying, not slowly, but with a sudden wide-open gaze under long, upswept lashes, the tear-

14

drowned eyes looked twice their size, and as clear and bright as newly-cut sapphires. Enormous eyes, defenseless, appealing.

"How can men be so cruel—so selfish," she breathed.

His face was so close to hers now that she could see where his growing beard showed like tiny splinters of gold, roughing the smooth polish of his young skin. She could see the faint quiver of his eyelids, and the slight pucker between his brows.

"Men are not all the same," he said, his voice deeper than it had been and a little harsh.

Not all the same? Was there a single man in the whole world who had never said exactly those same words? They were as alike as tom-cats, all striped with the same vanities, clawed with the same greeds. Here was this one, creeping forward inch by inch, as though he saw a dish of cream left uncovered.

"Men are not all the same," he repeated.

"Are they not?" She let her lids droop slowly, until the long, tear-wet lashes cast dark shadows over the brilliance of her eyes.

"There are men who can be faithful—who can be trusted."

The little wind of his breath was hot on her face. His hands slid up from her own to her waist, his hard fingers digging into the soft flesh of her sides through the thin stuff of her dress. She half-closed her eyes and drew her head back and away. She wasn't a "little woman," a mere dish of cream, was she? She was the Viscountess de Beauharnais, an aristocrat, a ci-devant. Besides, this man—he might be only an insignificant lieutenant, without money or position. Not unattractive, but ... cream didn't cost much, but that was no reason to waste it.

She turned her face away from him, put her hands against his chest, stiffened her arms against him.

"Don't" she said breathlessly. "Don't—you frighten me. And I—I don't even know who you are."

Obediently his hands dropped from her waist and he drew back. The weight of him was gone from her knees. He was standing stiffly erect before her, withdrawn to a distance of formal civility.

"Lazare Hoche," he said. "Recently General in the Army of The Republic, at present candidate for the guillotine. And the Citizeness's humble, obedient servant."

Quite proper and correct he was, and respectful. He must be very young, or very inexperienced. A General. . . .

She slid her eyes sideways under modestly lowered lids. She was in a little cell like her own, but cleaner, and with some furniture

in it. This chair she sat in, a real upholstered armchair, though shabby and worn. Over there was a three-legged stool, a wooden bench with crude washing facilities on it and, hung to the wall above, a mirror—a real mirror, bigger than the one the Duchess d'Aiguillon had broken. There was a pallet-bed, straw-filled like her own, but there was only one, and it raised from the floor on short wooden legs.

Beside her chair was a table with books on it, and in its middle a china dish full of peaches. Peaches! And she hadn't even seen fresh fruit for over three months. Paris peaches, enormous, luminous, acrid-sweet as honey. Luscious, ivory-flashed beauties, tight-clad in jackets of perfumed, red-gold velvet. What more could any one desire than to touch, to smell, to enjoy so all-satisfying a thing as that? Yet this young man, standing hungry-eyed before her—

A General. And since he had a room all to himself with real furniture in it, one not entirely without importance, prisoner though he might be; and since he had fresh fruit from outside, he must have money enough at least to bribe jailers. For the sake of the peaches alone, it would almost be worth— Besides, in this joyless place, it would be wrong, selfish, not to give a little pleasure when one could. And men were so easily pleased. Especially young ones. Poor lad. He was lonely. And not at all unattractive.

"You must forgive me," she said, low-voiced. "But you don't know what it is like to be a woman, alone and helpless. And I—I am so very much alone, now—and forsaken."

All the stiffness went out of him, like the dressing out of rainwetted taffetas. She raised her hands in a little fluttering gesture, and he stooped to catch them in his. Lovely, delicate little hands, lost and helpless in the compelling strength of his. He raised them to his breast, drawing her after them. Futile little hands, very pale against the dark stuff of his coat. Soft, weak hands, fragile between the hardness of his palms and the strong beating of his heart. His voice was a husky whisper:

"Not forsaken, my lovely—nor alone. Not now."

Smooth and hard as polished wood his hands slid over the bare skin of her arms to her shoulders. She pressed back a little against the urge of his grasp. But what could one small woman do against so big and powerful a man? Besides, she had had no food that day, and in the pent-up heat of the room, the scent of the peaches, heavy and sweet as incense, made her head swim and her knees shake.

16

She swayed a little, so that his hands slid down from her shoulders, and she was inside the circle of his arms. The cloth of his coat was rough beneath her cheek. She looked up at him without raising her head, so that her long lashes were folded back like the opening petals of a dark flower. She saw tiny beads of sweat prick out on his upper lip; and in his neck, where the skin was white just below the ear, a pulse throbbing with an uneven beat. She could feel his arms about her quiver, as though he were cold beneath the hot, thick stuff of his uniform. How funny men were! The honey-sweet scent of the peaches, making her head swim—

"I'm hungry," she said.

His face was pressed against her hair, she could feel the rasping of his beard-roughened skin again it, setting her teeth on edge.

"So am I hungry, my lovely," he said in her ear. "So am I hungry. Josephine—?"

Men were so shamelessly greedy, and so so selfish in their greed. But they were made like that, and nothing could be done about it. She sighed, and raised her face to him.

> "If in the first moment of my wrath
> I had written to you, my pen
> would have torn the paper....
> Now I can tell you coldly that you
> are the lowest of all creatures."
>
> ALEXANDER DE BEAUHARNAIS TO
> HIS WIFE JOSEPHINE, JULY, 1783

CHAPTER

❧ II ❧

SHE LAY ON HER PALLET, STARING WIDE-EYED INTO THE BLACKNESS. From the little window a shallow trickle of rain-cooled air spread over her, refreshing as a linen sheet between her body and the hot blanket of the night. She had heard the distant clock of the Hôtel de Ville strike two, but she was still awake. She thought Delphine was awake too, though the girl made no sound.

Delphine's silence wasn't irritating any more, since it was no longer a silence of mysterious and superior knowledge, making one feel stupid and gauche. She was Delphine's equal now—though she had been a fool before, not remarking how often, at the noon hour when the cell doors were unlocked, Delphine had turned back at the last moment to get a forgotten handkerchief or scarf, lingering behind by design as she herself had lingered by chance. The man, of course, simply turned straight back from the refectory door as though he, too, had forgotten something. The thing was obvious and so easy, once you knew how. Though, of course, it meant missing one's dinner—

She touched her lips with her tongue, searching on them for the last dim ghost of the sharp, sweet taste of peaches. Fresh peaches instead of dried herring and soused cabbage. Yes, she was quite satisfied with the exchange. She hoped the young man was satisfied, too. It was easy enough to satisfy young men.

The young man. Lazare Hoche. Lazarus. Certainly a name of good omen. It was as lucky to please a man with a fortunate name as it was to touch a cripple's hump.

General Hoche. She remembered now who he was. "The spoiled child of victory," the people called him. He wasn't getting much spoiling now, poor lad. A man of the people. That, too, had been refreshing. Oh, it wasn't the first time she'd met men who called themselves Jacobins, sans-culottes; but under the laborer's smock and striped pantaloons, they'd nearly always turned out to be only gentlemen, after all. It was disappointing. Like sitting down to enjoy a truly vulgar soupe à l'oignon and finding only chicken livers and truffles inside the rough, earthenware dish. Hoche was a surprise of a different kind. A real man of the people, but temptingly served in a clean skin, and elegantly garnished with good manners and polite speech.

General Hoche. Most decidedly a presentable and attractive young man, as these modern soldiers went. And hadn't people always said that if ever Robespierre and his Terror were overthrown, it would be by a soldier? This one, with the name of Lazare, would most certainly get out of this horrible tomb of a place alive, and if he did, he would as certainly not forget her. These men of the people set such importance on trifles that a man of the world wouldn't think twice about. Anyway, it was only through a man that one could ever get anything at all in this man-made world. This one could at least provide fresh peaches, no small thing in a place where cabbage and dried fish were considered to be edible food. And she wasn't one of these great ladies, too wrapped up in the importance of their own dying to think of giving a little pleasure while they were still alive.

Nor was Delphine. Alexander and Delphine. It was a consolation to know that Alexander had had his little pleasure before he—before he went out.

Poor Alexander! She wasn't one to bear a grudge, and she was truly glad that he had at least been successful as a lover. He'd never been very successful as anything else. Not as an aristocrat, or a revolutionary, or a General. Not even as a husband.

Especially as a husband. It hadn't been her fault, had it, that he'd wanted to marry her younger sister? Nor that Catherine had died, so that she'd been sent in her place? That was no reason for telling her she had neither beauty nor wits, and was already too old—at seventeen—to be taught how to behave in good society. Nor for saying even worse things when he wanted a divorce, after Hortense was born. But that had been five years later, when she wasn't too fat any more, and had begun to learn about her eyes. Some of the gentlemen of the Parliament of Paris hadn't been too old to understand the feelings of a young and misunderstood wife. They had been kind about the divorce, but it hadn't really done much good, Alexander always made such difficulties about the separation allowance he had been ordered to pay.

No, he hadn't been much good as a husband. Still, she wasn't vindictive. They'd been quite friendly again since the Revolution, when he'd become a General and she'd had to take care of both the children—Eugène, who Parliament had said was his, and Hortense, who had been given to her. She hadn't really disliked Alexander at all these last few years. Nowadays such unlikely people suddenly became powerful and important, one could never tell. But not Alexander. He'd only got his head cut off.

Not a successful man, Alexander, nor even a very pleasant one. Yet there had been a time—a brief time—when she was seventeen and he nineteen.... Those were the days when he was still trying to improve her mind, to teach her about politics, and philosophy, and Jean-Jacques Rousseau, and the American Declaration of Independence. And she crying because she couldn't learn. He would have done better to teach her how to cry without making a shiny, reddened mess of her face. But he'd left her to find out that sort of thing for herself, and by the time she had, it was too late. And now....

Poor Alexander! She'd never wished him any harm. Certainly

not the harm that came to him. He'd really only been conceited and selfish, and if you killed men just for that.... Besides, he was the father of her children. Yes, of both of them, in spite of the fuss he'd made over the date of Hortense's birth. Her children, her poor, fatherless children....

The tears rose in her eyes and slipped softly down her cheeks. Gentle, melancholy tears, as soothing to over-strained nerves as a warm bath to a tired body.

Poor Alexander....

So, with tears for Alexander on her lashes and the taste of ripe peaches on her lips, she slept.

> *"Josephine nearly always lied, but she lied with charm."*
>
> NAPOLEON

CHAPTER

❧ III ❧

THE CLOCK OF THE HÔTEL DE VILLE STRUCK TWO, THE NOTES COM-ing muffled through the heat-soaked darkness.

Lazare Hoche stretched his long body on his straw mattress, and cursed the intolerable atmosphere of his cell, that wouldn't let a man sleep. It seemed as though the heat of this unnatural summer would go on increasing in intensity until it ended by scorching the city of Paris off the face of the country. And perhaps that would be as good a solution as any other.

The starting of a revolution was easy enough, it was in the stopping of it that the trouble began. The Revolution of '89 had been a noble bonfire, for the purifying of vitiated air and the burning of old rubbish. The Terror of '94 was criminal incendiarism. That was what happened when you allowed an undisciplined mob to play with fire. It was more than rubbish that was alight now, it was the very fabric of the State itself. It wasn't the spittle of politicians that could quench that blaze. It needed the professional fireman. The soldier.

But what soldier? Carnot? A good officer was Carnot, an honest man and an able Minister for War. But there it seemed to end.

One would have expected him to do something when they started throwing his own Generals into the furnace—Custine and Houchard gone already, and now Beauharnais. Himself probably the next on the list. You'd think Carnot would take steps to stop such criminal wastage of good officers. Especially now, with the Battle of Fleurus just won, and even greater things over the horizon.

It was worse than the heat, this being cooped up here like any common criminal, all one's physical and mental powers deliberately put out of action, like spiked guns. And why? Because he'd been present at a military defeat, and because that conceited little lawyer, Robespierre, had decreed that it was illegal for a French General to be defeated. Illegal! As one might decree it was illegal to throw garbage into the street.

And for that he, Lazare Hoche, who had held Thionville against the Prussians, and routed the English at Dunkirk, was no better than a cheap pickpocket, because he had been on the field at the defeat of Neerwinden. Illegal! You'd think that even the law-abiding mind of a Carnot would revolt at such monstrous nonsense as that. But no. He was a soldier by education, not by birth. And military education didn't include the manœuvring of political parties, the assault of governments.

Whereas he himself, born the son of a kennel-man, a sergeant at nineteen, a General at twenty-five—what might he not be at thirty? Nothing, apparently, since at twenty-six he was already dead meat for the guillotine.

No, not quite dead meat yet. The little Beauharnais woman could answer for that. Not unattractive, the little woman. True, she would probably never see thirty again. Still, with that kitten's face of hers, the small pointed chin, high cheek-bones, and wide-open sapphire blue eyes—truly remarkable, the eyes—she wasn't without appeal.

She was a liar, of course, and a silly little liar at that. But after all, lies were the only weapons they had to protect themselves with, these poor little women. Everybody knew she'd been separated from Beauharnais for these ten years or more.

An incompetent fellow, Beauharnais. Not only as a soldier but as a man as well, apparently. It was always some man's fault when the silly little creatures went wrong. They didn't really want adventures, only security. They were only trying to make a living. And how else where they to do it? That's how she'd got herself mixed up with that gang of crooked politicians—Tallien, Fréron and company—trying to make a living in the only way she knew how. The cold-blooded killing of helpless little women like that made one loathe Robespierre, whereas before one had merely despised him. It was as cruel and senseless as tearing the wings off butterflies. Let him kill in the name of national security if he must, but to kill in the name of virtue! His own brand of virtue, too, which it was said he couldn't help. To arrest a helpless little creature like that as a loose woman—what barbarous rubbish! A loose woman? To the contrary. All she wanted was to cling as tightly as possible to some man.

He lay still breathing in the faintly acrid smell of rain on heated tiles and dusty paving-stones, listening to its steady trampling. A few men ran by in the street below, their shoes clacking on the wet stones. One of them dropped something that clattered sharply, swore, paused for a second, and ran on. A man of the National Guard probably, hurrying in out of the rain, and dropping his musket in his haste. That was the sort of thing a National Guard would do, keep his skin dry and let his musket get wet.

The clock of the Hôtel de Ville struck three. The driving charge of the rain swept on, but it seemed to him that, under its sharp clattering, there was a deeper, graver sound, coming from the direction of the Hôtel de Ville. He turned his head to listen. Any unusual sound, and at once the hopeless hope leaped up that one day Carnot would do something unorthodox. After all, they'd guillotined Beauharnais that afternoon, and Carnot couldn't have liked that. But no. The sounds, whatever they were, had died away.

He lay open-eyed staring into a darkness that was no longer quite opaque, but faintly luminous with dawn, like a heavy curtain across a lighted window. The clock of the Hôtel de Ville struck four. There was no other sound. Nothing. And Carnot, had he done anything at all, would have made more noise about it than that. There was nothing timid or furtive about him, God knew. Still if he, Hoche, ever got out of this place alive he would for curiosity's sake find out if anything unusual had happened on this night.

What night was it? He raised himself on his elbow, felt about on the floor for the day's gazette. He found his briquet, struck it, and looked at the date of the paper. The twenty-seventh of July —no, it would be the twenty-eighth, now. Year Two of the Republic, and of Our Lord, 1794.

He blew out his briquet, dropped the paper on the floor, and lay down. It was cool enough for sleep now.

The clock of the Hôtel de Ville struck five. His eyes jerked open. There were noises in the street outside again. Probably only the shop-keepers opposite opening their premises for the day. Still, it didn't seem fair that people who weren't allowed to live shouldn't be allowed to sleep, either. There were women's voices, shrill and excited. Somebody was whistling a strain of the Marseillaise—"Le jour de gloire est arrivé!"—over and over again, irritating in its senseless repetition. "The day of glory—" What glory could there be for a nation ruled over by an emasculate little fanatic of a lawyer? Still, there had been Valmy, and Wattignies, and Fleurus. Perhaps—

He got up and drew himself up to the window. Down below, on the far side of the street, was a little crowd, men and women of the people, all of them staring up at the high barred windows of the prison. In front of the group, apart, stood a woman in a white frilled bonnet and a striped skirt. It was she who was whistling "the day of glory." But that wasn't the whole of it. First with her right hand she spread out her dress, slowly, elaborately, as though displaying some fine piece of brocade. Then she raised her left hand and showed, balanced on its palm, what seemed to be an ordinary stone from the road. After that she dropped her skirt, raised her right hand to her throat, and drew her forefinger across it sharply from ear to ear. Then came the whistled bars of "the day of glory," and as she whistled, the rest of the crowd looked up at the prison walls, nodding, smiling, waving. Then the woman began her performance again—dress, stone, and throat. Again, and still again, insistently, meaningfully.

Watching, he clung to the bars until his muscles began to quiver and crack with the weight of his body. Then he let himself drop, but kept thinking of the woman. Her dress, robe, the stone, pierre—a finger across her throat, the guillotine. Robespierre. The guillotine. The day of glory. The 10th of Thermidor, the 28th of July. Day of glory. Suddenly he saw that his hands were shaking, as they would never have shaken if it had been he instead of Robespierre who was mounting the scaffold on that day.

"There are no longer any men in France, there are only events."

MALLET DU PIN, 1794

CHAPTER

IV

THE MAN IN THE GRAY SILK COAT SPREAD HIS HANDS OUT ON THE table before him and looked at them with aversion. They were lean, nervous, clever hands, but at the moment they were undeniably dirty. He frowned at them. Dirty hands were a thing that he found excessively distasteful. He moved his shoulders under the pale gray coat, and felt the sweat-soaked shirt sticking to his skin. That, too, was distasteful. In fact, the whole grimy business was in execrably bad taste.

Murder. Legal murder, that left men's hands not frankly bloody, but just that—grimy. Yet by now every journalist in Paris would be sharpening a pen the better to celebrate the noble band of heroes who had so courageously rid the country of Robespierre the Monster—until yesterday, on those same pens, Robespierre the Incorruptible.

He smiled thinly. He, Fréron, was a journalist, too. He was a good journalist. He would even have liked to be an honest journalist—though that, obviously, was impossible. Not that he particularly admired truth as a virtue, it was only that it was usually so much more purely dramatic than any invented drama ever could be.

His own hands, in Marseilles, had been frankly bloody enough. He hadn't especially disliked the place, nor even its inhabitants. But to destroy—to annihilate utterly—a whole great city! If he had been able to accomplish that, he would have produced the greatest, the most starkly perfect tragedy of modern times. But Robespierre hadn't seen it like that. He had no dramatic imagination at all. That was one reason why he had let himself be overthrown by these grimy fellows—because he had never been able to imagine such a thing.

Marseilles, that he could have turned from a dirty commercial port-town into a deathless drama that would have borne his name.

24

A pity. There would have been the one necessary touch of color in the dark grandeur of the thing, too. The girl. As lovely a little piece as one could possibly imagine. A little Corsican girl. Paulette Bon-something-or-other. He couldn't remember. He'd even thought of marrying the child at one time; because of the Roman matron of a mother she'd got, it was no use thinking of anything else. It would have been the perfect touch, that one drop of sweetness distilled from the bitter grapes of Marseilles.

But Robespierre had spoiled that, too, calling him back to Paris as he'd called all the other Deputies on Mission. There was true drama in that if you liked, the victim contemptuously summoning his own destroyers about him.

He raised his fine dark eyes from his hands, leaned his head back on his chair, and stared at the ceiling. From the tall windows behind him the already heat-faded light of dawn seeped into the room, curdling the dark shadows to a livid gray, like sour milk poured into wine. Light came into the room, but not air; and that already enclosed in it was heavy with the odor of tired bodies, bitter and rank, and with the tallowy stench of cheap, unsnuffed candles. They hung up there among the crystal pendants of a splendid chandelier, their smoky flames as incongruous as tawdry brass beads in a diamond necklace. As incongruous as were the men they shone down upon, disheveled, soiled, unkempt, in that noble chamber that had so little a while ago been a drawing-room in the royal Palace of the Tuileries, and that was now the Council Chamber of the Committee on Public Safety. They had managed to tarnish the beauty even of the theater they acted in, these dull, inefficient actors of a dull and artificial tragedy.

Bonaparte. That was the name. Pauline Bonaparte. Lovely enough almost to make a man regret ... still, it was probably for the best. The girl had a brother, a military fellow of sorts, who'd shown signs of going far in Robespierre's favor—and who would now of a certain go as far in the disfavor of whosoever took Robespierre's place. Who? That was a thing these fear-befuddled plotters hadn't taken into account—that in order to throw a ruler off his pedestal, you had yourself to climb up on it—and a damned uncomfortable place it could be. Who?

Without moving his head he lowered his eyes and from beneath drooping lids surveyed the other men about the table. A dozen or so of them: Charlier, the President, at the head—a weak-faced, elderly man, with a head that moved incessantly in a small, twitching jerk; next to him Carnot, a man with a hard jaw and a crimson scar on the flat of his cheek. He drew endless small maps on scraps of paper with short, sharp jabbings of his pencil, eyed them critically, then crumpled them and tossed them to the floor.

Next to him was Finance Minister Cambon, his hands clasped across the bold curve of his stomach, his head sunk as far forward on his chest as his short neck would permit. He made small wheezing sounds as his breath forced its way through his cravat-strangled throat. Beside him was an empty chair. Barras's chair. Barras of course was off making the only showy gesture of the whole sordid business. Giving the coup de grâce after it had been made quite safe for him to do it.

Then came Tallien. He was a coarsely handsome, yellow-haired man, at the moment more coarse than handsome. His cravat was unwound and hung like a dirty scarf about his neck. His waistcoat and shirt were unbuttoned, showing a ruddy-furred chest beneath. With one black-nailed forefinger he held a coin on edge, while he flicked at it with the other, endlessly spinning it, while his eyes followed as though mesmerized the small white transparent blur it made.

The men on his own side of the table he could not see without moving his head, and they weren't worth that trouble. They were, he knew, scribbling aimlessly, whittling at pens, biting their fingernails, fiddling with their buttons—and all the while endlessly sliding their eyes towards the closed doors behind the sleeping Cambon. A depressing crew. What was it Danton had said of them? "Ignorant bastards, patriotic only when drunk." Drunk with wine or with terror, it didn't matter. They had been patriotic, and they were still terrified lest their drunken assault might even yet have failed.

Not that Robespierre didn't deserve to be killed, bigoted little rat that he was. A rat. Then why not have set down a saucer of rat-poison, and been done with it? It would have been so much less fatiguing for everybody concerned, the rat included. But no, these men had consciences, that is to say, they were cowards. Yes, all of them in one way or another, from Carnot who was afraid for his beloved armies, to Tallien who was only afraid for his not very clean neck. So they had to set the terriers of the law on the rat, to hunt him from hole to hole, worry him, corner him, over two days and nights. And even then not be sure—

Tallien flicked clumsily at his coin, and it flew with a tiny

26

clatter across the table. Beside him Cambon sat up with a jerk, as though awakening from a nightmare. He frowned, and glanced angrily at his neighbor.

"Must you do that, Tallien?" he said irritably. "It's bad enough without your incessant fidgeting."

Tallien reached out a fleshy, ill-kept hand for his coin.

"It's all very well for you, Cambon," he said. "It wasn't you who threatened him with a dagger. It wasn't you who started the cry of 'Down with the tyrant!' It wasn't you—"

Fréron sighed. "Shut your mouth, Tallien," he said, without shifting his eyes.

"Shut your own, Fréron!" retorted Tallien. "You were glad enough for me to open mine yesterday, when none of the rest of you had the guts—"

President Charlier tapped hesitatingly on the table with his pencil.

"Citizens, Citizens!" he remonstrated with timid authority, his head jerking spasmodically.

Tallien turned his anger-flushed face towards him.

"It's your fault, Charlier!" he half shouted. "What did you want to send Barras for? Making a General out of a sod like that, just because he's showy and knows how to look at you down his nose. What's the good of a pantomime soldier like that? Two hours now he's been gone. Two hours to go as far as the Hôtel de Ville and bring the dirty vermin back here to the Tuileries. Two hours! Pah! Any cowardly gutter-rat could have done it in half the time."

"Then you should have gone yourself, Tallien," said Fréron pleasantly.

Tallien ignored him and leaned farther forward across the table, the better to throw his words in the shrinking face of Charlier.

"You and Barras! The President of the Committee, and the Commander-in-Chief of the National Guard! A pair of muddling fools! You'll ruin everything between you, you'll get us all killed, you'll—"

President Charlier tapped again with his pencil. His head twitched, his lips jerked into a contorted smile.

"You should remember the dignity of my office, Citizens, if not of my person," he said deprecatingly.

Tallien bared his big white teeth in a sneering grin. Then he turned to the square-shouldered man in uniform.

"Why didn't you go yourself, Carnot?" he said. "You may be a fool, too, but at least you're a real soldier."

Carnot went on with his map-drawing, not raising his head.

"That's why," he said. "Because I'm a soldier—not a gendarme, I don't hunt unarmed fugitives."

"Unarmed! That little viper with his poison-fangs, that filthy, green-eyed spider, that—"

"Hush! Listen!" interrupted a man at the far end of the table.

Every eye jerked mechanically towards the door. Tallien, his mouth still open, turned his head sharply over his shoulder. Cambon tried to do the same, but his stout neck was too firmly held in its tight cravat, so that he had to twist his whole plump body about in his chair.

A dull clatter of stoutly-booted feet came through from the antechamber beyond the closed door. The men about the table sat silent, unmoving, their faces grayer than ever in the already heat-thickened light of the growing day. Here and there a candle spat and went out, leaving a thin column of smoke. They sat staring with fatigue-reddened eyes at the closed door, waiting in haggard silence for what should come through it.

A man stood there. A big man, with a handsome head well-carried above a handsome uniform. The noble head of an ancient coin, still strongly-cut, but with the outlines a little dim, as though rubbed and blurred by life's over-usage rather than the passage of time. He stood now well-planted on his feet, looking from face to face of the men before him, smiling a little. Then he turned towards President Charlier, inclining his head with a slight gesture of dignified deference.

"It is done," he said gravely, his voice deep, slow, and pleasant. Then, turning again to Charlier:

"I have arrested the, er—criminal, and brought him here. Is it your wish, Citizen President, that I produce him before the Committee?"

President Charlier's face twitched in a sharp spasm of nervous fear and indecision. He glanced nervously about the table. No one spoke.

"For God's sake, no!" he broke out violently. "Doesn't the place stink enough already?"

Other men echoed his "No, no! Not in here!—not here!"

Barras smiled and inclined his head again. He spoke briefly over his shoulder, then came forward into the room.

From under drooping lids, Fréron watched him. A superior

fellow, Barras. In his elegant uniform and with the conscious affability of his manners, he might have been a staff-officer deigning a few well-chosen words on the course of hostilities to the poor devils in the trenches. The smiling condescension of him when he spoke—

"Then," he said, resting his hands lightly on the back of his chair, "Citizen President and Citizens, I will make my report as briefly as possible. In accordance with instructions given me by the Committee of Public Safety," he bowed slightly, "I, with a detachment of the National Guard, marched on the Hôtel de Ville, with the intention of arresting the, er—chief malefactor together with his accomplices, who had taken refuge there. He—the chief malefactor—had summoned the men of the Communes to his help—quite illegally, since he is no longer a member of this august body"—he bowed smilingly again.

"But the fortunate state of inclemency of the weather, together with the equally fortunate state of, er—inebriety of their leader, soon persuaded them that the true course of wisdom, if not of valor, was to, er—return to their homes. We therefore entered the Hôtel de Ville unopposed, and proceeded to arrest the outlaws. Nevertheless, an unfortunate incident took place. The chief, er—miscreant—"

Fréron smiled up at him engagingly. "Would it not be simpler, er—Citizen General, to say, er—'the man Robespierre'?"

A pompous ass, Barras, and therefore easily vexed. It was amusing to vex him.

Barras inclined his head stiffly. "I thank the Citizen Fréron for his suggestion. Very well, then. The man Robespierre shot himself, or was shot, through the lower part of the face, and was gravely damaged. Very unfortunate, Citizen Deputies, but"—he stretched out his hands, palms upwards—"not my fault, I assure you."

President Charlier gave a spasmodic nod. "No, certainly not—most certainly not your fault, Citizen—that is, General Barras."

"The lesser culprits," Barras continued, "I have left under guard at the Hôtel de Ville; but the, er—man Robespierre I have, according to instructions, brought here"—he nodded towards the door behind him—"where he has been accommodated on the table in the antechamber.

"He was in great pain, and I therefore took the responsibility of securing medical aid to relieve him—an officer of the Public Health I found in the corridor below, and an officer of yours,

Carnot, an Army surgeon I picked up at the Ministry in passing—
if you will forgive the er—liberty?"

Carnot nodded without looking up. Barras flicked his fingers
together, as though ridding them of some unpleasant substance.

"That, Citizens, is all I have to report."

He bowed, pulled out his chair, and sat down. Tallien turned to
him with a snarling aside.

"What did you have to call doctors to that carrion for?"

Barras pulled out a gold snuff-box and helped himself delicately. "It is the custom among civilized people," he said shortly.

Play-actor, thought Fréron. And a damn bad one at that.

Tallien bared his strong white teeth.

"Civilized?" he sneered. "And do you think *he's* civilized?"
He jerked his thumb over his shoulder. "He'd have had the lot
of us arrested in the next twelve hours, and guillotined in twenty-
four—for the crime of not liking him. Do you call that civilized?"

"True," said Barras, snapping his snuff-box open and shut
between his white fingers. "But, my dear fellow, he'd have done it
decorously, with a certain sense of, er—good manners."

"Good manners!" repeated Tallien. "He spat on me once—
spat on me! Do you call that good manners?"

Fréron bowed graciously to him across the table. "Not good
manners, no—but good taste. There's a subtle difference."

Tallien eyed him suspiciously, grunted, and began to spin his
coin again.

President Charlier tapped nervously on the table with his
pencil again.

"Gentlemen," he said. "That is—Citizens. I should like to eluci-
date the situation— That is, I should like—briefly. . . . In a few
words, I should like—"

Fréron raised his dark head and yawned.

"And I," he said, "should like to wash. Perhaps, therefore, the
Citizen President will permit the few brief words to be mine."

Charlier gestured vaguely. Fréron said, "I thank the Citizen
President," and went on.

"Briefly, then, the situation in this. The Dictator Robespierre
having threatened us all, Deputies and members of the Committee
alike, with more or less instant death, we, in a sudden access of—"

Tallien raised a scowling face. "We?" he queried truculently.

Fréron bowed to him across the table. "Your pardon. The Citizen Tallien, then, in a sudden access of panic-terror denounced
the said Robespierre as a tyrant and a traitor. Other Citizens too

numerous to name lent him their support, more or less vociferously. Still another Citizen, whose name I honor but do not remember, proposed the arrest of the tyrant, the motion being seconded by a Citizen whose name I have never known.

"The accused and his accomplices having, by means not yet ascertained, eluded their guard and taken refuge in the Hôtel de Ville, the Citizen Barras, with his customary courage and devotion to duty, volunteered—"

Barras raised an immaculate and protesting hand.

"Was ordered, if you please—was ordered."

Fréron bowed to him. "The Citizen Barras, then, was ordered to take command of the National Guard, to march on the Hôtel de Ville, and seize by force the persons of the fugitives. While he, with his customary zeal and—prudence, was carrying out these orders, we, on our side, were issuing a decree of outlawry against the monster Robespierre and his associates. That, briefly, is what has already been done. Remains, still more briefly, that which still has to be done."

"Kill them!" grunted Tallien.

Barras raised his eyebrows, and looked at him distastefully.

"My friend, you are a little, er—unpleasant."

"Not half so unpleasant as them," said Tallien. "Kill them. All of them. Now."

"Quite," interposed Fréron. "But let us at all costs be legal—and the law requires that an outlawed criminal be identified by an appropriate magistrate before he can be executed. In this case, by the Public Prosecutor. Therefore, at eight o'clock, as soon as the Revolutionary Tribunal is in session, the outlaws will be legally identified. And after that—well, after that we'll all be free to go home and wash our hands."

"Six o'clock now," said Tallien, taking out a handsome watch that had a ducal coronet in diamonds on its back. "Two hours to go. What about food? The Republic owes us at least a free meal—eh, Charlier?"

There was general applause about the table, an usher was summoned, orders were given. The strain had gone out of the atmosphere, as from an unstrung bow. Those about the table shifted their bodies, stretched their limbs, but gingerly, cautiously, like men released from the rack.

Carnot pushed back his chair with a rasping scrape.

"I, for one," he said, "prefer to eat in different company. And that sort of thing"—he motioned towards the antechamber—"isn't my affair. I have a war to get on with." He lifted his sword-belt from the back of his chair where it hung and buckled it on.

"But," he continued, "there is one thing that is my affair, and that I wish settled. The release of Lazare Hoche. Be good enough to see to it, Citizen President. Not later than today."

Charlier rubbed his hands nervously along the arms of his chair, and the polished wood squeaked under his sweaty palms.

"But—Citizen General—in the name of what authority?"

Carnot lifted his chair a few inches from the floor and slammed it down again.

"Good God, man! In the name of common sense. And on your own authority—if you're capable of using it without Robespierre's permission."

Charlier blinked and twitched with nervous anxiety.

"I—in my position—in the present circumstances—"

Barras stood up and faced Carnot.

"I, personally, will see that General Hoche is released," he said.

Carnot turned squarely towards him, frowning, bitter-mouthed, the scar on his cheek livid as a fresh wound.

"I thank you for your condescension, Citizen Commander-in-Chief of the National Guard," he said stiffly.

Barras smiled and waved an affable hand. "It is a pleasure to be of service to you, er—Citizen Minister, Commander-in-Chief of the Armies of the Republic," he answered.

Carnot muttered, "Nincompoop," snatched on his hat, and marched to the door. His footsteps rang hollow on the uncarpeted floor of the antechamber, going steadily, firmly, neither swerving nor pausing beside that which lay on the table in its center.

Barras sat down again, and flicked snuff from his coat with a lace handkerchief.

Fréron pushed back his chair, and smoothed his rumpled waistcoat. He looked across the table at Barras from under wearily drooping eyelids.

"While you're about it, old man," he said languidly, "you might see to the release of my haberdasher. Fellow of the name of Vilkers. Only man in Paris who can make a wearable pair of braces. It's been intolerable without him. Really, my dear fellow, quite intolerable."

It was a real pleasure to vex Barras, his reactions were so completely satisfactory. He became so aristocratic as to be scarcely human. Now he took out his elegant gold snuff-box and flicked it open with gracefully arched fingers.

"I scarcely think," he said, "that the release of your, er—worthy friend and others of his kind necessitates the intervention of, er—military authority. But doubtless the Citizen Tallien, for instance, would be glad to occupy himself with prisoners of his own, er—social standing."

Fréron lowered his heavy eyelids still further. Military authority! The dressed-up amateur comedian!

"Your pardon, Citizen General Commander-in-Chief of the National Guard. And I crave pardon, too, of the Citizen Tallien. I had not realized he was capable of signing his name."

> *"What France needs is a man of high intelligence, skillful, superior to all his contemporaries, and perhaps even to his century. Has that man been born into the world?"*
>
> CATHERINE OF RUSSIA, 1794

CHAPTER

V

EVER SINCE THEY HAD LEFT VOLTRI THAT MORNING, THE CORAL-PINK haze of dust had hung over them, for there was no wind to dispel it, and the two travelers moved slowly.

The lean, shabbily-clad young man who went in front was on foot, leading his horse by the bridle. It was so that an army traveled, on foot, with its baggage-train following after. He limped a little because the wound in his thigh still troubled him, though it was nearly six months old by now. That was because it had been badly treated at the siege of Toulon. Or rather, not treated at all. For when he had refused to let the Army surgeons amputate, they had shrugged and left him, to go and carry on their barbarous business elsewhere.

Some day he would do something about those ignorant butchers who, because they didn't know how to do anything else, amputated for a blistered heel or a hangnail. Some day . . . meanwhile there was the dusty pink Italian road from Genoa to Nice to be considered.

The traveler who rode behind was still younger, scarcely more than a lad. He slouched in his saddle as much as the tightness of his fashionable waistcoat would let him, and stared resentful-eyed at the angular back that plodded steadily on before him. He resented the back, he resented the heat, and the pink dust he had long ago ceased to try to brush off his dove-colored breeches.

He was resentful of the whole dull, tiring business, and felt he had good reason for it. He had looked forward to this secret mission to Genoa. He had imagined himself adroitly worming dark secrets from the fair young wives of aged Genoese statesmen, or hiding, at the risk of his life, behind shadowy curtains at secret conferences of Austrian Generals. But all that had happened was that he had been obliged to listen to interminable and incredibly dull discussions about roads, endlessly argued between his brother and a handful of unromantic, practical-minded old gentlemen of the Genoese Senate.

Who cared anyway whether they agreed or not to build a road from the coast town of Savona up over the mountains to the probably wretched little villages on the other side? Who wanted to go over their horrible mountains, anyway? Certainly not he. He had had enough of roads to last him a lifetime. If only he could get to the end of this one, and find himself comfortably home in Nice! But his brother refused to listen to sensible advice. He always did. So there was nothing for it but to trail along in a cloud of dust behind a man interested, or so it seemed, only in counting his footsteps between one town and the next.

"Eight hours you've gone on foot," he complained, "ever since we left Voltri this morning, and we're not at Savona yet. You'll only break your wound open, and then you'll have fever again. You always do. What good'll it do you to be laid up with fever? Tell me that!"

His elder brother did not tell him. He did not, in fact, hear him. He was gazing out where, to his left, the tideless Mediter-ranean lay flat beneath the weight of the oppressive heat, shape-less, opaque, like a great blue velvet carpet. A stretch of color solid enough, it seemed, to walk upon. If, walking upon it, you went far enough due south, you would come presently to that great, red-gold footstool of the gods, Corsica, set down upon it.

But it wasn't the foot of a god that was on it now, it was the jackboot of the English. Some day he would do something about that, for it was intolerable. It was true the English didn't enslave their conquered people. They only made servants of them. Corsica had been conquered before, but she had never accepted wages. Corsicans were aristocrats born, preferring the dignity of helpless slavery to the indignity of paid dependence. Intolerable. Some day—

The younger man shifted in his saddle, and winced. It was all very well when you were made only of leathery sinews and weather-tanned skin. But when a man had a bit of human flesh about him, that same flesh was apt to get sore, if sat upon for too long a time. These little inns never had anything but hard wooden benches to offer, either.

"Couldn't you stop and rest a bit in the shade? Half an hour won't upset your God-important calculations, will it? Though what importance there can be in six inches of dust on a damn-awful road—but I suppose you'll please yourself. You always do."

The thin man in front limped unheedingly on.

Infantry should be able to make a steady five kilometers an hour on a road like this, for eight hours a day. Ten or twelve, if required. And the best way to find out exactly what it could do when required was to do it yourself beforehand.

The road, of course, was bad. Most roads were, especially in Italy. The dust would be almost enough to suffocate an army on the march, if it should happen to be in the summer season. Even the King's pavé, in France. The jolting was so bad you couldn't move heavy stuff with any speed—munition-wagons, artillery. Engineers ought to be able to devise something that neither suffocated your infantry nor tore your wheeled transport to pieces. The Romans had known how to do it. Some day one would have to look into it.

In the meantime, the Genoese had promised a road of sorts over the mountains, passable at least by infantry. And where some men could take only infantry, others could take artillery as well.

"You'll only get your wind-pipe full of dust, then you'll start coughing. You always do. What'll mother say if you come back to Nice spitting blood again? She'll put leeches on your back, and you won't like that. But she'll do it. She always does."

The unresponsive back went steadily forward. He was looking to his right now, towards the north. The westering sun outlined his bleak profile so that it looked like a dark mask, sharp-cut, hard, deep-shadowed.

Up there to the north, glistening white and sharp as a wolf's fangs, the Appenines were tearing at the sky; farther along, a second range, the Alps. Between them a gap, as though a fang had been torn out. It was through that gap the Genoese had promised to build him his road, to make a pass of what was only a gap; a road passable by infantry. Robespierre wouldn't be able to deny he'd got what was wanted from the Genoese Council.

He had never met Robespierre. He had no wish to—had in fact refused. When one was eighteen and still thought of one's self as a Stoic, immolation of the individual on the altar of the State could—when seen from a distance—seem heroic and noble. But when one was twenty-five and had had the bloody victims thrust under one's nose, as it had been when Barras purged Toulon of three-quarters of its population and wealth, one began to feel uneasy. Robespierre and his Terror. Yet fear had served the country well, once—had united it against the Austrian invader. The Austrian was gone now, but Robespierre's Terror still remained. No longer a single sword, but a thousand guillotines needing a thousand tribunals to serve them. That was the trouble. Robespierre's servants. Whatever motive lay behind his methods, only the most degraded of men could execute them. That was why he, who at the age of twenty-five had been offered by Robespierre the Military Governorship of Paris, had refused. One could work with Robespierre—not for him.

"I don't suppose you'd notice if I dropped dead. You'd just go on thinking about yourself. You always do."

And it couldn't last. The people might endure the terrible justice of Robespierre the Incorruptible—but sooner or later they would rise against the terrible exercisers of it. Men like Barras, Tallien, Fréron. When that time came, Robespierre would have to choose between destroying his servants, or being destroyed by them. And was Robespierre a strong enough man to do that? Was he great enough to impose the only policy that could save the nation—alliance of the ruler and the people against the privileged class, call it aristocracy, the Jacobins, finance, or what you would?

Finance. There again. Robespierre's exchanging of gold for paper money was well enough, for if the nation was to win its war without entangling itself in the spider-web of foreign loans, it must sacrifice its gold as freely as its blood. Confiscation of

Crown and Church property, good. Confiscation of the fortunes of the guillotined—picking the pockets of the dead—no. That was where men like Barras and Tallien found their chance. That was what turned legal confiscation into robbery with violence. And that, too, couldn't last.

Yet there again—was Robespierre strong enough to rid himself of the men who used his method to their own profit? Yet who else was there? Robespierre was at least incorruptible. It was imagination that he lacked. He had tried to bribe the people with the Rights of Man, and it hadn't worked. He had tried to coerce them by terror, and that would fail, too. But let him appeal to the imagination of the people—let him show the people the glory of an Italy liberated from the Austrian, of his terror driven into Austrian hearts instead of their own throats, of gold won from Austrian defeat instead of pilfered from French corpses, and he would be invincible—if he was strong enough to hold his own pack of jackals at bay while he did it.

That was the only plan that could have any chance now of saving the nation from the Jacobin corruption that menaced it. Robespierre had seen it at last—admitted it—agreed to it. The first step had been taken—a military road to Ceva. . . .

If a man were to put an army up there, at Ceva, at Montenotte, he would be making of it a nut between the Austro-Sardinian nut-crackers. They'd never believe a man would dare to do that. But then the man who'd put his army there might make of it, after all, a spear-point thrust between the joints of their armor, wedging them apart, driving at the unprotected flesh behind. It would all depend on who that man was.

In the meantime from here, where the new road would branch off due north from the coast as far as Nice, one must study every meter of the old road, every twist and turn of its length, every stone and hollow of its surface. A knowledge of roads was as essential to a soldier as a knowledge of arteries to a surgeon.

"I don't believe you've listened to anything I've said. You never do. You might at least answer a man when he takes the trouble to talk to you. Are you dumb as well as deaf? Napoleon!"

The lean young man went steadily on, his feet in the dust of the road, his eyes on the mountain-tops, his imagination in the future. Then he half-started, and looked back over his shoulder.

"What did you say, Louis?"

"What did I say? I've been talking for hours. And you haven't heard a single word. You never do. You can't expect me to repeat everything I've said since we left Voltri, can you?"

"No," said the lean young man.

He turned back to his contemplation of the road, and to his limping progress along it.

> *"Barras ... who pushed knavery to the point of genius, and immorality to the point of perfection."*
>
> LOUIS MADELIN

CHAPTER

❧ VI ❧

"IT'S HOT ALREADY," SAID BARRAS.

He spread a fine cambric handkerchief over the stone balustrade in front of him before laying his hands upon it. His hands were almost as white and as fine in texture as the handkerchief. Tallien, standing beside him, glanced at them, and drove his own fists deep into his breeches pockets.

"It'll be hotter presently," he said.

Barras smiled. "We shan't have to wait for that. In a few moments, I'll show you what I brought you here to see."

Tallien spat over the balustrade into the dry moat below. Aristocrat, he thought. Robespierre had been right. Nothing but death could change them. They called themselves Revolutionaries, Jacobins, Terrorists—but they were aristocrats just the same. Count Paul de Barras, with his narrow white hands, that didn't look as though he'd even had to rinse the blood off them. He, Tallien, had scrubbed his, but that only made them look red and shiny and tight-skinned. Yet Barras' hands had been bloodier than his. Over half the population of Toulon he'd wiped out with those delicate fingers of his, whereas he, at Bordeaux, had spared thousands—literally thousands.

That had been Theresia's scheme. Earn gratitude and money at the same time by selling men their own heads while they were still alive to pay for them.

It had seemed a good idea at the time, only Robespierre had

found out, as anybody but a fool would have known he would—a fool who'd let himself be flattered and taken in by the clever tongue and selfish mind of an aristocrat like Theresia. Marquise de Fontenay! Pah! She'd let him take her out of the Bordeaux prison, hang her with jewels, smother her with money, save her friends for her, make her the idol, the queen of Bordeaux—and he without the sense to see that while it was she who was profiting, it was he who ran the risk. Not until it was too late. Not until Robespierre recalled him to Paris, on a charge of corruption. Under the guillotine he'd have been too, for all Theresia cared. The sweat pricked out on the back of his neck at the thought.

But there again Robespierre had been right. He'd known that when an honest man goes wrong, there's always a woman to blame. She'd been the first to go to prison. And in prison, for all of him, she could rot. He wasn't going to be caught and used again like that. He'd had enough of aristocrats and their dirty schemes, for which men of the people like himself had to pay in the end.

The others—Barras and Fréron and all the other Deputies on Mission—they'd been recalled, too. Their hands, too, had been corrupt with money as well as blood. And that was the only stink Robespierre couldn't stand, the smell of money. They'd all have been under the guillotine by now, except for him. It wasn't they, it was he who'd dared shove a dagger under Robespierre's nose, who'd dared to call him tyrant before the whole Convention. Barras'd only dressed up in his fine uniform and waited to be "ordered" to arrest a man already beaten, so that he couldn't be blamed even then if the coup failed at the last moment. Oh, he'd been careful enough to the very end, had Barras, not to run any risks. It was he, Tallien, who'd taken the risks, Barras and his kind who were profiting.

But they needn't think they were going to go on using him. No. He was going to have some of the profits himself. He wasn't just a cheap Deputy any more. He was Jean-Lambert Tallien, the hero who'd killed the monster. He was more important than they were now. It wasn't only Barras who could throw his authority about, give orders, grant favors. He'd thought himself very fine, giving Hoche to Carnot. But he could do it, too. He'd been just as fine, he'd just as offhandedly given a prisoner to Hoche. He was glad Hoche had reminded him of the little Creole wench. That was the sort of woman he liked. Not superior and contemptuous like Theresia, looking at a man as though he were something nasty she'd stepped in on the street. Yes, he was glad he'd released the little Beauharnais. Of course, she was an aristocrat, too. He'd paid a quarter's rent for her once in the old days, and she'd condescended to take it. Well, the boot was on the other leg now. He knew a thing or two.

He knew it wasn't for the pleasure of his company that Barras had asked him to walk in the colonnade of the Tuileries this morning, nor yet for the sake of looking out over the gardens to the Place de la Révolution beyond, deserted at this hour of the morning, except of course for the guillotine. They'd taken the blade away for sharpening after finishing Robespierre and his gang. Well, it would soon be back again. There were still a good many heads that would look a sight handsomer in the basket than on their owners' shoulders. But it wasn't to discuss trifles like that, that Barras was being so friendly this morning. He was only friendly with men who weren't gentlemen when he wanted to use them. Aristocrat! He leaned against the balustrade, and spat again into the moat.

"Be careful of your coat, my friend," said Barras. "This place hasn't been cleaned since eighty-nine, and the pigeons are, er—in excellent health. Such a handsome coat, too."

"Twelve thousand francs," said Tallien. He looked down at it. Rich brown velvet, such as you could scarcely get these days, embroidered in green, with just a touch of gold thread to liven it. Yes, it was a handsome coat, and the yellow satin waistcoat beneath made a rich contrast. A little hot for the weather, perhaps, but worth the discomfort. And a man in the public eye had to think of his audience.

He looked sideways at Barras. Barras, for all his birth and education, didn't appreciate the necessity for making a good appearance. A pale fawn lustrine coat with only cut-steel buttons by way of decoration, over a white piqué waistcoat. As he stood, from his steel-buckled shoes to his plain batiste neckcloth, he probably wasn't worth more than five or six thousand francs. Of the two he might be the better born, but he certainly wasn't the better dressed.

"My compliments to your tailor," said Barras.

"I owe him nearly a hundred-thousand."

Barras smiled. "My compliments to yourself."

Tallien frowned uncomfortably. You could understand what these gentlemen said, but not always what they meant—whether

40

they were being complimentary, or only unpleasant. Childish waste of time, anyway. He took out his watch, and looked first at its back with its diamond coronet. It had belonged to the Mayor of Bordeaux. When he'd been condemned, he'd flung it on his, Tallien's, desk, saying, "Better even you than the executioner." It was a good watch.

"Look," said Barras, and pointed out over the Place.

There wasn't much to be seen, even now. A cart—the executioner's red cart—creaking slowly over the paving-stones behind its lazily plodding horses. An execution? What of it? Did Barras think an execution could interest him, he who had had, so to speak, his own private guillotine at Bordeaux? Anyway, the knife wasn't in place. They'd forgotten that. They weren't even efficient here in Paris.

"Do you know what you're looking at, Tallien?"

Tallien shrugged. "Paris executioners who don't know their job."

"No, my friend. You are taking part in an historic event. You are witnessing the end of the Terror. Robespierre's Terror."

Through the already heat-drenched air the figures of the men who'd got out of the cart there in the middle of the Place were indistinct, and seemed to waver a little, as though seen through moving water. But one could see easily enough what they were doing—knocking out the wedges at the foot of the uprights, prising up the planks of the scaffold. They were dismantling the guillotine. Had the heat and the excitement of the past ten days driven Barras out of his mind?

"Are you mad, Barras? Man, we've only just begun!"

Barras spread out his hands and smiled. "To the contrary, my dear friend, we've finished."

Tallien glared in angry bewilderment. "We destroyed all the notes in Robespierre's desk, didn't we? Well, there's some men have got the same notes in their heads. Are we going to leave them their tongues to blab with? Exterminate them, I say. Exterminate them."

"No, my dear fellow, no. I appreciate your, er—energy, but believe me, it is ill-directed. In the silence of general disapproval, a single accusing voice is clearly audible—but in the clamor of popular applause, a hundred can cry aloud and remain unheard. We have our thousands of supporters ready-made in the prisons. Therefore it is not exterminate, but liberate, that should be our policy. Consider the power of public opinion."

Tallien grunted. "Public opinion! Who cares for public opinion?"

"I do. Robespierre didn't. That's why he's dead. In the eyes of public opinion we're not just Deputies who've managed to save our own heads, we are, er—white-robed angels of mercy, winged doves of peace. We are the Men of July. The slayers of the Monster."

Tallien frowned, and set his fists on his hips. "We?" he said truculently.

Barras laid a placating hand on his arm. "I said we—but it is you who are in question. And you must do something about it— unquestionably, you must."

"About what?" demanded Tallien suspiciously.

"About the final act of your little, er—comedy, my dear fellow. Oh, I agree that Robespierre's last cry of agony on the scaffold was the perfect ending to a well-constructed tragedy. But the people have no taste for austerity in drama. They like the cheap vulgarity of an, er—happy ending."

Tallien hunched his thick shoulders and shook his arm free from Barras' hand. He wasn't going to be anybody's clown again. He'd got himself safely off the stage, and he'd stay off. If there were any more comedies to be played, Barras could do it himself.

"What ending?" he asked, scowling.

"The usual one, my dear fellow," said Barras lightly. "Marriage. You must release your, er—charming friend from prison and marry her."

Tallien drew back from him. Decidedly the man's brain was addled. Marry her? Marry Theresia? After all the pains he'd taken to get rid of her, himself denouncing her to Robespierre, and getting himself spat on for his trouble! Yes, and coming within smelling distance of the scaffold, too. And who bothered to get married these days, anyway, let alone to that spiteful bitch, that scheming whore, that—

"Marry?" he demanded. "What for?"

"Because it'll be expected of the man who brandished a Spanish dagger in Robespierre's face in the name of his Spanish lady."

"Well," said Tallien aggressively, "whose idea was it?"

"Never mind that. You did it. You played the despairing lover. You were the hero-knight, riding to the aid of beauty in distress. And now that the Monster's dead, you can't just go home, leaving your, er—Andromeda still chained to her rock."

"Her name's Theresia," muttered Tallien sullenly.

"Very likely. But you are the hero of the piece nevertheless. It is, er—unfortunate, but there it is. You are the hero, the people's idol—love, romance and all the rest of it—and you mustn't disappoint them now. You must give them their happy ending."

"All very well—but what about my happy ending? You don't know Theresia."

Barras smiled. "Never mind. Marriage isn't a quicksand any longer—it doesn't bury a man alive. And you shall have your happy ending too. Listen to me, Tallien"—unsmiling now, his voice grave—"we—you, are on the crest of a wave of popular enthusiasm such as Paris hasn't seen since the fall of the Bastille. And you must stay there—at all costs you must stay there, until it carries you—" He broke off, and threw up his hand, as though he were tossing a coin into the air.

"Where?" said Tallien, narrowing his eyes.

"Supreme power. The seat of Government."

Tallien grinned knowingly, and wagged a forefinger. "Not I," he said. "People who sit on Governments get their heads cut off."

"My dear fellow," said Barras smiling tolerantly. "You're mistaken, believe me. Nobody ever sat on a Government harder than Louis XIV—and what happened? The people adored him. He oppressed them, but he gave them what they wanted—a spectacle worth looking at. Eight-horse coaches, royal mistresses, military displays—magnificence, splendor, glory." He raised a deprecating hand. "Not, naturally, that I expect you yourself to make so, er—vulgar a display. There are discreeter methods. There is what is known as the power behind the throne. The late, er—lamented King's brother—"

"Fat Provence?"

"Fat Provence, if you like. Louis XVIII in Royalist eyes, nevertheless."

Tallien slid a sideways glance at him. "You mean—make the people take back a king?"

"My dear fellow, I mean no such thing. I mean only that a powerful man should, and a popular man can, er—divert the energy of the people into safe channels. And think, Tallien—think what would be the position of a man who had not only the love of the people behind him, but the gratitude of the throne as well."

"Gratitude? Provence's human, isn't he? And after all, we—all of us—killed the man's brother, didn't we?"

Barras shrugged. "As you say, Provence is human. And if Paris was once worth a Mass, surely the whole of France is still worth a few Letters of Remission?"

Tallien gazed out over the Place. The uprights of the guillotine were gone now, and most of the planking was up. He scratched his chin with his thumbnail. It was true he was popular. Men shouted, "Vive Tallien!" and clapped him on the back, they even kissed his coattails when he passed. Women flung their arms about his neck and kissed him when he went into cafés or dance-halls. He wondered if even Louis XIV had been as popular as that. The power behind the throne—

He straightened his shoulders and raised his chin. When he pulled himself up, he was taller than Barras. People who liked a man with a bit of life about him would say he was better looking, too. But he wasn't going to play Barras' game again. At Bordeaux he'd played the dupe for Theresia's schemes, in Paris he'd been the bait that lured Robespierre into the trap, and had been lucky to come out of it alive. He wasn't a coward, but he wasn't a half-wit, either. Aristocrats never offered a common man something for nothing, they only did it when they wanted something more in return. But he'd learned to look for the string on the carrot now.

"Maybe," he said. "But there's more to this business than just offering a man the crown and saying 'How much?' There's people that won't like it. And we've got to keep the show going in the meantime."

"Of course, my dear fellow, of course," said Barras affably. "We must first ascertain what is the, er—will of the people in the matter. In the meantime we must, as you so admirably put it, keep the show going. We've destroyed the Terror, though, er —inadvertently, I admit. The people will be satisfied with just not being guillotined for quite a long time to come.

"As for the parties"—he waved a negligent hand—"we have only to play them as a juggler plays with his balls. Moderates going up as the Jacobins come down, Royalists going up as the Moderates come down. Then the Jacobins up again. No final victory for any of them, but no ultimate despair either, until— That, I assure you, is the whole art of successful government. Anybody can do it, with a little judgment and dexterity. And I am not

44

noticeably clumsy. You are standing in the portico of a royal palace now—you need only to take a few steps—"

Tallien glanced over his shoulder at the imposing western façade of the Tuileries behind him. He remembered the Hôtel Franklin he'd had at Bordeaux. Very fine, he'd thought it then. He remembered riding through the streets in an open carriage with four matched horses before and uniformed guards behind. He remembered sitting in the Mayor's box at the Opera, with an aristocrat for a mistress beside him. Yes, very fine he'd thought it all then. But Bordeaux wasn't Paris, the Hôtel Franklin wasn't the Tuileries, the Mayor's box wasn't the royal box. And Theresia wasn't—

"Why Theresia?" he said. "I know a little piece—"

Barras frowned, then smiled patiently. "My dear good man, have your, er—little piece, by all means. But not as consort, for the reasons I have already given you—and for a still better reason. Money. Your Marquise de Fontenay was born into the great financial family of Cabarrus. Her father's Finance Minister to the King of Spain. Through him, she has contacts with bankers the world over—and we need loans—gold—to put the country on a sound financial basis again.

"Robespierre's system of paper money secured on land is false, and with a solid gold backing we can destroy it. With real gold in our pockets we'll be able to force down the value of the paper *assignats* until you'll be able to buy a place like that"—he jerked his chin towards the great bulk of the Hôtel Crillon that closed the northern end of the Place—"you'll be able to buy that for the price of a laborer's cottage. You see?" He took out his snuffbox, flicked it open, and helped himself daintily.

"The bankers of Europe, my dear fellow, will lend to a daughter of Cabarrus, provided her influence in government affairs is assured. But they will not lend to a, er—you will forgive my frankness—to an ex-Jacobin, ex-Terrorist, and, er—Regicide. You see my point?"

Oh, he saw the point. People who'd been called patriots yesterday were to be called Regicides to-day. But he wasn't the only one who'd voted the death of the King, yes, and been proud of it, too. They'd all done it. Barras as well as the rest. Barras couldn't wash that blood off his hands. Not ever.

He drove his own fist deep into his breeches pocket, and fumbled at the wad of paper money at the bottom of it. *Assignats.* The

45

people's money, secured on the people's land. He shifted his feet uneasily.

"All very fine," he said. "But what of the poor devils who don't spend their *assignats* to buy hotels, or even laborers' cottages, but only a loaf of bread and a liter of wine. What about them, eh?"

Barras shrugged. "There will, of course, be a period of, er— discomfort, for certain people during the period of readjustment. But, my friend, no omelette without broken eggs, you know. And the people will have their share of the omelette of prosperity in time. One must be practical in such matters, not sentimental."

Tallien turned his head and spat over the balustrade—but his mouth was suddenly dry of saliva, the muscles of his face contracted and stiff. He turned back and stared at Barras from under lowered brows.

"Have you ever been hungry?" he demanded abruptly.

Barras raised his fine eyebrows. "I? I suppose so, like everybody else."

Aristocrat, thought Tallien. Dirty aristocrat, with your aristocrat's hunger that's only greed at the thought of the meal to come—not the retching sickness of desire at the memory of yesterday's crust, that was the people's hunger. Eat your gold and digest it too, if you can. Only leave us—the people alone. Gold? Danton once said you could always buy a good riot for five louis. You can get it cheaper than that. You can get it for a loaf of bread. Be careful what you're doing. The people aren't fools. They can't be had all the time.

Gold. He fumbled the greasy little wad of *assignats* between his fingers. It wasn't so satisfactory as clinking a handful of gold in your pocket. His shoulders slouched forward, the muscles of his jaws slackened. Barras was right. The people liked glory. And somebody had to pay for it, didn't they? His own glory, the glory of having killed the Monster—the people owed him more than a little back-slapping for that. Besides, if the gold didn't go into the pocket of his own breeches it'd go into somebody else's, equally well-tailored, equally expensive. Gold was an aristocrat, too. It didn't like shabby clothes. It never had. And there wasn't anything you could do about it, was there? Except to keep as well-dressed as you could.

He pulled out the handful of greasy, crumpled *assignats* and looked at them. Dirty little bits of paper, smudged here with the print of a blackened thumb, stained there with a splash of wine, dark along the folds from dingy pockets. Pah! Enough to soil anybody's fine new clothes. He crumpled them into a ball and tossed it over the balustrade into the moat.

Barras smiled slightly, and pulled out his watch. "After eight," he said. "The Citizens—or should I say, gentlemen?—of the Convention will be waiting for us. Let us go in and, er—assume the weight of our responsibilities."

Side by side the two men walked up the colonnade towards the main entry of the Tuileries.

Behind them a cart laden with a few shabby, stained, wooden posts and weather-beaten planks creaked slowly out of the Place de la Révolution.

> *"Let us do nothing for a few years except live."*
> TALLEYRAND, 1795

CHAPTER

⇒ VII ⇐

IT WAS SHE WHO WAS PUTTING ON HER BEST CLOTHES TO-DAY AND making up her bundle, getting ready to go out. But she was going out properly, into the real world, into Paris, into life. She would have jumped up from her pallet-bed and danced about the cell, save for the jailer who was watching, and one had to maintain one's dignity before the lower classes.

Leaning hip and shoulder against the wall, he'd watched her all the time she dressed, out of insolently amused eyes. Not that it mattered. Great ladies at Versailles, she knew, had sometimes been served in their baths by lackeys. And that was all this man was now. A lackey.

A small man. Not like Hoche. A small man, lean and brown and sinewy. Yet there was something about these gutter-rats of Paris—narrow-boned, flat-muscled, small jointed, neatly put together. There was something in the bold intelligence of the eyes, in the bitter humor of the mouth, as though the youngest of them were as old as the city itself—and as ageless, too. Rather like one of those ancient daggers, worn to a shadow of itself, yet still finely tempered, still with its cutting edge, its needle point. His brown bare ankle between the coarse stuff of his pantaloons and the clumsy wood of his sabots was as delicately slender as a woman's.

Paris gutter-rats. It was a pity that they were so unnecessarily dirty and that they spat. Yet beside Hoche, this man was as sophisticated as a black olive beside a green apple.

She stopped in her packing to look again at what he had brought her that morning. It was coarsely printed on cheap paper, and it had a dirty thumb-mark in the corner. But no scented love-letter had ever brought greater happiness to a woman's heart. Tallien hadn't forgotten the old days at Croissy after all—and was it likely that a man of his class would forget a real Viscountess?

Besides, it had been said that he wasn't really the son of the Marquis de Bercy's maître d'hôtel at all, but of the Marquis himself. That would make a difference, wouldn't it? Anyway, there was his signature, sprawling and ill-formed, and her name in his writing, after the printed words, "the release of...."

It must be he who was important now. Perhaps he'd even taken Robespierre's place. After all, that was what men killed each other for, wasn't it—to take their places? A sort of king. Not that there was anything exactly kingly about him, but he was at least a man. And that's more than Robespierre had been. Poor Tallien. He really wasn't so bad, when you came to think of it. His nails might be black, but his teeth were very white. His body might be smelly, but it was a strong body, and virile. His manners... after all, a certain robustness of manner wasn't unbecoming in a man, was it?

She tied her fresh white fichu, tucking in her chin to see the knot on her bosom. It was a pity she hadn't thought to take Hoche's mirror the day he left.

She put on her little frilled bonnet with the cockade, wondering how it looked over the short curls of her hair. It really was aggravating about the mirror. It was just possible Tallien would be at the prison door to welcome her. Why not? He wouldn't take the trouble to release her for nothing, would he? Yes, it was more than probable he would be there. It was almost certain. If only she had a mirror—

Hoche might be there, too. That would be amusing. The soldier and the politician. The Moderate and the Jacobin. The man of the people, and the man on top. And she between them.

Yes, it would be amusing. Two fine, big men. Towards which should she lean? Government men usually had more money than soldiers, but soldiers were easier to manage. More generous too, and less suspicious. Yet why choose, after all? It was easy enough for a woman to walk between two men at once.

She stood up, shook out the ample folds of her red and white striped skirt, and smoothed down the basques of her white piqué bodice with its frilled, elbow-length sleeves. She was ready. She had nobody to take leave of, for even Desirée had been released days before. She picked up her bundle, then on a sudden impulse threw it down again on the pallet. She would take nothing out of this place with her. She would leave behind everything that was soiled and sordid and old. She would be new and fresh again. She would come out of the door of this filthy place as clean and untouched as a water-lily, rising pure and unsullied out of darkness and mire.

She went slowly towards the door with swaying, languid steps. The jailer was still watching, out of the brilliant slits of his eyes. He did well to make the most of it—for the time when he and his kind could approach fine ladies was over.

Lackey! Not even that. A gutter-rat. What was the man looking at her like that for, with his long eyes insolent under dark lashes? He couldn't possibly think—he couldn't conceivably imagine—Canaille!

As she passed him, she took from her bosom her little silk purse. It contained a hundred francs in *assignats*—all the money she had in the world. But what was a hundred francs to a Viscountess de Beauharnais, a friend of Deputy Tallien and General Hoche? It was a badge of poverty to own such a sum. Madame la Viscountess de Beauharnais dropped the little purse at the jailer's feet and swept past without looking at him.

He didn't move either to let her pass or to block her way—hip and shoulder against the wall, immobile, only his eyes slipping sideways as she passed, incurious, but seeing even the grain of her skin.

Canaille! Gutter-rat! She felt his eyes on her as she went, like touching fingers, making her back tingle. Down the narrow corridor, remembering to keep her head up, her shoulders back, her elbows in, as all great ladies walked.

Behind her the jailer touched the little purse with his foot, then with a lithe sweep of his arm picked it up. He looked inside, lifted a contemptuous lip, and spat after her retreating back.

A group of released prisoners came up behind her, talking and laughing noisily. She stood aside to let them sign and pass out of the door before her. Water-lilies don't grow in coarse bunches, they appear in lovely dignity, alone.

The dark frame of the door stood empty, save for the heavy curtain of sunlight behind it, thick and yellow as honey. She stood there for a moment with closed eyes. Then she raised her head on the slim round stalk of her neck and looked up at the sky. She drew a deep breath through parted lips, so that the gracious curves of her bosom swelled above the low-tied folds of her white fichu. She took a step forward, then swayed and stood still, breathing quickly, looking down at her hands, twisting the wedding-ring on her finger. What else could she do, the young widow cast out helpless and penniless onto the streets of Paris?

She heard the sound of running footsteps. She'd been right, then. He—they had come. Tears rose in her eyes, just far enough to hang caught, sparkling in the sun, at the tips of her very long lashes. Dew-drops on the petals of the lily. . . . They were coming towards her, crossing the court, eager, hurrying. She looked down steadily at her hands. The running feet came up the stone steps. They were beside her. There was a hand at her waist, another on her arm. A voice, breathless with eagerness, spoke in her ear.

"Mother!"

She lifted her head sharply and looked. There was Eugène with his arm about her waist, Hortense clinging to her arm. Her children! Of course, her dear, sweet children, that she'd never stopped thinking of all these long months. How tall they were! Was it possible children could grow so much in so short a time? She'd thought of them as babies, and here they were— Eugène in breeches and stockings, and she'd left him in long pantaloons, held up by big buttons fore and aft. It was true he'd hated them, but he hadn't been of an age for breeches. He still wasn't. He couldn't be. Hortense in a queer, straight slip of a dress, just a sack really, tied with a ribbon beneath her bust. Yes, actually her bust. It wasn't believable in so young a child!

They clung to her, Hortense kissing her bare arm, Eugène her cheek. He was tall enough to kiss her cheek without standing on tiptoe. Some children, of course, did shoot up like that, far beyond their years.

"Oh, Mother! Mother!" How dear they were, with their eyes and thoughts only for her—as hers were for them, of course. She stooped and kissed them gently. Then she stood for a moment, with her arms about them. The young mother alone in the world with her fatherless children...the tears rose again in her eyes, but she smiled bravely. She took her children by the hand and came slowly down the steps. Eugène pulled his hand away, and offered his arm. She took it, and smiled at him. The dear child, playing the little protector already, at his age. It was touching—really touching.

"You came—alone, my pets?"

"Yes, Mother," said Hortense. "Aunt Desirée thought it would be nicest like that."

Just like Desirée. She was a sentimentalist at heart, even liking the children to call her "Aunt." Kind, of course—but not practical. To get home alone, through these crowded steets, with no man to help her.... No, not practical at all.

She bent down and kissed the top of Hortense's fair head, glancing to left and right under lowered lashes. She saw plenty of men's feet, in pairs, in groups, or with women's skirts bobbing beside them. But none coming towards her. She sighed, and raised her head.

"Of course, my dear," she said. "It's much the nicest like this."

She stood erect, and walked resolutely out into the rue Vaugirard. She was a young matron, attending strictly and bravely to her own affairs. And her affair at the moment was to get her children home to the rue Saint Dominique as quickly as possible. There she would see Desirée, and find out....Well, find out.

"Hortense, my lamb," she said. "Your dress—really, it makes you look like a girl of twelve."

Hortense raised candid blue eyes to hers. "But I am," she said.

"Nonsense!" How strange little girls were, always wanting to be grown up before their time. Why, Eugène was two years older than she, and that would make him— Quite absurd, of course.

"Don't you like my dress, Mother? I made it myself—Marie only helped me a little."

Marie, Marie Lannoy, who'd been her maid when one still had maids. Marie and her husband Jacques. How loyal they'd been all through the bad days! It was good to think that such loyalty could still exist in the lower classes, when it was considered patriotic to denounce your betters.

Yes, the Lannoys had been good and faithful, serving her for nothing when she had no money, taking care of the children while she was in prison. She owed them a debt of gratitude—and four or five months' wages as well. And of course there was the thousand francs she'd borrowed from Marie when Alexander had gone to prison and left her without any money. She'd pay them more than that. She'd pay them double. She'd give them a pension for life! Nobody could say that she was ungrateful, or that she didn't pay her debts.

"We'll cross the street here," she said to the children.

They stood for a moment, waiting for a gap in the busy, noisy, disorderly traffic of the rue Vaugirard. They crossed, and turned to the right, up the rue du Bac, that had been so rich and splendid in the old King's time. The street had changed since then, but not since she'd last seen it.

She looked at the women. Their dresses seemed very queer—like Hortense's, rather as though they'd come out in their night-dresses or their shifts. Just straight, skimpy gowns, without a waist, tied under the bust with a ribbon. They looked grotesque, completely ridiculous, without shape or style or elegance. Yet all the women were the same. Like lamp-posts with strings tied round them. It was she who was different. She was an unfashionable woman! It was impossible to be seen in the street like that—it was uncomfortable, almost indecent. She hurried her steps.

"Mother! Did you hear what I said? Mother, listen!"

"Yes, I'm listening. What did you say, Eugène, my lamb?"

"I said I'm going to be aide-de-camp to General Hoche!"

"Oh! You've—you've seen General Hoche? But, my dear, you're too young! What—what did he say?"

"Yes. He came to see us at Aunt Desirée's, before he went north to the army. He said I was very tall for my age." He looked at her sideways and grinned. Eugène was more—more sensible about that sort of thing than Hortense.

"Did he—did General Hoche say anything about me?"

"About you? Why, you're a woman, Mother. You can't be a General's aide-de-camp. But I can. A real aide-de-camp. With a uniform. And a sword. And to General Hoche, Mother. General Hoche himself!"

"Yes—of course. I just thought he might have—said something."

Men were so sentimental about children. They always thought women weren't intelligent enough to think about anything else. Of course, she was glad that Eugène should be pleased. Naturally. She was fond of her little son—very fond. Still—

"We'll cross now, my dears. Here's the rue Saint Dominique."

"Oh, but, Mother!" Hortense raised a face pink with excitement. "Couldn't we just go down to the river? Look, everybody else is going. They'll be driving along the quais. Any minute, now. Oh, please! I do so want to see the Spanish lady."

"Spanish lady? What Spanish lady?"

"Oh, Mother! Don't you know? It's like a fairy-story, really it is! He saved her from having her head cut off, and now he's going to marry her. Just like a story, and she's very beautiful, and now they're going to live happily ever after. They call her Our Lady of July, because it was in July the Monster was killed, and—and—"

"Don't be silly!" said Eugène scornfully. "It's Tallien's woman, Mother. He got her out of prison last month, and took her home to his mother till he could marry her. Tallien's supposed to have killed Robespierre to save her head. Which, of course, is just the kind of thing that uneducated people do say. It's easy to see what Tallien's after. Though they do say she's a handsome enough wench." He touched his upper lip with his forefinger, as though there might be a mustache growing on it.

The Spanish lady—Tallien's woman—taking her home to his mother! One hadn't really imagined people like Tallien having mothers, though of course they had to, like everybody else. One didn't imagine them getting married, either. Not to ladies. Not actually *married*.

"How can you say such awful things!" cried Hortense indignantly. "It was she who sent Tallien the Spanish dagger from her prison to kill the Monster with! Everybody knows it!"

"Silly child," said Eugène tolerantly. "She didn't send anybody anything from prison, for the simple reason she was kept in secret, and couldn't. If anybody gave Tallien the dagger it was Barras, or perhaps Fouché. Still, it might be worth seeing— the first State wedding since the Revolution. Ex-lackey Tallien and his ex-mistress—"

"Eugène! Not before your sister!" Children did, of course, pick up words they couldn't possibly understand.

"Do let's go, Mother! Do let's go!" Hortense was pulling at her arm.

She stood irresolute on the corner. Everything was so different —Hoche was with his army, Tallien was getting married—so what was the use of looking at him? Still, there was the woman—the Spanish lady. It would be interesting to see what sort of "lady" would marry a creature like Tallien. Besides, the children both wanted to go, and one shouldn't disappoint children.

At the end of the rue du Bac, where it gave onto the quais and the Seine, she could see a fringe of people already standing to watch the strange bridal couple. She began to walk slowly towards it. She was only the Widow Beauharnais, going dutifully with her children to witness a public show. Though why a show, just because a French lout was going to marry a Spanish harlot?

They were in the crowd that blocked the end of the street now. Mounted guards were pressing the people back. It was incredible! You'd think you were back in the old days, waiting to see the King drive by.

"Keep your eye on Tallien, Mother," Eugène said. "Believe me, he's the coming man. He's the man to watch. If I'm any judge of men and affairs, he's the next ruler of France."

She sighed. Why was it so difficult to know in advance which men were going to be worth while and which were not? As difficult as knowing which egg was going to be a hen and which a cock. Tallien ruler of France! He'd lent her some money once, and she'd only replied with a "Thank you." If you could only *know!* It might have been she instead of the Spanish woman the people were waiting to see if she'd only known and been a little more—grateful. But it was so *difficult,* when royal Princes were in exile, and lackey's sons in the Tuileries. "More than Queen," her old black nurse had told her—yet here she was, in these quite impossible clothes, standing on a street-corner to see another woman drive by in triumph.

Mounted gendarmes in plumed hats were riding by, then a detachment of the National Guard, on foot, with their music marching before them. People were shouting so that she was nearly deafened, jostling so that she had difficulty in keeping her place.

"Our Lady! Long live Our Lady of July!"

The horses of the carriage itself were just in front of her now. A scarlet carriage, with four white horses. She smiled. Tallien wouldn't know, of course, that of all the numbers of horses one could harness to a carriage, four was the only one that was quite impossible. A person of breeding might ride behind one, or two, or six—three even, though that smacked a little of vulgar eccentricity. But four was quite definitely the mark of the common social climber, and of nothing else. Naturally, one couldn't expect so ill-bred a creature as Tallien to understand such fine distinctions.

"Our Lady! Long live Our Lady of July! Our Lady of Mercy!"

The cheers were frantic now and from the other side of the quai, where the Pont Royal had its opening, the people who had been massed on the bridge surged forward and flooded about the carriage, bringing it to a halt. It was an open carriage, and the couple in it were plainly visible. Or at least the woman on the near side was. She was laughing like a school-girl with the gay excitement of the adventure.

She didn't look more than twenty—though of course she might be twenty-five or even thirty, you could never tell with these southern women.

You couldn't deny that she had looks. Yes, she was really quite handsome. Her skin was white with the luminous pallor that some southerners have. It was such a pity that complexions like that never lasted. A year or so, and they were as yellow and greasy as old cheese. Her eyes were enormous, dark, and shadowy. Her hair was black, startling—crude really—in its contrast with her white skin. She seemed to have vast quantities of it too, though of course you could never be sure, so many fine heads of hair from the guillotine had been sold in the past year or so. Yes, she was very handsome. No one would be ungenerous enough to deny it. She was of the voluptuous type that very soon runs to fat. Already the girl was well-fleshed. The dimples in her cheeks, that firm, wide neck, with the clearly marked neck-lets of Venus. No, not a lasting type of beauty, nor a very patrician one, either. Seeing her sitting there with her head thrown back, laughing in that hoydenish fashion, you weren't so surprised after all that she should be willing to marry a man like Tallien.

Somebody near her shouted, "Long live Tallien!" as the carriage swerved him into sight—and he only scowled, without moving his head. The girl beside him turned, put her hand on his arm, smiled up at him, said something. He stretched his mouth into a hard grin, without talking off his scowl. The crowd roared louder than ever,

"Our Lady! Our Lady of July! Our Lady of Mercy!"

The girl was evidently not only ill-bred, but tactless as well—

55

forcing her man to take second place in public! You could brow-beat and humiliate a man in private as much as you liked, so long as you let him be important before other people. Well-or ill-born, men were all like that, and you had to remember it if you wanted to keep them.

The girl was throwing flowers now, and the people were scrambling for them, as they used to do when the King's largesse was scattered from the royal coach. A pink rose-bud fell at her feet, and Eugène snatched it up eagerly. Then he flushed, and stood twirling it awkwardly between his finger and thumb.

"She—she's really not too bad, is she, Mother?" Trying to be nonchalant, but with the lobes of his ears scarlet as geranium petals. At his age—a baby like that! Certainly the Revolution hadn't been good for children, making them—notice things, when they ought to be still playing with their toys.

"Not bad?" shrilled Hortense indignantly. "She—she's *beautiful*. Someday I'm going to be like that, and ride in a carriage with a gentleman in white satin."

A gentleman? Hortense would certainly have to be taught the difference between a gentleman and Tallien.

"Come along, my dears. It's time we got home."

She turned away down the somber rue du Bac, filled with big, empty houses with the "For sale" placards hanging from their gates. She felt as abandoned and unwanted as this empty street of abandoned mansions. She hurried her footsteps, and turned into the rue Saint Dominique. Here the sun shone. A more cheerful atmosphere altogether. The houses were smaller, and people lived in them. Coming into it was almost like walking out of prison a second time, out of the sour atmosphere of a dead past into a living present that stretched out straight before her, sunlit all the way.

Here at last was the house—953, rue Saint Dominique. It wasn't a bad house to live in. A wide, white, stone house, flat-faced and flush with the street. There were little wrought-iron balconies before the windows, some with bright flowering plants in them, so that they looked like cages full of gaily colored birds. There were two steps up to the dark wood door with the brass handle, there was a brass knocker in the shape of a mermaid. They could have done with a little polishing, but service wasn't easy to get these days. No, not at all a bad house. It was true she had only the second floor, she and

Desirée together. But the rooms were spacious, and the very
best people lived in cramped quarters, and were glad to get
them.

Eugène opened the door for her, and she went in, the children
behind her. The same smell. The faintly spicy odor of ancient
wood, the thin acidity of dust, and just a hint that the Duclos,
on the ground floor, were having a roast gigot for dinner. Not
really an atmosphere that would have been tolerated in one of
those great mansions of the rue du Bac, but living and human
and, after the prison stench, sweeter and purer than incense.

She climbed the stairs, feeling under her hand the familiar
smooth mellowness of polished wood with its little surface grit
of neglect. She remembered that one always had to be careful
not to touch it in going out, it left gray smudges on one's fingers.
Coming home, of course, it was different. Coming home—she
hadn't actually realized that this was truly what she was doing,
coming home, just as naturally and surely as though she'd
gone out only that morning for a few hours' shopping. She
began to run, laughing and gasping as she went. There was
Marie waiting for her just inside the open door—Marie with
her hard black eyes, her hard bony frame, and her heart inside
it that was as soft as a powder-puff.

Being squeezed by Marie was a little painful, rather like
being squeezed by the two wooden arms of a sign-post. Marie
was holding her at arm's length, looking at her with the accusing severity that with her took the place of emotion; frowning
silently at her as though she were a naughty little girl who
had stayed out late and ought to be slapped.

In the salon was Desirée, kneeling on the floor, rummaging
among a mess of things half out of the bottom drawer of a
mahogany tall-boy. How lovely it was to see Desirée like that,
not in an austere prison-yard, but just as she'd always been—
surrounded by mess and muddle, bits of silk and lace and ribbon
that she was eternally "tidying" by scrabbling about in it like
a clumsy puppy.

Desirée looked over her shoulder, shrieked, scrambled to get
up, caught her foot and nearly fell headlong in her rush across
the room, trailing a length of blue satin ribbon from her ankle.
Then they were in each other's arms, laughing, crying, saying
broken sentences and unfinished words.

"Dé-dé, my precious! I thought I'd never—"

"Jo-jo, my sweet! So you've—"

Certainly Desirée was the best friend anybody could possibly have. With her, you didn't have to be anything special—not a Viscountess or a sorrowing widow or a devoted young mother—you could just *be,* without thinking at all. Desirée was standing back now to look at her, laughing and pointing a mocking finger.

"Oh, my dear! Oh, Jo-jo! I'd forgotten already how excruciatingly comic our clothes were!" She clasped her hands together and sighed like a bellows. "It's the greatest tragedy of the Revolution, my dear! There's never been anything so awful—never! The fashions completely changed in less than four months. Nothing in our wardrobes of the slightest use any more. It's impossible—but quite impossible, my dear, to be seen in anything but Indian muslin, thin silk, or gauze."

She stood on one foot and disentangled the ribbon from her ankle. "What we'll do in winter, God only knows! But there it is, my love—all our velvets and brocades—rubbish, my dear, so much rubbish! As for that sort of thing you've got on—nobody but kitchen wenches and milk-maids would be seen dead in them now. I assure you, my sweet, the most awful tragedy that's ever happened. How we're going to live, I can't imagine."

"But you—you've got one of the new dresses. Let me see—"

Desirée spun round to show off her dress, which didn't seem quite necessary, as it was apparently exactly the same back and front—a long, straight, narrow skirt of mauve and white striped silk, beginning just under the bust and ending at the ankles, with above it a tiny bodice only a few inches deep, and little puffed sleeves well off the shoulder. At first glance, quite without style or distinction—yet when you studied it more carefully, you weren't quite so sure. It was always like that with new fashions, of course. Look at vaccination, for instance. At first, everybody had thought it quite disgusting, and a hideous disfigurement. Yet after the King and Queen had their children done, you could see for yourself the piquant attraction of the small round scar on the otherwise faultless skin of a lovely arm. Something like a beauty-patch. This dress with its severity of unbroken line made even Desirée, who was plump—or, to be quite frank, dumpy—look slim and graceful. What might it do for herself, with her long, straight legs, the clear, firm line of her neck and shoulders, and her really perfect bust. Yes, on the whole she thought there were distinct possibilities in the new fashions.

"What do you wear underneath?"

Desirée gave a shriek of laughter. "My dear, how excruciatingly comic of you! Underneath? Well, I have on a shift, of course, and I wear stockings—in the daytime, that is."

"But—but where have you got your bones?"

"*Bones,* my sweet? Nobody has bones any more—literally nobody. They simply aren't worn. Feel!"

Yes, it was true, Desirée was quite soft all the way down. No bones! Yet after all, that, too, was an advantage. The width of her waist had really been her only fault—but even that would be an asset now, for undoubtedly well-marked hips would never do under that narrow, clinging skirt. Yes, a straight up and down line—except of course for the curve of the breasts, which must obviously be encouraged—was unquestionably an advantage. She was quite sure she was going to like the new fashions after all. Simplicity, even severity of line, nothing to detract from the well-displayed beauty of a perfect bosom.

"Oh, take it off, Dé-dé, and let me try! Let me see! Where does it fasten? Let me—"

A man in a livery-coat too small for him came abruptly in, carrying a tray with a carafe of white wine, glasses, and a plate of little cakes. He hooked a chair out of the way with his foot, set his tray down with a clattering thump on a small table, said, "There you are," turned his back and went out, slamming the door behind him.

"Who in the name of Heaven—"

Desirée snatched a cake and stuffed it into her mouth. She gestured vaguely with her hand while she swallowed it.

"Oh," she said at last. "He's Gautier or Gontau, or some such name. Our new lackey—I beg his pardon, 'domestic official' is, I believe, the correct term. You didn't expect such grandeur, did you?"

"But—but who's going to *pay*—?"

"Nobody." She pushed forward the plate of cakes. "Have a cake, my sweet, and don't gape. With ten thousand people let out of prison in less than a month, there's any number ready to work for a roof and a meal."

What would Alexander have said, Alexander who used to enquire into the antecedents of a new domestic for as far as three generations back?

"Out of prison! But he—he may be a murderer, or a thief, or—"

"What of it?" Desirée, curled up on the couch, a glass of wine in one hand, a cake in the other, laughed. "The best people are murderers these days. As for thieving—" She gestured with her cake about the room. "There's nothing worth stealing here, so he's more likely to bring things into the house than take them out. So that's all to the good. But speaking of paying. Have you got any money? I literally haven't a pierced sou."

There was her hundred franc *assignat*— Her hand went to her bodice. But no, she'd thrown it to the jailer, thinking— That's what came of being generous to the lower classes.

"No, I haven't a sou, either."

She sat down abruptly. Tallien riding through the streets of Paris in white satin with that girl, Hoche somewhere in the north with his army, and she here without the price of a meal, literally without food to put into her mouth. She stared at the little cake in her hand through a fog of tears. Really not bad, those little cakes with the cinnamon in them, almost as good as the pre-Revolutionary ones. She was an unhappy, forsaken woman who could starve to death, for all anybody— There wasn't even Alexander now. Alexander! She looked up and laughed.

"What a fool I am! There's masses of silver and things at the Ferté-Beauharnais. I'll sell some of that. After all, the château's my property now, isn't it?"

Desirée shook her head. "Not a bit of it, my girl. It's State property. Only the State inherits from guillotined people. You ought to know that." She waved her glass and bit into her cake. "But don't worry. We'll manage somehow. We always have. After all, Marie's Jacques earns something with his cobbling, and Hoche's taking Eugène off your— But it's I that am the fool. I completely and utterly forgot!" She uncurled herself so abruptly that the wine spilled over her dress. She jumped to her feet, and dropped the glass and half-eaten cake on the floor.

"Fool! Fool! Fool that I am!" she chanted, twirling about on her toe. "I forgot all about Hoche!" She dabbed hastily at the wine stain on her dress. "The only rag I've got, and of course I would— But Hoche! There's a fine figure of a man, my dear. My compliments!" She kissed the tips of her fingers. "But as I was saying—Hoche left a packet here for you, when he came about Eugène. Where—?"

She stood on tiptoe to peer into a tall vase. "I usually put things in there, but it's not— No, I didn't think— Now where—

Oh, there it is! No, there—look, under these things I was tidying in the bottom drawer. I knew I put it somewhere safe."

There it was, lying half hidden beneath a little heap of crumpled silk stockings. A flat, white packet, tied with green tape and sealed with red wax. Quite official and important looking. The red seals on one side and on the other her name, inscribed in the clear, careful letters of a hand still conscious of the art of writing.

"Open it, Jo-jo! Open it! There may be money in it. He wouldn't write you a letter as thick as that, would he? Or would he? But open it quickly!"

How could she be quick, with the yards of tape he'd put on it? Not just ribbon, but hard, thick, cotton tape that you couldn't use for anything else afterwards, and that you couldn't break, not even untie, because of the wax smeared all over the knots. How thoughtless men were!

"Haven't you any scissors?"

"Scissors? Of course. Where—? Oh, here they are!"

The scissors were loose and blunt, and gnawed rather than cut, especially if you were in a hurry. But they did at last chew their way through the tape. There— But no, another wrapping, with another tape about it. What an extraordinary amount of time men wasted! Then inside that there was a letter folded about the packet, and that had to be torn off, too. Then— There it was! The neatest little packet of fresh-printed *assignats* you ever saw. And dozens of them—literally dozens—hundreds! Money! Enough money to last a life-time. At least, for quite a long time. Anyway, enough to buy clothes fit to be seen in, and not worry about anything, not anything at all. Not even about Tallien. How that girl *could*—!

A pile of *assignats,* as thick as a book, and as neatly put together. Money wasn't meant to be kept tidily bound up like that, heavy and dull as a book of sermons. It was meant to be like poetry, light and alive and free—like that!

With a sudden flinging up of both her hands, she tossed the packet to the ceiling, and stood with upturned face and outstretched arms, laughing to see it fly apart like a bursting rocket, letting the scattered scraps of paper flutter down about her. Money! Money from the sky, like rain.

An *assignat* glided obliquely towards the open window. Desirée shrieked, and snatched at it as it sailed past. "Jo-jo, you fool!

You fool!" She pursued it across the room, caught it, and brought it back to the table.

"How much is there?" she asked breathlessly.

"How much? I haven't the least idea. Does it matter? There's lots."

"Of course it matters. Jo-jo, you *are* a fool! How ever are we going to know how much we've spent, if we don't know how much we had to spend? You're so *unpractical,* my sweet! Pick it up, and let's count it."

They picked up *assignats* from the floor, from the chairs, from the mantel-shelf, and laid them on the table. They made a much more satisfactory pile just thrown loosely like that; they looked twice as many. It made you feel really rich to see them just tossed casually—

"Jo-jo, there was a letter wrapped up with them. I'm sure there was."

"Was there? Well, I daresay we'll come across it some time. Are there any more?" There was one, under the couch.

They went down on their knees, laughing, feeling for the *assignat,* pushing each other's hands away.

"I've got it!"

"No, I've got it! Let go!"

"Don't pull, you'll—"

With a tiny, rending sound, the *assignat* tore in half. They looked at each other with consternation on their faces.

How comic Desirée looked, vaguely waving her torn bit of paper, looking as scared as a little girl who's torn her best Sunday dress! She giggled. Josephine giggled. They sat back on their heels, facing each other, and threw back their heads and laughed till the tears ran down their cheeks.

Gautier—or Gontau—thrust his head in at the door, and contemplated them without surprise or interest.

"Your supper's ready, if you want it," he said.

CHAPTER

❧ VIII ❧

SHE WONDERED WHAT BARRAS WAS LIKE. HE WAS IMPORTANT, OF course. More important really than Tallien. She'd had a narrow escape with Tallien. But she'd make no mistake this time, there was no possible doubt now that Barras was the coming man. And he'd asked to meet her; it was his idea, this luncheon-party at Croissy.

Paul de Barras—ci-devant Count. A real gentleman, not like Fréron, who after all was only an over-smart man of fashion. Yes, a real aristocrat, a frequenter of Versailles. She stirred a little uneasily. But after all, people could go to Versailles quite often and not actually meet each other, couldn't they? Still, one would have to be a little careful.

She wondered how he would like her dress. At first she'd thought of wearing something gay, until she remembered the exuberant gaiety of the girl she'd seen with Tallien. One didn't compete with that sort of thing, one contrasted one's self with it. To do that properly one had to have something very special. It had taken a long time to find, and a great deal of money to buy—or it would, when she could pay for it. But there it was, spread out on the day-bed, waiting. A perfect dress, simple as moonlight, and as subtle. Gauzy Indian muslin, with no ornament at all, save in the weave itself, that made half-invisible silvery stripes on the soft transparency of the whole, like a luminous mist shot through with shining rain. An April shower of a dress, neither gay nor melancholy, but a tender blending of the two.

A carriage rattled to a halt in the street outside, and there was a beating of the mermaid knocker. She heard a shriek, and a scurrying sound like a frightened mouse from Desirée's room. With infinite precautions, for it was very nearly as fragile as it looked, she slipped the dress down into place, but she couldn't

63

fasten up the hook at the back until Desirée came in to have her own done up. Desirée wore a dress of champagne-colored linen with sprays of violets all over it, a band of violet ribbon under the bust, and three more about the edge of the skirt. Not a bad dress at all. Not a work of genius, of course, but not bad, and suiting her simple style of beauty really quite well. Desirée hooked her up, then stood back to look at her.

"Ravishing, my love—truly ravishing. Barras'll—" She sighed. "If only I could wear a bodice like that! But considering my architecture, I'm obliged to leave something to the imagination." She laughed. "Still, men's imaginations being what they are, I don't do too badly." She clapped her hands, and spun about on her heel. "It's going to be a lovely party, a lovely party!" she chanted. Then, sobering a little: "That is, if Barras hasn't forgotten to send the food."

Desirée's little country house at Croissy sat as artificially demure as a Watteau milkmaid on its green carpet of lawn. All in white, with scarlet roses at its bosom and a rakish little peaked bonnet of pink tiles on top, it sat smiling in the sun, all innocence without, a baggage at heart. Ravishing little house, that they hadn't seen for nearly a year. It sat content in the September sun that was nearly as hot as that of August had been, but mellower, less brutal and crude.

On the white painted door there were the round patches of pink with little grains of red still sticking to them, where the seals had been torn away. That was Barras' doing—Barras who, because he wanted a luncheon party at Croissy, could flick away Government seals as he would flick away crumbs from a tablecloth. Assuredly, this time there could be no mistake.

They went inside. The house was as it had been. Odd bits of furniture, some brought from Martinique, some picked up in Paris, some of precious woods of the Islands, some painted to hide the coarseness of their grain. It was like a little harlot, dressed in fine silk and cheap glass jewels, and like a harlot, kind and warm and generous. Today it was tidy, which was unnatural. That was because of Marie and her Jacques, who had come down the day before to set it in order. They dropped their veils and cloaks on the floor, and stood looking at each other. A party, a party at Croissy! The first really dress-up party since Robespierre's Reign of Virtue which, actually, had spoiled things much more than his Reign of Terror had done.

64

After all, people were being killed all the time all over the
world, and that didn't prevent other people from being happy.
But Robespierre had made it unfashionable to be happy, and
you couldn't struggle against fashion, could you? Now the
fashion had changed again, and there was going to be a real
party, with distinguished guests and elegant clothes and delicate
food.

"Food?" she said tentatively, and looked at Desirée.

Desirée echoed "Food?" a little blankly, then laughed. "My
precious, what a frightful thought! Suppose Barras— Let's go
and see!"

They rushed down the hall that divided salon and dining-
room, and along a narrow passage to the kitchen. It was all
right. Marie was there with her Jacques, and so was the food,
spread out on the big white-wood table that stood under the
window, with muslin over it to keep off the flies. There were
grain-fed Bresse chickens that Marie had roasted the day before
to serve cold with salad, splendid tongue in jelly, dainty gray and
white soles from Dieppe, and black-armored lobsters still vaguely
alive, moving feebly in their nest of wet sea-weed.

There were cakes from Frascati's and tarts from Méo's, enormous black grapes that looked as though they came from the
King's espalier at Fontainebleau, fresh figs from the south,
cheeses from the Brie, from Port Salut and Pont l'Évêque. There
were nuts from Grenoble and olives, green and black, from the
Midi. And, of course, from their own garden there were great
waxen Duchesse pears and rusty-brown Reinette apples. And
there, most divine surprise of all, was a little linen sack of
coffee—but real coffee, in the bean, not just ground-up scorched
barley with a little chicory added. Undoubtedly, Barras was a
man who could be trusted.

"Enough to feed an army!" cried Desirée.

"Yes," said Marie sourly, "provided your army's willing to
eat its chicken in its fingers and its fish raw. There's not a
dish nor a plate nor a pan nor a kettle that's fit to use. I've done
what I could with the birds, but I can't do your fish in a leaky
bucket, and that's all there is in the place." She stood resigned
and resentful, her hands on her hips.

It had always been like that, even in the old days. You bought
a dinner-service, and somehow in a month or two it was gone—
just gone. As for kitchen utensils, it seemed a pity to waste
money on such uninteresting things. But they'd managed some-

65

how. They used to borrow from the Pasquiers next door. Of course, the Pasquiers!

"Marie, are the Pasquiers back yet?"

"The young couple are. He came out of prison two weeks ago. The father's gone. So's the brother."

"Oh, how awful! Oh, I *am* sorry! Then they'll be able to spare plenty of dishes, won't they? Dé-dé, did you hear? Two of the Pasquiers are—are gone. Oh dear, how sad everything is! Jacques, take a basket and ask the Citizeness—no, say the Baroness de Pasquier, if she would be so extremely obliging as to lend us a few plates and dishes. Say enough for—how many, Dé-dé?"

"How many? Let's see. There's the Talliens, Fréron and his creature, ourselves, and of course Barras. How many's that? Seven—"

"Ask for a service for seven people, Jacques."

Jacques nodded, picked up a basket, and made for the door. He had been married to Marie for so long that he, too, was hard, bony, and silent, though not as much.

"Oh, Jacques, and glasses!" Desirée called after him.

"And a kettle for the lobsters and a pan for the soles," added Marie. Jacques nodded again, and went out.

Oh, and there was the coffee, too—the divine coffee. "Jacques! Jacques!" she called. "And a coffee-service! And don't forget the spoons!"

"I knew we should manage," said Desirée. "We always do. Let's get flowers for the table."

Jacques came back panting and heavy laden with Madame Pasquier's compliments and her best dinner-service, and they set the table with fine cut crystal and heavy, crested silver. Nobody's table could have looked handsomer or more elegant. You'd never imagine there'd ever been a Revolution or that anybody had ever been guillotined. Except for the difference of dress, it might still be '89—and except, of course, that Alexander wasn't there. But he'd never been there very often even then. It was rather amusing, really—two hostesses and no host. A carriage—

"Dé-dé! Somebody's coming already, and my hair—! Who is it? Look, quick!"

Desirée peered out of the window. "Only Fréron and his— his— It doesn't matter. There's plenty of time. But we'd better go up and get tidy."

They went upstairs, leaving Fréron to take care of himself, Fréron and his—well, to be quite frank, people called her his dry-nurse. Her name was Céleste, and that's all anybody knew about her, except that she had once been the sort of actress that can attract very young men to a very cheap theater. And that had been a long time ago. But Fréron clung to her as some men cling to an old pair of slippers. Not that anybody else wanted Fréron, of course.

When they came down Fréron was in the salon sitting on the couch reading a paper. Céleste was sitting on a straight-backed chair, looking at him with the large, fixed stare of a cow at its calf. He was slumped down on the middle of his back, with his legs sprawled out in front of him. He didn't get up. He threw his paper on the floor, yawned, hunched his shoulders, and drove his fists into his breeches pockets. He was being a lout to-day, and he was trying when he did that.

"*Assignats* have dropped to fourteen-hundred," he said. "I shall do nicely over that."

Céleste rose, picked up his paper, folded it neatly, and put it on the couch to his hand. She sat down again. She said nothing. Fréron flicked the paper onto the floor again with his finger, swung his legs up on the couch, and leaned back with his hands behind his head.

"Damn' tiring drive from Paris," he said, and closed his eyes.

Desirée giggled. They both crossed to Céleste and said, "Good-afternoon, Citizeness." She said, "Good afternoon, Citizenesses," without shifting her eyes from Fréron. "The heat makes him cross," she said.

They looked at each other, and went out through the long windows to the little portico in front of the house. They stood at the head of the steps, smiled at each other, grinned, giggled. They laughed, they shrieked with mirth until they were obliged to sink helplessly onto the top step. They snuffled into their handkerchiefs, looked at each other, and choked with laughter again.

"Our fashionable p-party!" squealed Desirée.

" 'The heat makes him cross'!" quoted Josephine.

"I'm—I'm so glad we d-dressed properly," choked Desirée. "Did you see his c-cravat? Like a bandage for the scrofula!"

"Our distinguished guests? . . . . And here come some more of them. Look!"

Through the tears in her eyes she could dimly see the shape of a carriage coming up the road towards the gates of the drive. A scarlet-painted carriage, drawn by white horses. Four of them—Tallien. She blinked, and clutched at Desirée.

"Dé-dé! It's Tallien and his—his—"

"Wife!" supplied Desirée. And suddenly the idea of Tallien's wife seemed funnier even than that of Fréron's dry-nurse. They leaned against each other and sobbed weakly.

Tallien and his wife! Still, they were guests and after all, Tallien was still Tallien. One couldn't sit there and shriek with laughter in his face.

"Dé-dé, get up! Stop it, and get up!"

They stood side by side, still shaking and shuddering with internal laughter. The carriage with the four white horses turned into the drive. It seemed to have a procession following it. All the villagers and peasants from the neighboring farms clustered about it so that its horses had to move at a walk; all shouting, cheering, crying, "Long live Our Lady of July! Our Lady of Mercy! Our Lady of Succour! Long live Our Lady!"

The cluster of humanity was, in a fashion, scraped off by the gate-posts, and stood outside in the road, still shouting and cheering as the carriage came up the drive.

It drew up with the four white horses jerked back on their haunches. Tallien got out and stood mopping at his face with a lace handkerchief. Then, as though by after-thought, he turned and offered his hand to his lady. She too got out, and came up the steps towards them.

Desirée gave a snort, then coughed into her handkerchief. It was scarcely to be wondered at, for certainly nobody had ever seen a more extraordinary spectacle than this. She was dressed in the thinnest apple-green silk, a long flowing robe fastened with a wide gold belt, and over it a shorter tunic with a gold tassel at each corner. About her neck was a great emerald pendant—or at least, a stone the color of emerald. She had gold sandals on her bare feet, and a gold band about her hair, that was dressed now in a huge, pointed knot at the back of her head. The sort of dress you saw on Greek statues. Only she wasn't a Greek statue, she was very Latin and very much alive—almost indecently so, every movement of her body showing plainly through her transparent draperies. She was handsome, certainly, but equally certainly quite without taste. Gold and jewels and silk for the country!

68

She could feel Desirée beginning to quake beside her. She stepped forward hastily. "Citizen, Citizeness Tallien—"

The Citizeness Tallien turned her back and stood on the top of the steps, waving her hand to her crew of rustic admirers clustered about the gate, still shouting for their Lady of July. Some people, of course, might call her a lady. She smiled at them, waved. She turned a radiant face to her bridegroom beside her and said in the most agreeable voice, "Couldn't you smile, you fool? Are you obliged to look as unpleasant as you are?"

She kissed both her hands to the crowd, laughed, and turned to her hostesses. "My dears, I have heard so much. . . . I have so wanted . . . and now at last. . . ." She sailed past them through the long windows and into the room. She waved airily to Céleste, crept up to Fréron still prostrate on the couch, and tickled his nose with one of the gold tassels of her tunic. He opened languid eyes, grasped her bare arm, and drew her down to sit by him on the couch. Céleste watched stolid-eyed. Tallien, sweating in plum-colored velvet, stood scowling in the middle of the floor. Decidedly, she had been lucky about Tallien. Just imagine if—

"I have seldom enjoyed more distinguished society, Madame de Beauharnais," said Desirée mincingly.

"The enjoyment is entirely yours, Madame de Hostein," she replied with a stiff bob. They grimaced at each other. She crossed to the mirror over the fireplace to rearrange her hair, disturbed by the breeze of out-of-doors. Presently the reflection of Tallien's hot, flushed face appeared beside her own. From behind her, with a sideways jerk of his chin, he said,

"What do you think of—her, eh?"

She pulled a curl away from her brow. "I think she's the loveliest woman I've ever seen. My congratulations, Citizen."

"Ha! She treats me like dirt, and looks as though she wanted to have a bath every time I touch her."

That was natural enough, wasn't it? Who wouldn't want to have a bath? She lowered her lashes, then half-raised them, looking at him under her lids in the glass.

"Oh, no! She's probably just timid. After all, you're—a great man now, Citizen Tallien."

Tallien grinned. "Timid? She's as timid as a she-cat. She's no gratitude. No manners nor morals, either."

Anybody could see that without being told. She took a little rouge-pot out of her reticule, and dipped her finger in it. She tilted up her chin and threw her head back, the better to see her lips as she dabbed at them. Her hair almost brushed his face. She had touched it with a drop of essence of jasmine. His nostrils flared, the red of his face deepened.

"I like a woman that's kind," he whispered hoarsely. "That's gentle and well-spoken. I like a woman that's—that's a lady. That's what I like. A lady. And I can pay handsomely for what I like. It's true, what you said. I'm somebody, now."

She could feel the heat of his breath on the back of her neck. Pah! It smelled of stale wine, and that disgusting pipe-thing he smoked. She smiled at his reflection. If only one could be quite certain, really certain. It was so easy to make a mistake, and even now— She let her lashes sweep down on her cheeks. She felt his body touch her own, the hot velvet of his coat against the bare skin of her arm. The things women had to endure—

"Present me, Tallien, there's a good fellow."

Tallien's pressure slid away, she saw his face jerk sideways, then disappear from the mirror. There was another face there in its place, a handsome, faintly-amused face under carefully waved, freshly-powdered hair. She stared into the mirror, then turned about.

The man before her was tall, well-made. Not too young. He wore a straw-colored coat of silk, but so dull it might have been linen, save for the suppleness with which it clad him. He had plain, very white batiste at neck and wrists.

Tallien had drawn back. He was scowling again. He hesitated a moment, then jerked his thumb at the newcomer.

"Barras—Josephine," he said, and slouched away.

The man before her bent his head, so low that she could see the knot of black ribbon at the nape of his neck. Without conscious thought, she sank in a reverence, as she hadn't done for these five years past. The man straightened as she swept upright. They looked at each other, and suddenly they were both laughing.

"Our friend's presentation is a little, er—Republican," said Barras. "But I trust that, nevertheless, it may be effective."

"I, too, with all my heart, Citizen Barras."

"'Citizen'?" He raised his eyebrows and smiled. "Surely, Madame, you and I—we can discard these childish formulas of

70

the new order? Especially now that you have so exquisitely re-minded me of the graciousness of the old."

She did curtsy well. She'd learned to do it at the Convent of Panthémont, while she was getting her divorce from Alexander. She'd watched the great ladies who were in retreat there, and learned a great many things.

Barras. She was talking to Count Paul de Barras, the future master of France. And she'd been right to put on the old-fashioned clocked stockings. They went well with his powdered hair. She swept down her lashes and laughed softly.

"But," she said, "I am afraid there is little of graciousness in a hostess who permits a guest to find his own way while she rouges her lips."

"No guest who is permitted to find his way to so charming a spectacle can have anything but gratitude in his heart." He looked at her steadily out of his handsome blue eyes in which mockery was but the thinnest of veils over his admiration.

She had forgotten that such men existed, men who could look at a woman as though—well, as though she were a woman, but with nothing in their eyes of the frank desire of a Hoche, the coarse lust of a Tallien, or the insolent appraisal of a Fréron. She looked down at her rouge-pot, and dropped it into her reticule.

He laughed. "We are both of us er—gracious persons, well-met in a singularly ungracious world." His smiling gaze rested on Theresia Tallien, still beside the recumbent Fréron, bending down so low to whisper in his ear that her bosom touched his coat; upon Céleste, who had slipped her feet out of her shoes, and was wriggling her cramped toes; on Tallien, glowering out of the window with his back to the room.

"Ah," she said, "but in these days, one cannot always choose one's company."

"To the contrary, Madame. I flatter myself that I can, that I have indeed, er—done so."

She was the Viscountess de Beauharnais, stepping from her coach for a few hours of tolerant amusement in the company of Count Paul de Barras among the vulgarities of a popular fair. Presently she—they, would drive away again, and—

"Mesdames are served," Jacques, in the livery-coat whose sleeves had been too short for Gontau's arms and were even shorter for his own, stood in the open door.

Desirée sprang up from where she had been sitting beside

71

Céleste, as though released from a penitence. "Without ceremony! Without ceremony!" she cried. "Everybody to seat themselves as they please!"

Theresia jumped to her feet, dragging Fréron with her.
Céleste, struggling with her shoes, said to nobody in particular,
"She'll make his head ache if she jerks him about like that."
Theresia and Fréron rushed hand in hand through the door,
with Céleste following anxiously after. Desirée smiled at the
morose Tallien, and put her arm through his. Barras inclined
his head and offered the back of his hand. She put the tips
of her fingers on it. More than ever she felt a looker-on, a
tolerant audience of the crude pleasures of that section of
humanity that didn't know how to be informal with courtesy.

She took little part in the conversation at table. She was the
Viscountess de Beauharnais, sitting opposite Count Paul de
Barras at a table that happened also to accommodate a flashy
man of fashion whispering improprieties into the ear of a
married strumpet, an aging drab who watched her man with
the eyes of a kicked bitch, and a half-drunken lackey with
sweat-stains under the arms of his velvet coat and dribbles of
sauce on his lace jabot, who sought her little satin slipper under
the table with his clumsy foot. How vulgar they all were! Except,
of course, Barras. The meal finally came to an end, and every-
one but she and Barras fled unceremoniously into the garden.
He was looking at her across the table, thinking, perhaps. . . .
Desirée, of course, had been too obvious, like a bourgeoise
mother leaving her daughter alone with the desirable young
man. She got up and walked towards the window, hesitating
there a moment. Barras was just behind her.

"Perhaps a little more, er—restful here than with the others,
don't you think, Madame?"

She started. "Oh! I'm sorry. I hadn't noticed— Yes, perhaps
you're right. These—affairs are a little fatiguing, don't you
find?"

She sank languidly into an easy chair by the window. He
brought a cushion and adjusted it at her feet, pausing for the
fraction of a second while his gaze lingered on them. She had
no need to be ashamed of her feet, even in the unflattering shoes
of the day.

Marie brought in coffee on a silver tray and set it near them
on a small table. Outside, Theresia tossed the emigrette, shrieked
with pleasure when she caught it, tossed it again, and shrieked

with even greater delight when it struck Fréron on the ear. She looked like a Romany woman in those garish silks of hers, only Romany women didn't show their legs like that. And her breasts, when she ran, under that flimsy covering that was no support at all.... And she needed support, however young she might be.

"Madame Tallien is very lovely, don't you think?" she said.

Barras shrugged very slightly. "She has the charm of all very young things—and their gaucherie, too. Young boys like green fruit. But for myself, who am old enough to shrink from crudities, I prefer the subtlety of maturity."

He sat close to her, attentive, concentrated, but without touching. It was strange how she hadn't realized—or had forgotten—how much more exciting the restrained intentness of a man could be than what was called the frankness of manners of today—the pawing and nudging, the rudeness that didn't even know it was rude, the insolence that thought it was wit.

She sipped her coffee. "It's good to taste real coffee again," she said, "after the imitations we drink now."

"Imitation coffee for an imitation society," he said. "For that is what our new society will be. A cheap imitation. Unless—" He glanced at her, then out of the window.

"*There* is the material out of which we have to make it. Tallien, son of a lackey, who has forgotten the virtues of his own class and cannot learn those of any other, successful through sheer force of brutality. Theresia Tallien, Spanish financier's daughter, married at sixteen, divored at eighteen, whose life from then until now has been equally divided between prison and Tallien's bed. Fréron, a clever, degenerate school-boy of forty. You, Madame—you, who remember Versailles—" He spread out his hands, and gave her the half-smile of his brilliant blue eyes.

Versailles. She looked sideways at his face from under lowered lashes. Was it after all a natural understanding that lay in his small smile, or was he adding her mentally to his imitation society? Did he know that she had never seen the palace save from outside, except once, when she had stood behind a wooden barrier and watched the King and Queen at their dinner?

She lowered her eyelids still farther, till they shadowed the limpidity of her eyes—then raised them with the suddenness of tiny up-flung wings, turning the startling blue of her gaze full on him. Men often forget what they were going to say when she did that, which was at times a useful thing.

His smile didn't change. "I can see what you are thinking, Madame. You are wondering why you never met me at Court— and if I am another imitation member of society. It is true I was seldom at Court—though only because most of my youth was spent with His Majesty's forces in India. But reassure yourself, Madame. The Blacas, the Castellanes, the Pontèves, are not ashamed to call the Barras cousin."

She made a small, protesting gesture. "I assure you, Monsieur, that no such thought was in my head. Besides, one can always recognize one's own kind, as it were, instinctively, don't you think? Especially—" She glanced out of the window. Fréron was in his shirt-sleeves now, Theresia's great knot of hair had sagged down onto her shoulders.

"Precisely," said Barras. "One's own kind. And because of that, Madame, you will permit me to speak, er—frankly, without restraint?"

"But of course." How frank was he going to be, how unrestrained? After all, even the strictest laws of good breeding didn't require a man to go on being respectful forever. She looked down at her hands.

"The Revolution," he said, "is finished. Remains now the task of reconstruction."

She moved her hands impatiently in her lap. How bored, how unutterably wearied she was by the Revolution! How unspeakably sick she was of forcing a smile to her mouth and animation to her eyes when men talked politics. As though it mattered! All that mattered was for everybody to be happy and to have plenty of money, then there wouldn't be any need for politics and revolutions, would there? You'd think men would have the intelligence to see that for themselves. Perhaps they had, and they did it on purpose, because it was one of those odd things they so inexplicably enjoyed doing. She turned her face to him, her mouth eager, her eyes expectant.

"Ah, yes, reconstruction. How passionately interesting a task!"

"Yes. And difficult. The Revolution, do you see, failed because the men who made it tried to turn the social structure upside down, the few at the bottom, the many at the top, like a pyramid balanced on its peak. It has of course quite simply fallen down, and all the stones of its different layers are inextricably mixed. Hence the necessity for an, er—sample of

74

each, to help match up the others by." He nodded towards the window.

She said, "Of course," and wondered what time it was. She watched the others in the garden. It might be vulgar to tear about on a lawn and shout, but it was more amusing than politics. And if you had to waste your time, as well do it pleasantly.

"Tallien, do you see, can draw the lower orders together, being himself of that ilk. Fréron can appeal to those who call themselves thinkers, for he, middle-aged buffoon though he may seem, has a sting at the point of his pen that a hornet might envy. Madame Tallien will collect the financiers about her, for she was born with her father's gold in her veins, and gold attracts gold, always."

Gold. Their thirty-seven louis—no, twenty-four. What had Desirée done with them? They had been—they must still be on the little bed-side table. And with Gontau alone in the apartment— Had they locked him inside? And the cat, too. Had they locked the door at all? Oh dear, that was the sort of thing that happened when Marie wasn't there. The cat, and Gontau, and the front door, and—

"How clearly you explain," she said, "so that even I can understand."

"Even—?" He raised protesting eyebrows, then leaned towards her. "As soon as I saw you, Madame, I recognized in you not only a woman of singular charm and beauty, but one, too, of intelligence and discernment. Otherwise I should have paid my compliments and searched elsewhere. As it is, I see that I have no need to do that, having already found perfection. · Yourself, Madame."

"I?" She started a little, and interest awoke in her eyes that were getting a little weary of being animated. He leaned still closer to her, his forearms on his knees, his loosely-clasped hands just touching the stuff of her skirt.

"You. If you will bear a little longer with my explanations? Theresia Tallien is opening a salon in what she calls her, er— 'Chaumière,' in the Allée des Veuves."

She smiled a little. Theresia would, of course, think it smart to give the name of cottage to a mansion on one of the most fashionable thoroughfares of Paris. He answered her smile with the quick understanding of his own.

"Gold must be tempted back to France. That, Madame, was

Robespierre's true crime—not that he killed a few thousand people, but that he denied the economic law of gold. Financiers, as is well known, are all artists at heart. But though they may admire a painting for its beauty alone, their admiration is much increased by a gilded frame. Madame Tallien's Chaumière will supply that frame. But, important though such a task may be, there remains a greater. We still have to restore to our social pyramid its upper layer, its supreme peak. The aristocracy."

"Ah!" She felt excitement moving within her. The peak? More than Queen. . . .

"For the peak, Madame, it will not suffice to choose haphazard among our stones. When all is said and done, they are all more or less of a shape, of a size. But the peak is different. If it is to fit, it must have its own particular form, made up of birth and breeding, of intelligence and charm.

"What I ask of you, Madame, not as a man to a woman, but as one patriot to another, is this. As Madame Tallien has consented to act as hostess to the lesser society of finance, I beg that you will condescend to do the same to the superior one of birth. That you will receive, entertain, welcome those members of the aristocracy that the clemency of the new Government permits to come out of hiding, or who may be tempted by it to return from their exile. Do you consent, Madame?"

Would she consent to offer hospitality, refuge, welcome, to those people who had refused her even recognition in the old days? If she were a vindictive woman, she would refuse. But she wasn't. She would receive them gladly, generously, without rancor for the past. They could come to her, poor souls, the Rohans, the Noailles, the Richelieus, the de Muns, her home should be open— Her home. This miserable little house at Croissy, with its two rooms below-stairs and its four above, the apartment of the rue Saint Dominique, with Desirée's litter in every room, and Gontau perhaps at this very moment taking down the curtains to pawn them. Could one receive even a Caulaincourt, a Montesquieu, in a room with Desirée's stockings on the floor and no curtains at the windows? Tears of vexation rose in her eyes. It was unfair, unjust. If Alexander had only had the good sense to make proper provision for her while there was still time!

"The necessary means would, of course, be, er—provided," Barras continued. "There is a little house—quite a charming little house, rue Chantereine. It belongs to Julie Carreau, Talma's wife. The lady being in financial difficulties, it seemed to me that an, er—discreet manner of offering assistance would be in renting her house for a year. I did so, little thinking"—he looked up at her and smiled—"that my poor crust of charity would be so soon returned. For there is the house, complete with all the amenities, save only a worthy tenant. There are delightful reception-rooms, and adequate stabling."

"Oh! But Alexander—my husband—took both our carriage horses to the Army with him. And lost them when he ran away from Strasbourg."

"Your horses were lost in service with the Army? Your husband had two carriage-horses, you say? Doubtless he had saddle-horses as well, certainly at least four, since he was a General. And, naturally, he was obeying superior orders when he, er—made his strategic retreat from Strasbourg, so they were lost on active service. The, er—Republic will of course replace the carriage-horses, Madame, and reimburse the cost of the others—together, of course, with that of the carriages, harness, saddles and equipment that a man of General de Beauharnais' position would naturally have possessed."

"You—the Republic is most kind—though, of course, one doesn't grudge any sacrifice made for the Nation. He—my husband, had some—most of our family silver with him as well. And of course the Ferté-Beauharnais confiscated—"

He bowed his head gravely. "The silver shall be replaced, Madame. As for the château—one must, of course, abide by the law. In any case, it would be well first to study the movement of land-values."

He put his hand very lightly over hers on her knee. "Believe me, Madame, you will not find the, er—Republic ungenerous if you will consent to render this service. As for myself—if you should still further deign to accord me the honor of your, er—consideration, you will find in me your most humble, devoted servitor."

How delightful was the delicacy of approach of this man of the world after the hot pressure of Tallien's body against her. "I can pay for what I want." "The honor of your consideration." No difference? There was as much difference as between swilling wine from the neck of a bottle and sipping it out of crystal. She straightened in her chair and said with dignity:

"The honor will be mine, if I can be of service to—to the Republic."

He raised her hand and kissed it, bending his handsome head very low. Still holding her hand, he drew her to her feet. "I have already kept you unpardonably long from your guests," he said.

PART II
1795

*"The ivy twines itself about the first tree
it finds; and there, in brief, is love's history."*

CAPTAIN BONAPARTE

*"Who is this General Bonaparte?
Where has he served? Nobody has
ever heard of him."*

JUNOT, PÈRE, 1794

CHAPTER

❧ IX ❧

HE READ SLOWLY, WITH FIXED ATTENTION FOR THE SHAPE AND
meaning of every word. He could, when he liked, absorb the
essence of a page almost as rapidly as he could draw his thumb
down its margin. But this was no "thumb" reading, this was
an imprinting on the memory for future reference. For very soon
that was all he would have left of his book, the pages of memory.

A book was worth more than a meal, of course. But when
one has already eaten one's meals and not paid for them. . . .
No book was worth a debt. Not even Montesquieu. Nothing
was so shameful, or so crippling to a man, as debt. So Montesquieu must follow Rousseau and the others to Fauvelet the
second-hand dealer, and Justat the wine-merchant must have
the fifteen francs that were his due.

It was strange that Rousseau could provide as much food for
the body as Montesquieu—Montesquieu, the only French writer
from whom no single word could be deleted without loss. Of
course, in one's youth one had intoxicated one's soul with
Rousseau, as had every other very young man with a soul
worthy of the name. But one sickened of it in the end. With
what relief one turned from that syrupy-sweet liqueur to the
clean, dry wine of Montesquieu.

He bent lower over his book. He coughed rackingly, with
a twist of pain between the shoulders. The advancing tide of
the night seeped into the room, spreading its first tenuous wash
over the page, graying the paper and blurring the print. He
bent still lower, his forehead pressed between his fists. Long
familiarity made it still possible for his eyes to grope their
way from word to word.

Outside, a clock struck five. At the last stroke he stirred, raised
his head. His hand went to his waistcoat pocket, and checked.

He had had thirty francs for the watch that had been his father's. To live, he had pawned his father's watch, while a man like Tallien, scarcely capable of reading the time, publicly flaunted the jeweled watch of a man he had murdered. Murder and corruption. The air of France reeked with it. Perhaps after all it would have been a cleaner thing to have squeezed out of it through the little window of Fort Carré, where he had been imprisoned—to have died quickly with the watch still in his pocket. He sat quite still, his hand at his waistcoat pocket, his eyes staring before him into the darkening shadows of the room. Everything was darkening. Soon the whole world would be as dark as blindness about him. Soon. . . .

He tautened his body, drew his empty hand away from his pocket. A man of courage despises the future. And in times of revolution a soldier had no reason—no right to despair. A soldier? He still had his uniform, his sword. His life, too. He'd been too insignificant for killing by a government that called itself merciful. Too important as well. Insignificant as a man, important as a soldier—an artillery man. You could stick a pair of epaulettes on the shoulders of almost anybody of reasonable intelligence, and make an infantry officer of him. But the artillery was different. It took six years to make even a Second Lieutenant of Artillery. So they'd let him out of prison.

Thrown him out, rather. Without trial. Without an opportunity to answer the charges against him, or to make charges of his own. They would spare a man for his physical skill or mental ability, but his spiritual integrity they would murder without hesitation. They hadn't declared him either innocent or guilty, but just ordered him to Paris.

Junot had come, too. A decent fellow, Junot. It would have been good to be able to see something of him, but one couldn't do that, for he had a little—a very little money that his father sent him. Junot, père, had been annoyed with his son, but he hadn't quite cut off supplies. Junot—indignant, resentful—had shown him the letter. "Why have you left Major Laborde? Why have you left your regiment? Who is this General Bonaparte? Where has he served? Nobody has ever heard of him." The old man was right. Nobody had ever heard of General Bonaparte. Probably nobody ever would.

Toulon? Any trained soldier—even an infantry man—would have known how to do what he had done. When your commanding officers were respectively a doctor and a painter, it was easy enough to seem to be a military genius by comparison. The painter and the doctor had been impressed. Nobody else had.

The proof—hadn't they, the new Government men, when he reported in Paris, offered him the job of pacifying the Vendée? He, an artillery man, to use his training and experience for the rounding up of a few poor devils of Royalists and priests? Work for the gendarmes. Naturally he had refused, as any other self-respecting soldier would have done. Since then the doors of the Ministry for War had been closed to him. Every door was closed. Even the door of his own home in English-occupied Corsica. At twenty-six he was struck off the active list like any doddering old veteran of seventy, while Pichegru beat the Duke of York in Holland, Jourdan drove Clerfayt out of Cologne and Coblentz, and Dugommier overwhelmed the Spaniards in the Pyrenees.

Outside, the quarter-hour struck. He turned his head to the right and stared out of the window against which he sat. All day, in the misty cold of mid-February, the Cathedral of Notre Dame had loomed gray and hard as iron. Now, as the setting sun guared redly through the fog, it glowed dully like a cooling ingot in a dying, smoky fire. The soul of France might be in Rheims, with the aspiring surge of its upward-rushing spires, but the heart of it was in Notre Dame, blunt-towered and strong-rooted. It was here that the Kings of France should have received their crowns. Rheims was of the spirit, aloof and mystic. Notre Dame was human, robust, and tolerant, without scorn for the market-women who haggled over their cabbages at her feet, or for the beggers who leaned their scabby backs against her skirts. The Revolution had dubbed her Goddess of Reason. But she was still Our Lady of Paris, unreasoning, patient, and very wise.

Ha! It was a long time since he had written poetry, and now wasn't the time to begin again. The time— Notre Dame had at least a reasonable and law-abiding clock at the service of those who had no watches. Half-past five. Fauvelet's shop would be closed by now. So, whether he wished it or not, he must remain the owner of Montesquieu and debtor to Justat for at least another twelve hours.

He stretched his cramped shoulders, rubbed his cold-numbed fingers together, and closed his book. The economic law forbade the lighting of the lamp at this hour. When one's ration of oil was limited to four hours' burning a day, one made the utmost possible use of one's supplies. Hence, the first hours of darkness must be used for the taking of exercise, of nourishment, and of relaxation. Then, after the final shutting of the door and window for the night, the lamp would serve not only for light, but for heat as well. That was one advantage of so tiny a room on the top floor of the Hôtel du Cadran Bleu—even a cheap reading lamp could give some faint semblance of warmth in so restricted a space. An even greater advantage was its price of three francs a week.

He got up, straightening his stiffened knees slowly. He coughed, and felt in his coat pocket for his handkerchief. With it, he pulled out a little slip of paper. He had forgotten that. Talma's theater-ticket. A fine actor and an honest man, Talma—suffering now because last year he had had the honesty and good taste to be revolted at the idea of celebrating on the stage the an- niversary of the murder of the King. He was out of favor over that, but still able sometimes to give a free ticket to chance acquaintances even less in favor than himself. A fine trait in a man, to give the little he could when there was no hope of return. Some day one would remember that. Some day. But it was the night that was coming now.

He stamped his feet to restore the circulation of his blood a little. He would go as far as the Palais Royal—Palais Egalité they called it now—and see whatever play his ticket admitted him to. At the Variétés Amusantes he would have at least a few hours' warmth and light for nothing. Warmth and light. The greatest gifts one man could give another.

There was food too, of course. He thought for a moment of his stomach. Undoubtedly he was hungry. Dine first? No. Since his stomach was already completely empty, it could not be more so in a few hours' time. Besides, by filling it as late as possible, it might not be entirely empty when he woke in the morning. He had no idea how long digestion took. At the Café Mécanique one could, by dropping one's coin into a slot, obtain little meat pies or slices of pâté, already neatly wrapped in paper. At the Café Corazza they didn't frown on clients who brought their own food—so there, with a cup of coffee added to the contents of one's little packets, one could dine very well for quite little.

He found his way down the narrow, creaking, unlighted stairs of the hotel, stumbling as he went in his boots that were too large for him. Impossible to get ready-made boots to fit. Some day he would have them made to his size.

84

He followed the rue de la Huchette to the rue Saint-Jacques, that in its turn led to the Petit Pont. He crossed the Parvis Notre Dame, and glanced up at the great bulk of the Cathedral. Only the tops of the squat towers were stained now with the sunset light. Dying torches held aloft above the darkening city. It was no longer towards Our Lady of Paris that the people looked for light, but to Our Lady of July—Our Lady of Mercy, and her satellites. Mercy, in that bloodstained crew? Barras, Tallien, Fréron—Theresia Tallien, who had been Queen of Bordeaux, and was determined, at all costs, to be Queen of Paris, of France?

He coughed in the foggy night air, and pushed his hands into his breeches pockets to find warmth. He had had as much as sixty-five francs for his overcoat, with his gloves thrown in for good measure. He crossed the northern branch of the river by the Pont au Change, then north along the rue Saint-Martin. There was traffic here, and one had to be careful of passing vehicles. When one's clothes had already been brushed to the very thread, one couldn't risk getting them splashed with melting slush. . . .

He turned into the rue des Lombards. Lombards. Money-lenders. There, of course, was where they would look for help, to the greater Lombard Street of London. They would pawn France to the money-lenders with far less compunction than he had pawned his father's watch. So far, they were living by the printing-press. The value of the *assignat* had shrunk so much that salaried people could no longer live on their earnings. Oh, the gentlemen of the Government managed well enough, of course. They had simply doubled their own salaries.

He turned into the thick shadows of the maze of little streets about the Central Markets. The air was heavy with the earthy smell of vegetables and the acrid tang of meat. Products of the land—of the peasants. Little enough of it, though. For the peasants were like other earth-rooted things, and they needed a well-regulated political climate or they wouldn't produce. Men like Barras and Tallien were apt to forget them. Yet the surface waves of political unrest could never die down until the great depths of the peasant-folk below were calmed and reassured.

He turned into the rue du Pelican, crossing the rue des Bons Enfants. A little farther along, and here was the Variétés. He paused and looked at the bill outside— "The Night of the Ninth of Thermidor." The thing had been popular last summer, just after Robespierre's death, while the people were still hysterical with relief over the end of the Terror. It was being kept alive now to bolster up the popularity of Barras and Tallien. Its own popularity was waning. The people were beginning to say that if they had been poor under Robespierre, then at least he had been poor with them—that if he had drained the country of gold, it hadn't gone into the pockets of speculators and thieving army-contractors. The people were beginning to say a great many things. They were hungry.

Still, whatever the piece might be like, there would be light and warmth inside the theater. And he was cold. Shudderingly cold. He found a coin, and bought a gazette of a vendor outside the theater. In the foyer was a great porcelain stove, ruddy with heat. He set a chair beside it, and sat down to read his paper.

More rats thrown to the terriers—Billaud-Varennes, Barrère, Vadier. There couldn't be many left that it would be safe to sacrifice. Treaty of peace between France and Tuscany. There would be peace everywhere soon. There had to be. War had been declared in '89 as a threat against Monarchy in general. It had been continued by the Jacobins to distract the attention of the people from home-affairs. It would stop now because foreign financiers wouldn't lend to a France at war. Not for patriotic reasons. Money has no nationality. But because the Republican armies of France threatened the very foundations of their system—loans and usury.

Prussia was ready for peace. She could afford to cede a little territory along the Rhine, if it left her free for another partition of Poland. Yes, there would be peace soon. Except perhaps with Austria. It seemed impossible that even a Government under Barras would permit Austrian troops to remain in occupation of northern Italy. Some day perhaps his plan for an Italian campaign would be read at the Ministry for War. Carnot was an able and an honest man. But honest men were at a discount for the moment, and with the advent of peace, even military ability would no longer be required.

The spectators were beginning to come in now. It was as he had thought—the people were no longer interested. This was a fashionable audience, or what passed for such in these days—women who threw aside sumptuous wraps to show the muscular arms and chests of washerwomen above the flimsy wisps of their dresses, and whose faces were better covered than their bodies with paint to hide their cold-grayed lips and cheeks;

86

young men who carried themselves like doddering cripples, their coats padded across their shoulders to make them look hunchbacked, their breeches fulled on the outside of the knee to make them look bow-legged, their enormous cravats swathing the whole lower part of their faces like slovenly bandages. Under the Monarchy, young men had powdered their hair in imitation of the gracious dignity of old age. These poor oafs tried to deform their bodies in imitation of its senile decay. There was a great deal to be learned from the dress of a people.

Everywhere in the crowd, of course, were Fréron's Muscadins —though there was little of the musk-scented sweetmeats from which they had taken their name about these young men— swaggering bullies in their caped, gray overcoats, their hats pulled over their eyes, their great clubs of sticks well in evidence. Safe behind the badge of their green satin cravats, they were at liberty to bully, torment, do violence to anybody they pleased. Sure sign of an impotent Government, that privileged class of legal brutality.

He found his way to the topmost gallery. That was the warmest place in a theater, and one could be alone, for none of that fashionable crew would deign to penetrate higher than the boxes —though most of them, a year or two ago, had been glad enough of the free spectacle of a Punch and Judy show.

The lights went out, and there was nothing left to look at but the stage, so one must look at that. The piece was of an incredible stupidity. Was it possible that men's memories could be so short, their understanding so limited, that they could accept that contorted parody of a public event that had happened not even a year ago? He heard a noble Barras spouting patriotic inanities, he saw a lofty-souled Tallien offering up his life for the good of his country. He watched the idiot caperings of an imbecile Robespierre, gibbering with guilty terror before the immaculate idealism of his murderers. He listened to the frantic applause of an audience that, a year ago, had cringed for the favor of a seat in the Jacobin Club wherefrom to applaud the Incorruptible. He felt a little sick.

Outside the night air was colder than ever, but it was clean. It stabbed at your lungs, but it didn't turn your stomach. He crossed the fore-court of the Palace, went through the portico and into the main gardens that were bordered on three sides by galleries which an impecunious and practical Duke of Orléans had lined with little shops to let. Here were light and animation and a babble of voices, for this was one of the favorite promenades of a promenade-loving Paris. He, too, joined the endless round of people, pausing here and there to stare in at a shop-window, to read a bill-of-fare posted outside a restaurant.

Here was the Café Foy, on one of whose chairs Camille Desmoulins had climbed to raise the mob for the storming of the Bastille in '89. Near to it was the Café of the Thousand Columns. He peered in, the better to see the mirror-lined walls that endlessly reflected the twenty columns the place actually contained. That was how mass opinion was formed; artificial repetition, until for one man's idea you got the fanatical creed of a nation.

Here was the cutler's shop in which Charlotte Corday had bought the knife for the killing of Marat. Surely of all political stupidities, political assassination was the least intelligent. Perhaps that was the meaning of the myth of the Hydra. Here was the Café Hollandais, with its hanging sign of a little gilded guillotine. The sign had been turned upside down, making of it a guillotine overthrown. Surely as simple and economical a way of changing one's political colors as could be devised.

He went on the Café Mécanique. Here he changed two hundred franc *assignats* for metal discs the size of silver franc pieces. He examined the cupboard-like compartments that lined the room, each with a notice on the door describing the nature and price of the contents. Many of them were empty, bread for sandwiches being unobtainable. The little meat pies were the best value for one's money, though apt to become a bit monotonous in the end. He dropped his coin into the slot he had chosen. There was a whirr of mechanism, and the cupboard disgorged two little paper-wrapped packages into the basket hung beneath to catch them. He picked them up and dropped them into his pocket.

He went out again into the arcade. He stopped in front of a brilliantly-lit eating-house, and stood reading the bill-of-fare posted outside. Here one could have a dish of hot Paris ham with eggs for 750 francs, a helping of turkey for 900. A forced peach cost 575, a cup of coffee 200, and seventy-five must be paid for salt. There were a hundred items at like prices to be had by those who could pay. Every day there were those hundred different items, for that was the boast of the proprietor. Was even the gaming-house next door quite as shameless as that, in a city where the bread-ration was down to a quarter of a pound a head?

88

And there were fifteen such places in the Palais Egalité alone. Yet there was something to be said for these new eating places, these restaurants as they were called. They might yet prove to be one of the few useful things that had come out of the chaos of the Revolution. This one—Robert's—belonged to the ex-chef of the Archbishop of Aix. Many other chefs of great men, left to their own resources when their masters emigrated, had followed Robert's lead, putting their skill at the service of the public, instead of one man only. They profiteered shamelessly, of course, but there was something in the idea. Suppose one opened restaurants in the popular quarters of the city, and equipped them modestly, on premises with low rents. He took out his notebook, balanced it on the polished brass rail that protected the restaurant window, and began to set down figures.

He thought of his mother's great stone kitchen in Ajaccio, filled with the rich, warm smell of figs boiling in honey-syrup, and at the end, the kettle to scrape out with a wooden spoon. Yes, even at seventeen, when he was a Lieutenant with an epaulette on his shoulder, he had had the kettle to scrape out. Nine years ago. Nine years had brought him from the sane occupation of pot-scraping in the rich simplicity of a Corsican kitchen, to the madness of planning, in a bitter cold Paris night, how to fill ten thousand stomachs when his own was empty. Still, better to concentrate on the filling of other men's stomachs than on the impossibility of filling your own.

> *"Josephine would drink gold from her lover's skull."*
>
> BARRAS

CHAPTER

X

HER KNEES MADE TWO LITTLE PINK AND WHITE CORAL ISLANDS above the perfumed water of her bath. She amused herself by alternately raising and submerging them, making small tidal-waves that rushed in miniature fury from side to side of the bath.

A real bath, of pale marble that you could actually lie down in full length. She'd never imagined that the "amenities" of her little house would include so breath-takingly modern a luxury as that. In the whole Palace of Versailles there hadn't been such a thing. The Queen herself had had to sit crouched in a tub on the floor, while people brought her hot water in buckets. French people didn't understand the real pleasure of bathing. They took baths from a sense of duty, or because the doctor ordered it. Not oftener than necessary. Never for the joy of the thing. Islanders were different. Perhaps because their island itself lay eternally luxuriating in its ocean bath. Even at the end of six months it hadn't begun to pall. She'd had it completely lined with mirrors. That had cost a good deal, of course, for the best mirrors come from Italy, and prices had gone up because of the war. But it never really paid to buy anything but the best.

After she'd finished doing the bathroom and her bedroom, there hadn't been much money left for the rest of the house. She'd had such original ideas too for the salon and dining-room. Well, it wasn't her fault if they hadn't been carried out. Barras wasn't always as generous as she'd expected him to be. He liked to examine bills and add things up. She sometimes wondered if he were quite so well born as he pretended.

Still she had the bathroom and her bedroom, both admirably furnished. She couldn't very well ask Barras for more money just yet, since the furniture-dealer—an intelligent, understanding type of man—had listed the mirrors and the fur carpet on his bills as dining-room and salon furniture. So that those two rooms she'd had to do as best she could with the odds and ends she'd had at the rue Saint Dominique apartment. She was sorry to have had to take the things; they left a good many blank spaces in Desirée's rooms.

Some day she would have to try to go and see Desirée; she wasn't one to neglect her old friends. But when one was prac-tically earning one's living, one couldn't give up much time to pleasure, could one? Anyway, Desirée would understand. She was a very understanding person—though just a little frivolous, of course. She'd given up the furniture without any difficulty. And after all, if you were going to entertain aristocrats, you couldn't do it in a salon with no furniture in it—not even if the aristocrats were returned emigrés who, for the past two or three years, had been living abroad on the thinnest kind of charity.

Not that a great many aristocrats had come back. Somehow they didn't seem to like Barras much more than they'd liked Robespierre, which wasn't very intelligent or very grateful of them, since he'd made it quite clear they wouldn't be guillotined. Up to now, at least, her salon of breeding hadn't been quite so successful as Theresia's salon of wealth.

Out there in the bedroom a sweet-scented fire of pine wood was burning, and before it, stout and snoring, was Fortuné. Fortuné was a pug, with a snail-shell tail and a face that looked as though it had been made of crumpled velvet and not properly stuffed. When you held him up against your own face the contrast was amusing. Several people had remarked on it.

Louise was moving about in there, laying out her things for the evening. She was sorry to have lost Marie, but one couldn't take everything away from Desirée, could one? Besides, Louise was smart; she wore a dainty lace cap and a tiny muslin apron no bigger than a handkerchief. She knew how to dress hair and how to do a complexion, and she said "Madame," instead of "My dear," or "My love," as Marie used to do.

Of course, she'd never forget the gratitude she owed Marie— nor the money, either. Was it a thousand, or two thousand francs? She'd give her double whatever it was, anyway. Nobody could accuse her of forgetting her friends, however humble, or of not paying her debts. Though just at the moment, when she hadn't enough money even to furnish her house properly....

"It is time, Madame." Louise, holding up the huge bath-towel that had been warming in front of the fire. Oh dear, how fatiguing life was! If only one could go on lying eternally in warm scented water, how perfect everything would be! But when one was actually earning one's living—well, one had to earn it, didn't one, however exhausting it might be. And Theresia was incapable—but literally incapable—of arranging a dinner-party by herself. Tact was a thing Theresia lacked entirely, so that the most unlikely people were seated together. Otherwise, once you really got to know her, she was really a sweet child. There was no affectation about her; she was perfectly frank and understood frankness in others. And she'd been very helpful over the bills....

She sat before her mirror, watching Louise do her hair. Yes, the effect was good. Charming, but at the same time dignified.

Rather like the wigs of Louis XV's time. As a final touch Louise sprinkled on gold-dust from a little silver pot like a pepper-caster.

Then she brought the dress—a new dress. She had to go on having new dresses, otherwise she'd have no money to spend. This one, for instance. The little gold stars embroidered all over it were of tinsel thread, but the dressmaker—a very sensible woman—would charge for real gold thread on the bill. Then when Barras paid, there'd be something left over, wouldn't there? Barras complained that she was extravagant in her clothes, but it wasn't her fault. If he gave her more money she wouldn't be obliged to buy dresses she really didn't need....

Louise went to the door in answer to a knock.

"There's a young officer downstairs asking for you, Madame. A messenger from General Hoche."

Hoche! She hadn't thought of Hoche for months. It would be awkward if he.... The white fur carpet, the sumptuous bed....

"Does Madame wish him to come up?"

How stupid! It wasn't Hoche himself, only a messenger. An officer. A young officer.

"Go down and see what he's like first, Louise. Some of these Republican officers—"

Hoche. Men were so funny about some things. They talked a great deal about liberty and equality, but when you took them at their word, they didn't like it. And she didn't owe Hoche anything, did she? It was Tallien, not he, who'd got her out of prison. He wasn't even paying the rent of this house. Of course, she hadn't stopped him sending the money, because that would mean explaining, and explanations were so difficult by letter. One didn't want to hurt the poor man's feelings. But he wouldn't be difficult to manage when the time came. Soldiers weren't. Still, she must think of something to tell him. Nothing that wasn't true, naturally. But there were so many different ways of telling the truth.

"He is quite a presentable young man, Madame. Madame has an hour to spare."

"Ah! Well— Yes, send him up."

Louise picked up Fortuné. He snarled and wriggled, but couldn't reach her hand, because she held him prudently by the scruff of the neck.

"Oh, poor Fortuné! Louise, must you—?"

"Madame knows that he always bites Madame's gentlemen," said Louise firmly.

So he did—jealous little darling that he was! It had been amusing while he was still a puppy, but now there were some men who didn't like it. Especially men with silk stockings. Louise went out with him dangling at arm's length.

She got up from the toilet-table and wrapped her dressing-gown about her. It was a nice gown, white velvet, and velvet was so difficult to get these days. She wondered whether Gontau —was that his name?—had managed to sell Desirée's curtains for her. It seemed so long ago, all that sordid haggling and bargaining. So undignified and insecure. Well, she was secure enough now, so long as Barras—

She reclined on a day-bed drawn up before the fire. She arranged the folds of her gown. The skin of her ankles and insteps was as white as the velvet itself. The little gilt mules barely covered her toes, but she had no reason to hide her feet.

"The young man, Madame."

Louise stood aside to let him enter, then went out and closed the door behind her. Yes, he was quite presentable. Even attractive. And very young. Not more than twenty, probably. He was tall, and his uniform became him very well indeed. She lay back against the cushions, and her gown slipped open a little. She drew it together slowly, and held it to her bosom. He stood awkwardly stiff, fumbling with his hat, staring, then turning his eyes hastily away. She saw the blood rise under the sun-darkened skin of his face.

"Monsieur—?"

"Captain Plessis, aide-de-camp to General Hoche. And—and the Citizeness's—Madame's obedient servant." He bowed with a sudden, angular jerk, like a crane spearing a fish. Not used to polite society, the lad. Yet he was doing his best, and that was more than you could say for most of them. He was looking at her again now, but clung to his post by the door, as though it were a sentry-box.

"I—I am late, Madame—I see the—the hour is inconvenient. But I went first to the rue Saint Dominique—General Hoche told me—"

"Yes, yes. I've moved, you see. Just moved. I haven't had time yet to notify all my—friends. You have a message—? Suppose you come a little closer—then we won't be obliged to shout at each other across the room, will we?"

He came forward, walking across the white carpet as though it were glass. They were really rather charming, these simple, naïve boys. He stood at the end of the couch. She moved her foot in its little gilt mule. He glanced down at it, then raised his eyes hastily to her face.

"General Hoche's compliments, Madame—and he hopes to be in Paris within two weeks, and will do himself the honor of paying his respects."

She'd always said that soldiers were easy to manage. Two weeks' warning— She smiled. "Why then I shall see him, shan't I?—so that I needn't bother you with questions—about him. Need I?"

"No. No, Madame."

He had a long, oval face, gray, dark hair and eye-lashes. From the Touraine, probably. They produced good-looking men in the Touraine. Gentle, too, and with a natural courtesy that didn't come from teaching.

"You are from the Touraine, Captain?"

"From Amboise. Yes, Madame."

"What is it like, that part of the country?"

"It is very—beautiful. I haven't seen it for three years. Not since my last leave. After Valmy."

Oh dear, now he was going to talk about Valmy. Every man in France seemed to have been at that battle, and every man wanted to talk about it. You'd think they'd want to forget things like that, wouldn't you? But men were so funny, and you had to humor them.

"You were really at Valmy? I've always wanted to meet— But bring a chair, sit down, and tell me all about it—all about it."

He brought a chair and sat at the foot of the couch. She lowered her chin a little, opened her eyes very wide, and fixed them on his face. If you did that, you could give the impression of concentrated attention without really having to listen at all. After all, you had to let men talk about the things they imagined to be important. Her mind wandered...what was he saying now?

"But you should have seen Wattignies, Madame! There was a soldier's victory. It was beautiful, Madame. Beautiful."

"You were actually at Wat-Wattignies? Oh, but you must tell me—you must explain it all to me."

He told her. He leaned forward, elbows on knees, eyes brilliant, and told her. She could see the clock over his head. An hour, Louise had said— He was very attractive in his eagerness of a young fighting male. It was almost worth having to listen, for the pleasure of watching him. If only they didn't keep on and on so. She smothered a yawn, and glanced at the clock. Still he went on—

"What a day, Madame! Quite perfect. Beautiful."

He seemed to find beauty in a good many strange and not very interesting things. She let her hand slip from her bosom to her lap, and her gown opened a very little.

"Then you find everything in the Army—beautiful, Captain?"

His eyes darkened, and his young brow was wrinkled by an anxious frown.

"It was, Madame. But now—now we're afraid—" He spread out his hands, then let them drop between his knees again.

"Afraid? I thought soldiers were never afraid."

"Of battles, no, Madame. Of treachery—yes. We have fought for over three years—for the Republic. Now there is talk—it is said—that the new Government, when it is set up, intends to recall the Bourbons. The old King wasn't killed just to make room for his brother. We'd—we'd rather have had Robespierre than Barras, Madame, if he's going to do that."

"Robespierre! But he was a murderer, a—"

"Maybe, Madame. He killed people. We can understand that. But he didn't sell them for his own profit. He didn't sell the Republic—the armies— That's what we're afraid of. And because we're afraid, the war isn't—isn't—"

"Beautiful?"

"Yes, Madame, that's it. You are understanding. The war's not beautiful any more, if we don't know what we're fighting for."

Not know what they were fighting for? Why should they know? You didn't tell your cook why you were having a dinner-party, did you? That's what all this talk of liberty and equality did for these lads—put ideas into their heads that did them no good, only tormented them and made them unhappy. There were more—beautiful things in life for young men of his age to think about than Republics. She moved her foot sideways a little, so that the toe of her mule touched his knee.

He flushed darkly, withdrew his knee, and said, "Pardon, Madame."

She looked down at her hands, then let her lashes sweep up,

without raising her head. She swung her foot gently, and the little mule, held only by her toes, fell to the floor.

"Oh!" she cried. "My shoe! Captain Plessis, would you . . . ."

He groped on the floor for it with his hand, but his eyes didn't shift from her foot. Well, it was worth looking at, wasn't it? Quite a perfect foot, really.

"Captain Plessis, be good enough to put on my shoe. My foot is cold, it is—"

"It—it is beautiful, Madame. Beautiful!"

These poor lads of soldiers, cut off from all human contacts. . . .

Whatever they said, a Republic couldn't be a very inspiring thing to fight for. Perhaps he'd find his war a little more satisfactory now. At least, she'd given him something better than politics to think about, something more—beautiful.

> *"Until then, women had never been*
> *kind to me. Madame de Beauhar-*
> *nais was the first to encourage me.*
> *It intoxicated me. I addressed my-*
> *self incessantly to her, and fol-*
> *lowed her everywhere. I was pas-*
> *sionately in love."*
>
> NAPOLEON

CHAPTER

❧ XI ❧

MOODILY HE FOLLOWED THE RIOTERS ALONG THE RUE SAINT-Honoré. Not that he liked riots. It was only that today he felt he would like to insult Deputies, throw stones at them, threaten them with bodily injury. Deputies were men. You couldn't insult a woman. Not in her own house. Though she apparently could insult people under her roof. Shrieking with laughter in his face. Mirth seemed to be the only emotion he could awaken in women. To them, he was comic. Very well then, he was comic, and that was an end of it.

Beside him, the torrent of angry men poured on towards the

Tuileries. Some whirled their leather belts in the air, shouting, "The empty bellies against the putrid bellies!" Some shook labor-soiled fists above their heads— "The black hands against the white!" A broad-shouldered laborer snatched at an apprentice-lad standing pressed back against a wall, and dragged him into the angry flood. "If you have no weapon," he cried, "then dig up your father's bones for a cudgel to break their heads!"

Fitting symbol. For that was what they were doing. Digging up the rotting past to threaten the present with. Jacobin rioters, Royalist plotters. They never had anything new to offer in place of what they destroyed. They tore down something evil, perhaps—but because that was the end of their imagination, something even more evil took its place. For evil always acts more promptly than good, as poison works more quickly than medicine. They tore down the King, and got Robespierre in his place. They tore down Robespierre, and Barras had climbed up. Now they were trying to tear down Barras—and what would they get in his place? They had nothing to offer but the bones of their fathers—Royalist bones, Jacobin bones—things not only dead, but rotting and stinking with the reek of vengeance.

But these people couldn't even destroy any more, for every riot led to a further scattering of the bones of the dead. Every upheaval brought exile and death to such of the old Royalist and Jacobin Deputies as were still left above ground.

At the Church of Saint-Roche the mob swung left and towards the Tuileries. This was a very spider-web of narrow streets and alleys, with here and there an important building caught like a fly in its meshes. The mob had flooded through into the Tuileries gardens, and was massing before the Palace. He stood on the Terrace of the Feuillants, looking down upon it. The sentries at the top of the steps crossed their bayonets. They were buffeted and driven aside as the river of humanity poured endlessly into the gardens. Then through the open door of the Palace another figure appeared, black-coated, and puny as a beetle at that distance. A Deputy of sorts. He was speaking, but his voice was inaudible over the roar. He was raising his arms, spreading out his hands. The usual gesture of the placatory politician. Still, the fellow had courage—

Those in the forefront of the mob halted to listen, but those behind pushed on, crying, "Bread! Bread, not words!"

Then from somewhere, starting with a single voice but echoed

97

and re-echoed until it rose to a dull, rhythmic thunder, the terrible battle-cry of the Paris streets—"Kill! Kill! Kill!" A tossing, angry wave swept up the steps, engulfing the gesticulating speaker. For a moment there was a surging whirlpool of furious movement. Then, high above the tossing surface, on the end of a pike, a head—

The mob howled with delight, and swept on into the Palace.

The bitter taste of nausea rose at the back of his throat. They had won their horrible little victory, but—what then? They wouldn't even know what to do with it. And a man was dead. Not dead purposefully on a battle-field, but kicked by wooden sabots to a death that could profit nobody, accomplish nothing.

What else but death could be accomplished? The Revolution itself was dead. The "putrid-bellies" who had gorged on its body clung desperately to power because they must rule or die. As for the people—they must starve to death, or call for help on a dead king or on the corpse of Robespierre. The whole nation was gripped in the twitching paralysis of death.

Yet, since twitch it did, the heart still beat. The strong, vigorous, fighting heart of the Army. The Army was still alive. And some day, because it was the only healthy, disciplined force still left in the country, the "putrid-bellies" would be obliged to call upon it to protect their miserable lives and their filthy loot. When that happened—when thieves and assassins called in the police to save them from their victims—then something might be done.

He turned his back on the Tuileries and began to walk along the Terrace des Feuillants, that was like a raised boulevard between the Palace gardens on his left, and the maze of narrow streets and jostling buildings on his right.

Already they—the "putrid-bellies"—were beginning to shake the dice for that last dangerous throw for power. Oh, he hadn't been deceived by the affability, however carelessly-friendly it might seem. He knew that the lion doesn't call on the mouse unless it knows itself to be inextricably netted. Barras hadn't deceived him with the apparent casualness of his meeting, the cordiality of his greeting. He had passed Barras many times before in the corridors of the Ministry for War, and might have been a chair for all the interest he'd aroused. Until that particular day. A week ago today.

The first visit he'd paid to the Ministry since they'd definitely struck him off the active list. He wouldn't have gone then, save

98

for the utter desperation of his need. He had gone from office to office. In some he'd been listened to with indifference, in some with amusement, and in some not at all.

It was outside the last door that he met Barras—a Barras who held out an affable hand saying, "Ah, but surely it is, er—ah, of course, General, er—Bonaparte. We last met, if I remember rightly, at Toulon." The cynical effrontery of the man—saying "We last met when I was engaged in wholesale murder," as calmly as though he said, "When I was on my summer holiday."

"You have been bearding the, er—beaureaucrats in their dens, General? But there's little to be had from them. They demand their printed forms, their rubber stamps, their signatures, eh? But if I can be of service—such little influence as I have, as Commander-in-Chief of the National Guard—"

A Commander-in-Chief who didn't even know how to protect the seat of Government against a handful of half-starved rioters!

"Soldiers should stand by one another in a civilian world, should they not? Just now, urgent affairs— Shall we say then, at Madame Tallien's, a week from to-day? You will have only to command me, General, er—Bonaparte—"

A soldier, that?—making his appointments in a woman's house ——and another man's wife at that? A shameless, brazen-faced politician, not so fit for authority as the youngest drummer-boy in the army.

"A week from to-day." Oh, he had gone. One may starve for the sake of one's spiritual integrity, but one can scarcely go naked. The first has dignity, the other is simply—comic. There was dignity in standing on your own feet. There was none in being obliged to stand because, when you sat, you displayed a darn on the left knee of your breeches. So he had gone.

He came to the end of the Terrace des Feuillants, and stood, elbows on the balustrade, looking out over the Place de la Révolution to the wooded Champs Elysées beyond. There again, a mass of trees whose curving paths gave not more than a hundred yards of vista in any direction. An army could ambush there unseen. If one ran a broad avenue straight up the slope of that wooded hill and on its crest placed perhaps some imposing monument— It would be handsome in the extreme, impressive. And from the Palace one would have a clear line of vision—or of fire—for at least a couple of kilometers.

He had gone. He had been announced, and shown into a great salon on the ground floor. A room all gray and blue and mauve.

99

A beautiful room, and apparently simple. But he knew the price of such brocades and silks, such deep-piled carpets. He had made it his business to inform himself. Prices were the fever-chart of an ailing nation. The dozens of candles in the crystal chandeliers, at the fifty-five francs the pound they cost, would alone have kept a poor man's family in food for a month.

The room was full of people—men and women sitting talking to each other, sipping at liqueurs or coffee, or strolling about, cup in hand. There was music, a woman singing, accompanying herself on an instrument of sorts—harpsichord, clavichord, piano-forte, he didn't know which. One of those tinkly things.

Because the music didn't stop when he went in, he stood there by the instrument, waiting. The singer had a small voice, but sweet in a strange, husky fashion. She was singing a sentimental Italian love-song, such as gondoliers sing on the Venetian canals, under the moon—insipid, smooth, and shapeless as a sucked lollipop. He stood awkward, uncomfortable, waiting for it to end.

"*—ti amo, amo, amo, si amatissimo amante,*" sang the slight voice, and sank to silence. Then it had lifted again.

"General Bonaparte—you who speak Italian—is my accent very dreadful?"

He had said, "Yes." Just "yes," not anything more. He didn't even know at the time that he had said anything at all. For as she spoke, she slowly raised her eyes and looked at him.

Her eyes were blue. Or he thought they were. Violet. A color unique, indescribable, without a name. Like the sky over Paris in the evening, when there was no moon and the stars were out. Profound but luminous, brillant but tender. They were like— But why try to compare what was incomparable?

Looking into those eyes he had felt— He didn't know what he had felt. He remembered once, as a boy, he had seen from the crest of the Corsican cliffs a ship close in to shore, one of the new French frigates, all strength and speed and grace, the loveliest thing afloat. The exquisite shock of it had made the scalp tighten and tingle on his head. But it wasn't like that, a thing of the senses alone. This was something behind the senses, deeper, graver. . . . He remembered, at seventeen, giving for the first time, of his own authority, the order to fire—and hearing his own voice answered by the crashing thunder of the guns. Accomplishment, the shock of power. Not like that either.

Something more profoundly intimate. Like— Like a new-forged sword, white-hot and plunged suddenly into cold water. A shock like that. The shock of tempering, of fulfilment. Dead iron turned to living steel in an exaltation of pain, unbearable and beautiful. A thing incomparable and nameless, since it had never happened to any man before. It couldn't have, or there would be a name for it.

He didn't know how long it lasted. Such things are timeless as well as nameless. It ended with another voice, a voice that said, "There's the truth for you for once in your life, Josephine. ... Now come and tell the truth to me, too, General."

Josephine—

She had smiled faintly, risen from the instrument, dropped him a little curtsy, and moved away to mingle with the company. Moved was the word, not walked. The firmly delicate onward movement of the ship through water. It was only then— only when she was gone, that he remembered the brutal crudity of his "Yes." And not even the truth. Her accent was like gentle water, rising and falling softly, without ripple or wave.

Madame Tallien touched his arm, and said again, "Come...."

The sun was setting now behind the trees of the Champs Elysées. It glowed hotly through the chinks in leaves and branches, like live coals in a brazier. He clasped his hands behind him and turned back along the way he had come, treading slowly on the heels of his retreating shadow. The gardens were empty now. The small bubble of popular anger had burst and dissipated in a little wisp of steam. But it couldn't go on. The bubbles would go on rising and bursting, until at last the pot boiled over, and then—

He'd sat before Madame Tallien's couch, forgetting the darn on his knee, not thinking even to cover it with his hand. He'd sat there listening but not looking, his eyes, over the back of the couch, searching the crowd, among which, somewhere, she moved—Josephine....

Madame Tallien had talked, and he had answered—questions about his youth in Corsica, about his brothers and sisters, about his army service—what he had done in the past, what he hoped to do in the future. The future. Somewhere, hidden in the crowd of people, Josephine....

"...Barras—so many calls on his time. You will understand his absence, and forgive. But any service he can render you— through me. You have only to ask—"

Not seeing her, not conscious of her save as a vague, questioning voice, all his own consciousness out there among the crowd, searching, he had answered. He had named the urgent necessity, the desperate need, that had brought him there.

It was then that she had laughed. A laugh vulgar, strident, insulting, thrown in his face like the dregs from a wine-cup. The stain and sting of humiliation, jerking him back from his quest to the woman who mocked at him with her laughter. He could only stare at her, numbly immobile, as he had seen wounded men stare at their hurts.

"You want— But how comic, how sublimely funny! Your modesty, your almost indecent modesty! Everybody else, an army corps at the very least! But you—" She laughed again, stretched out her hand, and touched the darn on his knee. The touch of her finger, like the sting of red ants on lacerated flesh. The numbness left him, and he jerked to his feet.

"Oh, there's no need to look so fierce, General. You shall have them, your breeches—word of honor of Theresia, you shall!"

With the ceasing of her laughter all other sounds in the room had ceased too. All about him was a malicious, listening silence. All about him were faces, turned towards him—not openly laughing, but narrow-eyed with mocking amusement. Eyes that flicked over him from head to feet, then slipped aside to meet other eyes in silent laughter.

He was ten years old again, he was at the French school of Brienne, ringed in by the jeering faces of his school-mates. He was a foreigner, a curiosity, of strange race, with a strange name and strange speech. Something different, alien, not of the pack, and therefore to be baited, tormented, harried. You could smash your fist against jeering school-boy mouths, and could bloody sneering school-boy noses. But these people—

The discreet smile hidden behind a fan, the veiled amusement of hastily averted eyes— He was caught, trapped in a cage of polite mockery, courteous cruelty, and he didn't know the way out. He could only stand with pride stripped naked and ashamed, while fleering eyes looked sideways—

Then she was there, shielding him with the gracious serenity of her presence. The light touch of her hand on his arm, the sweet breath of her voice in his ear.

"General—so hot in here, don't you think? It has made me quite faint. Be so good as to escort me out into the garden."

He had never believed before that there was any special virtue in womanhood. He believed it now. Her frail dignity was stronger than clenched fists could ever be. Before it the doorless wall of humiliation vanished, and she moved on as though it had never existed. He beside her, she with her hand on his arm—

With her, there was no more difficulty in crossing a salon than if it had been an artillery-yard. Even the complicated manœuvre of leaving it was as simple as a conscripts' drill.

They were out in the moon-silvered garden, walking among flowers. She herself a flower. No. If you trampled on a flower it became ugly and broken. But she had suffered the rough trampling of his rudeness, and it had only made her lovelier and more fragrant than ever. For a time they walked in silence. Then she had raised her face to his, and said, "Tell me—"

He had talked then. He hadn't imagined there was so much talk shut up inside him. Yet after all, six months was a long time to be silent and alone in the middle of a noisy and crowded city. Here in the little quiet, empty garden was companionship and understanding. Josephine....

No, he never wanted to go back to that house again. But he knew he would. Though all the women of Paris laughed in his face—he would go. Even if, behind the gracious veil of her kindness—listening to the pent-up flood of his words—she had probably found the naked soul he'd shown her not even interesting, but just—comic.

> *"Tallien ... in '92 you were head of a gang, and in '94 you seemed to be the hero of Thermidor. Today you are only a sorry scarecrow to frighten women and children."*
>
> "CENSEUR DES JOURNAUX," 1795

CHAPTER

❧ XII ❧

TALLIEN PULLED THE BELL-ROPE, THEN STOOD, BACK TO THE EMPTY fireplace, rocking from heel to toe, so that his spurs clicked rhythmically on the marble hearth.

He looked complacently about the room. He would have it done over now, more to his own taste. Theresia had been niggardly with the gilt. Those little fine lines about the white wood paneling—you could hardly see them. Why use gilt at all, if it wasn't to be seen? The furniture, too. Theresia'd had the run of the Royal Warehouse, but instead of taking his advice and getting something with a bit of meat to it, good virile Louis XIV stuff, rich dark woods and velvet, she'd listened to Josephine and taken all this effeminate Louis XV rubbish; chairs a man didn't dare sit down in properly, carpets that'd be ruined if you happened to spit on them by mistake. All pale grays and dusty pinks and washy blues. Nothing full-blooded about it. Still, changing a little furniture at the Chaumière wouldn't be much for a man who'd just done what he'd done at Quiberon, would it?

He rocked back and forth and smiled to himself. They thought he was finished, did they? Finished—physically, as well as politically. These giddy spells he'd been having. Too much soft living, that was all. Now he'd been five days in the saddle coming from the Breton coast, and was as fresh as a sea-breeze—the breeze over the Quiberon beaches. Barras wouldn't be able to squeeze him out of the new Government now. Not after what he'd done at Quiberon. A year ago he'd saved the Republic from the Jacobins. Now he'd saved it from the Royalists. He'd done it. In batches of twenty on the Quiberon beaches.

He pulled at the bell-rope again.

Barras wouldn't like it. He wouldn't be able to give the heroic coup-de-grâce to somebody else's kill this time. It was too far away. Quiberon—

Hoche hadn't liked it, either. Hoche with his "word of honor of a soldier." He had had to learn that the civil authority was above such sentimental trimmings as words of honor. Just as Barras'd have to learn that men of action came above politicians. He'd given them action. In batches of twenty, on the beaches of Quiberon. He'd been Tallien of the September massacres, Tallien of the 28th of July. Now he would be Tallien of the Quiberon beaches.

He'd tell Theresia about it first. Then, when he was rested, he'd see—no, he'd send for Barras. Theresia. Theresia Tallien. His wife. After all, whatever people said, being married to a woman made a difference. A wife wasn't just a woman to go to bed with. You had to give her more than just a gold piece left on the corner of the dressing-table. He could give it to her now, the power she wanted. Theresia. They made a handsome couple, didn't they, he and Theresia?

What was the matter with those damned lackeys? Was he or was he not the master in his own house? Did they think he rang the bell for the pleasure of the exercise? Lazy bastards, living on the fat of the land, and too fine to answer a bell. He jerked savagely at the rope, and lurched a little as he turned back. He steadied himself against the mantel-shelf. He'd have the whole lot of them out of here, driving the blood to a man's head with their insolent incompetence.

He stood glowering at the door. Damned airs and graces, any-way—a man having to be announced to his own wife in his own house. He'd put a stop to that high-faluting nonsense, too, he'd—

"Monsieur desires?"

A pale blue and white livery with, inside it, the icy contempt of a servant for a master of his own class.

"Monsieur desires to be answered when he rings, d'you hear?"

"Madame had not informed us that Monsieur would be in residence—again."

"In residence! Who else do you expect to be in residence in this house—eh?"

A shrug of the pale blue shoulders, so slight that it might have been only a deeper breath.

"Announce me to your mistress."

"Madame is in conference with Monsieur Barras in her boudoir, and gave orders that she was not to be disturbed."

"It's I who give orders here. Announce me!" he roared.

"But assuredly, Monsieur." The man raised his eyebrows a hair's breadth, but otherwise did not move.

What did a man—a gentleman—do? A fellow in striped waistcoat and apron you either kicked in the behind, or tossed half a louis to. But a thing in blue satin that looked at you with the blank eyes of a stuffed fish—

He'd go without being announced, then. He'd put a stop to all this damned nonsense once and for all. Anyway, this announcing business—less likely to be good manners than just a common precaution. "In conference with Monsieur Barras," was she, at this hour of the morning? He marched towards the door. He staggered a little. His spurs in the thick pile of the carpet, of course—

He knew something about conferences in boudoirs himself. Barras wasn't the only one who'd been about in high society. He mounted the stairs. Not that he was jealous. No. He knew quite well that Theresia went to the highest bidder. That was one of the beauties of the thing. To be able to prove he was the highest bidder. And he was. Again. He'd bid money in Bordeaux, popularity in Paris. Now he'd bid power in France.

He walked softly the last few steps to the boudoir door. Not that he was jealous, but it would be the final touch, if he could— He would be able to blast them with his righteous anger. No, he would apologize and withdraw courteously, in the grand manner.

The grand manner. He remembered Barras walking calmly into the Committee-room at the Tuileries, tossing his hat negligently on the table, and saying quietly, "It is done." There was an impressive dignity about that. The other could wait.

He retraced his steps a few yards, then came back heavy-footed, making his spurs ring on the inlaid flooring. He turned the handle firmly, and stood for a moment at his full height in the open door.

They were there, sitting decorously on either side of the table, with papers, pens, and ink between them. Theresia was in negligée, but Barras was dressed to the last thread. In gray linen, too. He wouldn't have worn that last night. He was particular about correctness of dress, was Barras. But never mind that sort of thing for the moment.

He advanced firmly into the room. He'd left his hat downstairs, so he couldn't fling it onto the table; but he laid his hands on the back of a chair, and leaned negligently against it.

"It is done," he said hoarsely.

Barras, carefully marking the place on his paper with his forefinger, looked up with polite interest.

"Ah, my dear Tallien. Back from your, er—diplomatic mission?"

"It is done," Tallien insisted still more firmly.

"I'm glad of that. But then, that's what you went for, isn't it?"

The thing didn't seem to be going quite right. What was Barras up to now? Making sure the enemy was quite dead before striking a heroic attitude over the corpses? Very well then, he should have his corpses—and a good week dead by now. He smashed the flat of his hand down on the table.

"I have done it. The Royalists asked for eight hundred bodies. I've given them a thousand. Shot. In batches of twenty, on Quiberon beach."

Barras rose very slowly and stood, his finger still on the paper, leaning forward across the table. He spoke tensely, in a voice of strained incredulity.

"You have—*shot* the Royalist prisoners of Quiberon?"

Tallien shifted his feet uneasily. Barras was over-doing the play-acting. Did he think that he, Tallien, was a fool?

"You said so yourself—what else did I go there for? You wanted the Royalists finished off. I've finished them—once and for all." He banged his hand down on the table again.

Barras straightened, resting the tips of his fingers on the edge of the table. He looked down at them, smiling a little.

"Finished, my dear fellow," he said softly. "Not massacred. There's a difference, you know. And the thing was done—they did it themselves." He glanced up. "Don't you see? A thousand French Royalists, landed on the coast of Brittany from English ships, with English money in their pockets and English weapons in their hands. The Breton Royalists themselves couldn't stomach that. They were beaten—beaten by their English friends before they ever set foot in Brittany. They were no more than a set of feather-brained adventurers. They were utterly discredited. And you—you had to make victims and martyrs of them." He stood erect, and his voice hardened. "Good God, Tallien! Have you no political understanding at all—have you no imagination beyond massacre and death?"

He rubbed the palms of his hands together. They were hot, but dry as scorched paper. Martyrs? Barras hadn't talked about martyrs when he'd dealt with the people of Toulon—not only a thousand, either, but tens of thousands who'd been guilty of nothing but having a little loose change in their pockets. And he, Tallien, hadn't made a sou over this business, not a sou. He'd done it from sheer patriotism. He'd saved the Republic. Barras couldn't deny that—he couldn't—

"Set of traitors, they were. Coming here with their English friends, wanting to hang us. Lot of dirty exiles, coming back by force. That's death. The law says so."

Barras sighed patiently. "And the law says too that a treaty made by a General officer on active service must be respected. Those men surrendered to General Hoche on his word of honor that their lives be spared. And you—" He shook his head. "I blame myself that, knowing you, I didn't warn you. But it never occurred to me—I never imagined that you—that even you could—" He threw up his hands, then let them fall limply to his sides.

"Man, don't you see what you've done? Dishonored French arms, the Government itself. You've given the people reason to fear that the Terror can come back. You've given Europe reason to believe in a return to Jacobinism—violence—chaos. You've undone all our work of the past year." He half turned away, and shrugged.

Tallien jerked at his cravat, that felt too tight. He'd saved the Republic. In batches of twenty. On Quiberon beach. He'd saved them all from hanging. Nobody could deny it. Barras couldn't deny it. Theresia couldn't—

"Theresia—"

She got up from the table without looking at him or speaking, and crossed to the window, her back to the room.

Barras straightened some papers on the table.

"Well," he said, "the thing's done. As you say, you did it. The responsibility's yours. You've destroyed a thousand young men—and I very much fear, yourself as well. It is unfortunate, with the elections only a month away. Very unfortunate."

Tallien gripped hard at the back of his chair. His mouth felt too small to hold his tongue, his head seemed enormous, so that the thoughts inside it darted and circled about like flies in the middle of an empty room.

"You mean," he said thickly, "you mean you—you won't—"

Barras raised his eyebrows. "I? My dear fellow, I can do nothing. I am only a simple Deputy, with no more power than yourself. But the new Government, that must at all costs inspire confidence at home and abroad, can scarcely—you must see it for yourself, Tallien—it can scarcely start its career in collaboration with a, er—forgive me, my dear fellow—an assassin and a Terrorist, and under the auspices of the massacres of September and Quiberon. It would scarcely be tactful, or even safe, would it?"

Not safe— Tallien contracted his brows. The flies of his thoughts, that had nowhere to settle— He could see them now, small black specks that circled and jerked, darting about each other so rapidly they made him giddy to watch. If only they had somewhere to settle—Barras, flicking his white hands at them, throwing senseless words at them— It only made it worse. Theresia—silent and still. Theresia—

"Theresia—"

He lurched heavily towards her, stumbling as he went. These thick carpets, they caught at your spurs. Not safe. He would have all that changed—changed.

"Theresia—"

She stood staring out of the window, her back turned towards him. She neither turned nor answered. Her fingers were jerking at the silk fringe of the curtain. The black specks of his thoughts were lost against the black masses of her hair.

"Theresia—"

"Well?"—without turning or looking at him.

"Theresia, I saved you—twice. In Bordeaux and Paris. I saved you—"

"And for what reason?" she said coldly over her shoulder. "Because you were corrupt—mentally, morally, physically. And you thought you could corrupt me too."

The blood suddenly rushed hot through his body. He was firm on his legs again, the black specks were incandescent, like sparks streaming up from the black smoke of her hair.

"Corrupt?" he said. "But for me, you'd be nothing but corruption—rotting corruption, worm-eaten, putrid. Stinking meat. That's what you'd have been."

Her fingers clenched on the silken fringe. "Must you stay in this room? It is impossible to breathe."

He snatched at her wrist, and jerked her about to face him.

She stiffened away from him. "Don't touch me. Your hands are filthy with blood."

He pushed his face close to hers. "But for me, my girl, your neck would have been bloody enough."

Her neck—white and round, with the great rope of pearls, white and round, about it. He remembered the pearls. In Bordeaux. He'd brought them to her straight from the Revolutionary Tribunal. She'd been talking with friends in her—their salon. He'd tossed them into her lap. She'd said, "Thank you," and dropped them carelessly into her reticule. He'd thought the gesture very distinguished at the time—a fortune in pearls, dropped into her reticule, not looking at them, not even checking her conversation. And not wondering, either, from what other woman's neck they were still warm.

His jaw was shaking so that his teeth rattled. The sparks had blurred together into a ruddy fog, blinding and choking. Through it her face showed luminous and pale, like a lantern— a swung lantern, rushing towards him and brightening, drawing away and fading. Theresia. Theresia went to the highest bidder. He could feel her hand pulling away from him, and with his fingers slimy with sweat, he couldn't hold her. Theresia went to the highest bidder—

Barras. He couldn't find him, because of the wavering mists that were rising behind his eyes. Barras, the dirty aristocrat, the cheater of the people, the— Then of a sudden he saw him very clearly, even to the delicate stitching on his coat, the gauzy weave of his cravat. He saw the noble head on the stately body, the handsome eyes under the fine dark brows, the elegantly powdered hair and well-kept hands. There was nothing about him that he couldn't see. Nothing—

"Aristocrat—you?" he said very slowly and distinctly. "The very lice on your body have a right to spit in your face."

He stood erect and very still for a moment—then, like a fire-rotted wall, crashed suddenly forward on his face.

Barras looked down at him, half smiling. He knelt, and turned him over on his back. He rose, dusting his fingers lightly together, as though to rid them of some unpleasant substance.

"The falling sickness," he said. "I have suspected it for some time past. Regrettable. But he has worn himself out, for crime, and by crime."

He stepped over the body, and reached for the bell-rope.

"We must, of course, have a doctor for the poor fellow at once. Though I think there is no cause for, er—undue alarm."

He crossed to Theresia where she still stood pressed back against the window. He put his hands on her shoulders.

"My dear," he said, "I very much fear that your husband's unfortunate state of health will debar him from, er—public life, for some time to come."

He bent his tall body, and kissed her lightly on the forehead.

> *"An event! Alteration in the style of hair-dressing effected by Mesdames Tallien and Beauharnais."*
>
> NEWS ITEM, PARIS DAILY PAPER,
> 1795

CHAPTER

❧ XIII ❧

SHE PUSHED THE BILL INTO HER DRESSING-TABLE DRAWER, CLOSED IT softly, then quickly turned the key. It didn't really do any good, of course; still, it gave one the feeling of having trapped the thing, imprisoned it, so that it couldn't follow one about any more. But it was no good. As well try to exterminate a swarm of ants by catching them one at a time and shutting them up in a patch-box. They just kept on coming.

A patch-box. She wondered if it mightn't be amusing to revive patches. Better not, perhaps. The fashion wasn't old enough yet. People would just think she could remember. People were so—

Did she look as though she could remember? She rested her elbows on the dressing-table, and leaned forward towards the mirror. She was quite alone. She preferred to prepare for bed by herself. Louise was apt to be irritable so late at night, and to skimp things. Besides, it wasn't always convenient.... Though tonight she was quite alone, save for Fortuné—and Fortuné, a little black lump of ill-natured devotion at her feet, didn't count.

She'd taken off her complexion with a soft sponge dipped in Aphrodite's Balm, and she was quite alone. So she could look at her face—really look at her face, not just at herself. She could be absolutely frank and honest with herself. She was thirty ... well, only so little over thirty that it didn't really count. Suppose she said twenty-eight. Did she—quite honestly—did she look twenty-eight?

She stared at her reflection in the mirror. Yes—being quite honest with herself—she looked almost twenty-eight. Though only without her complexion, of course. It was worrying. When a woman was—was in the middle twenties, she wanted a little security in life. Oh, she wasn't ambitious, like Theresia. She didn't want men to give her political importance and power. Just to pay her bills. It wasn't much to ask, was it?

How could you help being worried when a man like Barras began making such obvious excuses about election expenses? He must take her for a fool if he thought she didn't know there wasn't going to be any election. Oh, there would be voting of course, but that wasn't at all the same thing. No. She knew perfectly well that if a man like Barras said he couldn't afford a thing, it really meant he didn't want it.

As for Hoche.... She felt the tears rising in her eyes. She watched them well up. They made a sheen over the deep blue of her pupils, like moonlight over still water. Holding her head at just that angle, a little tilted forward, they ran down gently over the length of her lashes, like pearls slipping down black silk threads—and falling, clear and round, without touching her cheeks. With her head at just that angle, they wouldn't upset the complexion in the very least.

Hoche. She'd thought he at least was secure. She'd been so certain of him. It just showed you could never really trust any man. Looking at her with his red-brown eyes gone as opaque and hard as chestnuts— "Madame"—as formal as though he'd never met her before— "Madame, I have a lackey who is an even finer specimen, physically, than Captain Plessis."

How petty men were! She herself had never given Captain Plessis another thought. She'd even forgotten his name. But it was her own fault, really. She ought to have known that a young country lad like that would be too flattered not to boast a little—she ought to have realized that a man of the people like Hoche, great General though he might be, was still only that—a man of the people. His polish was only cheap varnish after all, it cracked and peeled off at the least provocation. Still, she had been upset, hurt, that he could say such a thing to her—she who'd never been anything but kind to him.

And of course there was Eugène to be considered. Poor child, he'd been so disappointed. But one couldn't possible leave a young—a very young lad under the influence of a coarse-minded man like that, could one? And naturally she couldn't have him here doing nothing, it wouldn't be good for him. So he'd had to go back to school. It was only fair that Hoche should pay for that, since it was his fault anyway that the expense had to be incurred.

She shook a few drops of Cleopatra's Wine of Pearls into the palm of her hand, and dabbed it on her face. It made the skin marvelously luminous.

There was Barras, too. He was always at the Chaumière now, never here. She'd cried to him about it, and he'd said he had to make himself agreeable to rich people. Naturally he did. But she would have entertained his millionaire friends for him, no matter how vulgar they were. There was nothing of the snob about her. She couldn't see what difference it could possibly make who Theresia's father was, he couldn't be much, considering the way Theresia behaved. Shameless, vulgar— But that was probably it. These new, ill-bred millionaires were probably attracted by their own kind. Though what Barras himself could possibly see—

It was very worrying and it didn't seem fair, did it? She'd had the shabby aristocrats, now she had to have the shabby soldiers.

Of the two she preferred the aristocrats, for the soldiers only talked about themselves, while the aristocrats talked about each other, which at least was amusing.

She removed the Wine of Pearls with a linen handkerchief soaked in Cupid's Tears. It was made of rose-water, but not just ordinary rose-water. It had been subjected to an electric current for exactly twenty-three minutes. That little Corsican with the curious name, for instance. Of course he was funny, but that was no excuse for laughing in his face. It was unkind. Besides, Barras was particularly interested in him. Though what he could see—

She dabbed Night of Love on her face. Though that was a stupid name—for, thick and sticky as it was, you couldn't possibly—

She'd really felt quite sorry for the poor little man. Although of course he was mad—but utterly mad. Never in her life had she heard a man talk so much, nor such complete nonsense— though she had listened to the ideas and ambitions of a great many men at one time or another. But never yet had she been alone in a moonlit rose-garden with a young man who talked exclusively about roads and mountain-passes and splitting the enemy in two, or some such barbarous Corsican method of fighting. It made one feel quite ill to think of it. That, and his passionate despair at being refused—the Army of Italy! Though how a man could excite himself to the point of trembling over an army— Especially an Italian army, when everybody knew the French ones were so much better.

She'd said something encouraging to him—something the Negroes of Martinique used to say, about the darker the night the brighter the stars. He'd looked straight before him then, straight into her eyes—and for a moment she'd thought he was going to be sensible. Then he only laughed, shrugged, and said, "When I was born, the sun was in mid-heaven." Yes, he was quite mad. Or perhaps just Corsican. For Corsicans weren't really quite civilized, were they? And it was probably the first time he'd ever met a woman of breeding. Naturally, one could quite understand that that might go to his head.

So she wouldn't really have minded if it had ended there. She'd felt sorry for him, and she'd listened to him. But that was the trouble with these provincials—if you were just reasonably polite, they thought you were really interested. For a whole month now it seemed as though she couldn't take a step in any direction without first having to walk around General Bonaparte. It was embarrassing. Not that people could think— They couldn't possibly, could they, a comic little down-at-heels oddity like that? But they smiled, and that was worse. For what was he after all but a Corsican refugee of no importance and without any money at all?

She painted her eyebrows with a little brush dipped in olive oil. Nothing was better than that for the lashes, though of course with a few drops of attar of roses to take away the smell.

She didn't want to be unkind to the poor little man. Besides, there was something a little exciting in an odd way about him. And Barras—after all, you couldn't possibly call him exciting. He was rather like one of those expensive Persian cats, elegant, handsome, more sophisticated than the sophistication that had bred him. The little man Bonaparte was more like some wild creature out of the forest, shy and savage at the same time. That was what was exciting about him. It somehow gave you a queer sense of power, a wild creature that came of itself to your hand— and a little of apprehension too, not quite knowing what it would do if you really tried to touch—

A Corsican half wild, strayed into a civilization that bewildered him, and coming to your hand. It was touching in a way. You couldn't be unkind, you couldn't just stamp your foot at him and drive him away. Besides, these days you could never be quite sure about men. Even Corsicans.

Still, without wanting to drive him away, you didn't want him to drive other people away, either. She'd tried to discourage him as gently as she could. She'd told him about Alexander whose memory would, of course, always be sacred to her. She'd even told him about her two young, very young, children. But it hadn't been any good. It only made him look at her as though she were one of those—those experienced women that always attracted naïve young men.

She felt the tears rising in her eyes, and blinked them back. It would be a nuisance to have to do her lashes all over again.

She sprayed her hair with Secret of the Stars. The man who made it had to cast your horoscope first, so that he could brew the ingredients when the stars that influenced the growth of hair were in conjunction or something with your own planet. She slipped on a pair of cotton gloves—for it stained the skin as badly as ordinary henna-water—and rubbed it well into the roots.

114

She hadn't really got a face like that, had she—the face of an experienced woman? She looked at it again in the mirror. Her hair was standing up all over her head in loose, damp tendrils and curls. One little ring was stuck flat against her cheek, just in front of her ear. She looked at it. She stuck another one just above it. Then three, one small and two a little larger, across her forehead. She lowered her head a little, opened her eyes very wide so that the lashes rayed out about them, and looked again. With her little three-cornered face, the eager innocence of her eyes, and her hair like that, she had exactly the head of a little boy who's been out in the wind and the rain.

She smiled—her new smile, with scarcely parted lips, because of her teeth. Something had happened to them in prison, and nothing she'd tried had been any good—not even that new stuff, the powdered lava brought specially from Mount Vesuvius. Her teeth were still dull and lifeless. She'd been upset about it at first, until she discovered the new smile. It was a very good smile. Mysterious. Enigmatic. Yes, that was the word. Enigmatic.

And with her hair like that— Theresia might have hair down to her feet, but its enormous mass would look positively coarse beside that delicate, fragile little head. And Barras who, after all, had taste and an appreciation of the finer things of life couldn't possibly help but see it.

She loosened her dressing-gown. The innocent, almost sexless boy's head above the voluptuous perfection of a woman's bosom, and her enigmatic smile between—it was an exciting discovery, quite breath-taking. It wasn't as though she'd even been thinking about that sort of thing, either. No, she'd been quite seriously considering her financial position. If she hadn't just happened to glance at herself in the mirror at that exact moment— But that's how things—important things, often were discovered. Just by the merest accident. It really did make one believe in some sort of supernatural power, didn't it?

*"Bonaparte, a little Corsican soldier
of no account, who will give no
trouble to anybody."*

BARRAS, 1795

CHAPTER

❧ XIV ❧

HE WONDERED HOW HE HAD EVER COME TO LIKEN THERESIA TALLIEN
to a snow-laden cypress. Half-naked as she was now, she had
more of the soft fleshiness of a carnivorous orchid about her.

Nevertheless, she was undoubtedly one of Nature's master-
pieces. She was admirable. Provided, of course, that you admired
Nature. For himself, he'd always found it just a shade vulgar,
and more than a shade fatiguing. Above all, fatiguing. He
glanced down at his uniform and sighed. He looked about
him, and sighed again.

He disliked bedroom scenes, both in art and real life. And
this one smacked more of the popular theater than anything
else. Josephine's bedroom had a little stately air of formality
about it, belonging to the days when ladies held court at their
toilettes. Theresia's was a bedroom, and nothing more nor less.
He wished she would either finish undressing, or else put something more on. A lace chemise. She was, after all, a bourgeoise
at heart. Her idea of an illicit love-affair was a man in a woman's
bedroom, and a woman in a lace chemise. It was years since he
had been even remotely interested by a woman in a chemise.
Josephine was never that. She was never anything less seemly
than a lady in negligée. He leaned back in his chair and closed
his eyes.

"Another cup of coffee to keep you awake, Barras?" said
Theresia a little sharply. "It's scarcely going to be a night for
sleep, you know. And by the way, what should one call you
now—Director, or General?"

"Call me your obedient servant, my dear," he said without
opening his eyes.

"Rubbish, man! I've told you, there's no need for that sort of

116

thing with me. And you've never yet served anybody but your-self." She set his cup down with an irritating little clatter.

He frowned. Josephine would never on any account say "Rub-bish!" to a man, no matter what she might think. One could talk as one liked to her, and she'd instantly and most tastefully display interest in the shop-windows of her eyes, and breathe, "How clever," or "How wonderful," or "How brave you are!", never missing her cue. There was something stimulating about it, even though you knew perfectly well she hadn't understood, hadn't even vaguely tried to understand what you were talking about.

Josephine. There was a connoisseur's piece for you, if ever there was one. She was a work of art from the tips of her polished toenails to the last strand of the studied disarray of the quite delightful hair-dressing she had recently adopted. Love, with Josephine, was like a minuet—a thing of infinite grace and elegance, but of no emotion whatsoever. Theresia was quite different. Fatiguing. Excessively fatiguing. It was unfortunate that one had had to dispense with Tallien not only politically, but in his, er—private capacity as well. He could hear Theresia moving restlessly about the room, clattering with the coffee things, snuffing the candles, stirring the fire. She had no repose whatever. A clever woman, but exhausting.

Josephine, on the other hand, was as restful to have in the room as an exquisitely painted picture. Getting rid of Josephine would be as painful as being obliged to part with a Botticelli one had one's self discovered in an attic, and bought for a song. But that was the trouble. She could no longer be had for a song. Giving money to Josephine was like giving grains of sand to the ocean. If one were rich enough, it would be amusing to see how much she could absorb without ruffling the placid surface of her acceptance. But he was not rich enough. Yet. Therefore—

The ideal arrangement, of course, would be a husband suffici-ently wealthy and sufficiently, er—broad-minded—

"One thing is certain," said Theresia tartly, "you'll never get yourself called Director at all if you don't do something quickly to earn your title of General."

He opened his eyes and looked up at her. She was vibrant with energy, blazing with the desire for activity. Activity! She hadn't yet learned that true success doesn't lie in activity, but in an ability to persuade other people to be active in your place. The way to dominate a crisis—especially a crisis of physical

117

violence—was not to attack it, but to cause somebody else to attack it, and then either support or disavow him, according to the results obtained.

It was Tallien and Fréron who had attacked Robespierre, and for a time he had supported them. It was Tallien who had massacred the Royalists at Quiberon, and that of course had been indefensible. It was Fréron who had raised a band of young louts to intimidate the Jacobins, and who would soon, in consequence, be taking a well-advised holiday in the south. It was he, Barras, who had avoided, er—exertion, and who therefore remained. You'd think Theresia would see that.

"Aren't you going to *do* something, man?"

It was this incessant prodding that got on one's nerves.

"Yes, my dear," he said. "I shall drink my coffee." She clicked her tongue impatiently, jerked away from him and, going to the window, flung it wide open.

"Listen! You can hear it, even at this distance."

He could hear it quite plainly, but he could see nothing to be gained by listening to it. It was a low mutter of sound like summer thunder, and possibly—though not probably—as harmless. The distant murmur of an angry multitude, not yet quite sure what to do with its anger.

She drew away from the window, and planted herself before him. He really did wish she would cover herself just a little more. Large expanses of naked flesh, however beautiful, had a certain crudity that was distasteful.

"This isn't just a riot, Barras. This is insurrection. The Faubourgs have risen to a man—forty or fifty thousand of them—armed, and angry."

"They do appear to be, er—vexed," he admitted. "Though why, I cannot conceive. They've done their voting. And of the half-million or so votes that were found to be, er—valid, we have frankly admitted that some thirty thousand were cast against us. They could hardly expect more of us than that, could they?"

"They'll expect a great deal more—they'll expect your heads, if you don't do something about it soon. That's what comes of this feeble policy of yours, this balancing of one party against the other. Now you've got them all—Royalists, Jacobins and Moderates—together in one side of the scales against you. While in the other—"

He pressed his finger-tips together and smiled at her over them.

118

"Believe me, my child, whoever may be found in the opposite side of the scales, it will not be I. Of that I can assure you."

"But if all the parties are united against you, you can't oppose one against the other. You're bound to oppose them yourself. You can't avoid it."

"That's where you're mistaken, my dear. I can." He sat up a little, and leaned towards her. "What, exactly, is the position? The present, er—unpleasantness is, as you so rightly say, no common riot, but an insurrection bent on destroying the new Government before it's even in power. As Commander-in-Chief of the National Guard, it is my duty to, er—discourage that idea. I have therefore sent my Second-in-Command, General Menou—"

"Menou! A blatting sheep—"

"Quite. I have sent General Menou to reason with the gentlemen of the Faubourgs, to persuade them to lay down their arms. Now, as the majority of the Guard are themselves with the insurrectionists, it is possible—it is just possible that, by force of habit, they will obey the orders of their commander. If they obey, the rest of the crowd will probably follow suit. The people, in the aggregate, are extraordinarily sheep-like in their actions, my dear Theresia. In which case all I shall have to do myself is to go before the Convention with the simple announcement, 'It is done.' If not— Why, then I shall, though reluctantly, be obliged to arrest General Menou, and set another Second-in-Command in his place. This time a man not of words, but of action."

"And where do you expect to get your man of action at this late hour of the day?"

He took out his snuff-box, and helped himself delicately. "My dear, why do you imagine we have been lavishing our food and, er—Josephine's charm on half-pay officers these three months past? Not, certainly, for the pleasure of their company, but in order to have on hand a good supply of professional soldiers, unsuccessful enough to be manageable, experienced enough to be useful, poor enough to be desperate."

"But he'd be a Regular Army man, Barras! And you can't risk that—you can't risk a Government that depends for its very existence on the support of the Army! You can't—"

He sighed. "My child," he said, "you are twenty-two, and you jump to youthful conclusions. I am—well, I am a man of not inconsiderable experience. Believe me, I am quite sure of what

I am doing. There is no question of the Army. The force to be used is the National Guard, or such part of it as has not, er—lost interest in its duties, supported by the police, and my own Sacred Battalion made up, as you know, of unfortunates who have for many years past suffered in prisons and galleys, and who are in consequence the natural enemies of, er—everybody else.

"As for the young man in question, it is he who will be dependent on us, not we on him. If he succeeds we will give him a reward far beyond any to which his merit or his length of service might entitle him—say, the Military Governorship of Paris. Thus he will have against him the hatred of the people whose blood he will have shed, and the resentment of his brother-officers over whose heads he will have been promoted. A man in his position will naturally, er—cherish the only support he has—ourselves. You see? A little tact, and—" He spread out his hands.

"Yes," she said thoughtfully, "that's not so badly planned... But if he fails?"

"If he fails— If he fails, my dear, we shall be deeply shocked at the brutal and unauthorized action of a young officer who has, on his own responsibility, taken it upon himself to shed sacred French blood. And we shall be obliged, in the interests of common justice, to take, er—disciplinary measures against him. So you see—" He leaned back in his chair again, and stretched out his legs before him.

She looked at him thoughtfully. "And the hero-elect—who is he? Are you certain he won't be—troublesome, afterwards?"

"Quite certain. I am never mistaken in my judgment of men. He is a little Corsican soldier of no account, who will give no trouble to anybody. A certain General Bonaparte."

> *"Bonaparte, a little General who
> was unhesitatingly dubbed a fool
> by all who met him."*
>
> MADAME DE CHASTENAY

CHAPTER

XV

He leaned forward on the wooden bench, rested his elbows on the barrier before him, and stared down at the scene below. From up here in the spectators' gallery, the Assembly room of the Convention was very like a theater: the brightly-lit stage of the Speakers' rostrum and the President's desk, with the more dimly illuminated horseshoe of the audience rising tier on tier before it. Higher still, the gallery, unlit—for the present management was loth to provide that unimportant section of the public with candles at sixty francs the pound.

The play being enacted down there was just such another of those dreary obscenities that the present semi-illiterate "society" of Paris mistook for comedies. At the theater one had a husband cuckolded by a cynical lover, here was a nation cuckolded by a cynical Government. But at the theater the play drew inevitably to that end, however ignoble, which its author had designed for it; while here something had gone awry with the last act. The nation had ignored its cue. Deceived and hoodwinked it might have been, but complaisant it resolutely refused to be. The plot was too grossly clumsy even for so tawdry a farce as this—263,000 votes admitted out of a voting population of at least three or four million! The nation would have had to be not only complaisant, but imbecile as well, not to recognize the smoke of burning ballot-papers rising like a fog of corruption from a thousand secret counting-chambers the country over.

"—union, fraternity, concord between all Frenchmen—these are the true means of saving the Republic!" declaimed the weary actor on the stage below. Thread-bare platitudes, pitiful gagging in a desperate hope of even yet bringing the curtain down on a happy ending. Yet surely a little clumsy, this appeal for unity from a new Government that had just registered a vote of almost

121

ten to one in its own favor? An actor at the Comédie would have been more adroit than that.

A new Government? No. The same shabby crew. At the best, honest men worn out mentally and physically by three years spent under the threat of the guillotine; at the worst, scoundrels who had no other choice than seats in the Government or on benches of the galleys. What more than weary or frightened ineptitudes could you expect? Yet it scarcely mattered. The audience wasn't listening. It was attentive enough, but with that strained attention of men who, knowing that a fire is blazing behind the scenes, try to persuade themselves that there is no danger. Oh, they were attentive enough, listening with every nerve for a crackling more sinister than the turning of the speaker's notes.

"—the will of the people. And we will see that that will is obeyed, though we have to impose it by force."

The will of the people isn't being stammered out in your cheap play-house, it's being roared full-throated under the open sky in the Faubourgs Saint-Denis and Saint-Martin. The people. Not the Royalists or the Jacobins or the Empty Bellies. The People. That was the miracle Barras had performed with his cynical juggling of party hatreds. He had united the people. For, imprison men in the same condemned cell and hate each other as they may, they will unite in trying to batter down the door.

The people united in their will to batter down the door. The tragedy of it was that the open door could lead only to chaos and anarchy, worse even than the corrupt rule they now had. For there was no decent, honest authority left in the country, save only the Army. There were plenty of leaders in the Army who could seize hold of a momentarily united people and bind them together before they had time to split again into fratricidal factions. Yes. The Army could do it, but Barras would never permit that clean strength to compete with his rotting power. He knew how to choose his scapegoats, as he had chosen Tallien for the evil affair of Quiberon. This time it was that poor brute Menou, a known Royalist, who could always be accused of treason at the convenient moment, no matter whether he failed or succeeded—

One wondered what steps, if any, "General" Barras had himself taken for the defense of a Convention that had placed itself under his protection. The Tuileries was defendable enough for anybody with an ounce of military or even common sense.

Staring down from the gallery, his eyes no longer saw the gesticulating figure on the rostrum or the strained audience before it. It was as though a luminous map unrolled itself like a geometrically figured carpet, hiding everything else from sight. There was the long, narrow shape of the Tuileries running due north and south. To the west, the gardens. To the east, the two unfinished wings jutting out towards the great bulk of the Louvre.

Between the wings of the Tuileries, flanking the eastern façade, were three high-walled courtyards. Those death-traps of court-yards in which, when the Tuileries had been assaulted before, in '92, incompetent authority had caged the Swiss Guard to be helplessly slaughtered. Incredible, that day's work. Cannon boxed up behind blind stone walls so that they had no target until the mob was upon them. Infantry placed in doors and windows so that their angle of fire could not clear their own artillery below. Incredible.

No. The mob should never be permitted to get inside the enclosure of the Palace at all. Therefore it was here, at the northwest angle of the building, that the batteries should be placed, with the open space of the gardens behind, the wide vista of the rue Saint-Roch before. Here was the only point at which guns could find any range at all, and an enemy could be kept at a respectable distance from the Palace itself. It would be so easy for a man with any spark of military imagination.

The focus of his eyes shifted. The map thinned and dissolved. His taut jaw-muscles relaxed, his strained shoulders slackened. He leaned back, sliding forward on the wooden bench until his knees were jammed against the barrier before him. He buried his fists in his breeches pockets and stared up at the ceiling above him. It was dark up there. Dark as a midnight sky. The darker the night, the brighter the stars— Her eyes— Yes, that was it. Her eyes were like stars reflected in the sea, when you stared down into it from a Corsican fishing-boat on a moonless night.

But there were no stars. And impossible for the night to grow any darker than it was. There was no longer even the dreary twilight of half-pay. His name was struck off the Army Lists altogether. He had irritated the gentlemen of the War Ministry. They were tired of the importunities of a man who wanted the right to work honestly at his profession. He had made application to join the new military mission being sent to Turkey. They were sick of the sight of his name. So they struck it off.

He might not work at home, he might not offer his services abroad. He was a discharged lackey, refused a "character" to find employment elsewhere. There was nothing more a man in his position could do. Nothing.

Unless— There were the men of the Faubourgs. They wouldn't ask for a "character." Forty thousand armed men, waiting to be led. Properly commanded, forty thousand men could seize not only the Tuileries, but the whole of Paris—France. Properly led— He saw again the courtyards of the Tuileries on that hot summer's day of '92, when the Swiss Guard had been slaughtered. Never since, on any battle-field, had he had the impression of so many bodies—the bodies of soldiers, of disciplined men, not only horribly killed as though by wild beasts, but stripped naked, outraged, insulted, obscenely mutilated.

That was the sort of thing that happened when undisciplined force took charge of the ship of State, and no decent man could take part in it. Admitted, the ship of State was a rotten hulk that should long since have been broken up. But she was afloat and in mid-stream. There was no salvation for anybody, save in obeying such authority as there was until she could be driven ashore on firm land. Driven ashore. And not even a star to guide her by.

Stars. There was no harm in worshipping a star, so long as you didn't imagine you could snatch it down. It was incredible, though, that other, less scrupulous men hadn't snatched at her long ago. Incredible. But no. She was too high-set in the heavens to be touched by men's desires, too high even to know that such desires existed. Yet it made one shudder to think—knowing what men were—

He'd never known that there were women like that in the world. He'd always thought they were either virtuous and stern, like his mother, or charming and corrupt. He'd never dreamed that charm and virtue could inhabit the same lovely person. She was Woman personified. She was the feminine mercy that paired with masculine justice, the grace that balanced strength, the kindness that softened virtue.

Kind. He had never before known a woman who was kind, with no other motive save that of kindness itself. She was intelligent, too. You could see it in the grave interest of her eyes. True feminine intelligence, made up of sympathy and understanding. A woman, and kind. And to crown all, the dignity of motherhood like a halo about her head. No, there was no harm

in worshipping, so long as you didn't permit yourself to imagine—

"—union, fraternity, peace between all Frenchmen—"

Good God, the man had got back to the place he'd started from without knowing it. Or another was re-reading his speech by mistake. Even the actors of the Comédie were more resourceful than that.

He leaned forward again, and looked down. The audience was still sitting as rigidly attentive as before. Strained, motionless. Though if somebody coughed too loudly, or kicked a chair— It would be amusing to try. But it wasn't his affair. It must be past midnight, and he had nothing to wait for. Nothing.

He got up and, in the darkness, began a stumbling search for the door. He struck his shins against benches, tripped over stairs. That was what he was like. A man in the dark, trying to find the door, checked and balked by invisible obstacles every way he turned—

Somebody opened the door, and a wedge of light cut through the gloom. He moved towards it, and the man in the doorway stood aside to let him by. He hadn't looked at the man, was scarcely aware of his presence, until he felt a touch on his shoulder.

"General Bonaparte?"

He swung sharply about. The man was obscurely dressed in shabby black, a soiled cravat about his neck, a round hat low-drawn over his eyes. A furtive, soft-footed, shadowy creature, with the stink of the secret police about him as rank as the garlic on his breath. What was the trouble now? Unlawful wearing of the uniform? They couldn't expect him to go wrapped in a bed-sheet, could they?

"Yes. What of it?"

"Only thank God I've found you at last. Before it's too late."

"Too late for what?"

"To save my job. General Barras's been waiting two hours already, and he's not—"

"Waiting for what?"

"Why, for you. He said to me, 'Duprès, bring me that little—' He said, 'Find General Bonaparte, and bring him here.' I've looked for you everywhere—in all your usual haunts—the theater, the café, at your lodgings—everywhere. So if you'll be good enough to follow— He's in the antechamber of the Committee-room. Two hours he's been waiting, and he won't be pleased. So if you'll be good enough—"

The man was literally trembling in his nervous anxiety. Well, he'd probably made plenty of decent citizens tremble in his time. It wouldn't hurt him. It was loathsome to think of having been followed, tracked, run to earth, even touched by one of those unclean jackals. If this was arrest again—and it could scarcely be anything else—then rather Barras, who was at least physically clean, than—

"If you will be good enough to follow."

"Very well."

He followed the man along the corridor, down the stairs to the central hall below. To the right were the open doors of the Assembly-room, with the droning monotony of the speaker's weary voice trickling through them. To the left was a door marked in black letters, "Committee of Public Safety." The man knocked timidly, opened it, said, "General Bonaparte," drew back hastily to let him pass, and shut it behind him with a cautious finality that was a sigh of relief.

It was a small room, scantily furnished. It had a few wooden chairs, a huge framed copy of the "Declaration of the Rights of Man" on the wall, and a long, narrow, baize-covered table down its center. He walked forward as far as the table, rested the tips of his fingers on it, and stood waiting.

The antechamber of the Committee. It was here the wounded Robespierre had been brought. It was here on this table he had lain all the long last night before his death. There were dull brown stains on the green baize. On this table—staring hour after hour at the Rights of Man that his virtue had created, that his terror had destroyed. Robespierre. Enigma. Monster and fanatic, but the Incorruptible nevertheless. Incorruptible—

Barras came through the opposite door from the Committee-room proper and faced him across the table that was marked with the blood of the Incorruptible. Very imposing he was with his tall body well displayed in the somber elegance of his General's uniform. He stood gracefully at ease, negligently dusting his fingers together. But there was a quiver of anxiety about his fine eyes, his smooth brow was taut with strain.

He smiled, the corners of his mouth twitching. "Ah, General, er—Bonaparte. It was good of you to come. I had begun to be afraid it might be too late."

Too late for what, in God's name? To save Barras' job as well? Barras with his uneasy hands and twitching smile, looking at him across the table.

"General Bonaparte, you are a man of, er—intelligence. I have no need—and indeed, no time—to make lengthy explanations. You know the situation—that the people of the Faubourgs are, er—displeased, disposed to violence—that the Convention, alarmed for the, er—dignity of the State, paid me the signal honor of placing itself under my protection. As far as that you are informed?— Good. My first move, then, was to send General Menou to, er—reason with the malcontents, to—"

"To *reason* with them?"

Barras took out his snuff-box, looked down at it, then up, without raising his head. "What else? A new Government, my dear General, is ill-advised to cement its corner-stone with the blood of the governed, if it can possibly be avoided." He took snuff, and raised his head. "However, there is no time for political argument, only for facts. General Menou, then, obtained the promise of the insurgents that they would disarm, if he in his turn withdraw his troops. This he accordingly did, but—"

"He withdrew, in the face of—"

Barras tapped his fingers on his snuff-box, and frowned. "I beg of you, General, no discussion. Menou withdrew, save for those of his men who, er—preferred the company of the rioters. But such is the good faith of the, er—people"—he laid his snuff-box on the table and softly dusted his fingers—"that no sooner was he gone, than they prepared to march on the Tuileries. That was the position—the regrettable position—two hours ago. And two hours is a long time, General."

"And during those two hours you have done—?"

Barras smiled and laid the tips of his fingers on the table-top. "I have been looking for you—for the purpose, General Bonaparte, of asking you to accept the defense of the Government."

"Why me? You have here in the city Bernadotte, Hoche—"

Barras raised his hand. "I beg of you, General Bonaparte. Believe me, I have adequate reasons for not wanting to employ the services of those gentlemen."

"But you, yourself—?"

Barras shrugged slightly. "It is true that, nominally, I am Commander-in-Chief of the National Guard. But I am not so fatuous a fool as to imagine that military rank of itself bestows military ability. I know myself to be without that ability. But you—I am sufficiently aware of your past services, I am a sufficiently good judge of the characters of men—to believe you to be competent to deal with this matter." His eyes across the table were steady, but his fingers shifted ceaselessly about his snuff-box. "General Bonaparte—will you undertake the defense of the Tuileries?"

He looked at the firm eyes, then down at the uneasily fidgeting hands. Barras knew how to choose his scapegoats—

"Do you accept, General Bonaparte? I give you three minutes to consider." He took out his watch and stood holding it in his hand.

Three minutes. He looked at the brown stains on the green baize, he looked at Barras' fingers that twitched as he held his watch. He turned his back, and walked to the long windows at the end of the room, standing staring out into the night. Up there in the gallery of the Convention he had theorized like a collegian. Now he must think clearly and quickly. Three roads lay open before the nation, and he had three minutes to reconnoiter them. He clasped his hands behind his back, and leaned his forehead against the smooth coolness of the window-pane.

The Revolution had been made, not in the name of a Republic, but in that of Constitutional Monarchy. A monarch who recognized himself as King by the will of the people would bring the Revolution to a triumphant close. But one who imposed himself by divine right would strangle it. He would wipe out in a day the liberties and rights that the people had won by five years of struggle and agony. That was what Provence proposed to do. The old order restored, the new obliterated. No.

Counter-revolution. A return to '92, when a King had been afraid to shed a thimbleful of blood in defense of his legal authority. The bodies of the Swiss Guards asprawl on the spattered paving-stones—the smoking pools beneath the scaffold. Blood, starting with a trickle that a handful of mud could have stopped, rising to a torrent that could sweep away a nation. No. The handful of mud, though it might soil the fingers, was better than that.

The new Government. New in name only. The same dirty pack of cards reshuffled. Yet nevertheless a pack of cards, with system, cohesion, organization. It was the Government, however debased. And, in time of crisis, a patriot must support the Government. No Government should ever be overthrown by violence, for that meant that violence itself ruled. He turned away from the window to face the man at the table.

"I will do it," he said.

Barras put away his watch, smiled, and flicked his fingers. "Rest assured," he said, "that you will not regret it. You will be rendering the State a service that it will—"

"What forces are at my disposal?"

"Why—the National Guard, such of it as is still, er—disposed to serve. The police. Colonel Murat's Chasseurs. Some couple of thousand men of the city garrison. And of course my, er—Sacred Battalion—"

"Brigands and cutthroats. Artillery?"

"There are forty pieces. But they are out at the Sablons Artillery Park."

"Why?"

Barras shrugged and spread out his hands. "My dear General, because we have no horses to bring them in. Even the Directors—we ourselves have been obliged to use hired cabs to—"

"Colonel Murat's Chasseurs."

"But I doubt—I really doubt if Colonel Murat would consent. Light cavalry. However—"

"It was not my intention to consult the wishes of Colonel Murat."

"Oh, quite, quite. The arrangements are entirely in your hands. It it not my custom to interfere with my, er—subordinates. You will use your own methods, take your own decisions, your own, er—responsibilities."

Barras knows how to choose his scapegoats— From somewhere outside a clock struck one. An hour after midnight already. Barras had been looking for him for over two hours, and during that time he had done nothing—not even brought in the guns. If the insurgents had the intelligence of gnats, they would be on the way to the Sablons Park by now. Two hours lost already, another three to bring in the guns—if they were still there to bring. Five hours. Even an undisciplined mob could do much in five hours.

"From now on then," said Barras, "I leave everything in your hands—everything." And he lightly dusted his own hands together.

Everything. The risk of the lighted match held to the fuse, of the explosion of mob-fury, insurrection, civil war. Everything. While Barras gently flicked the dust of responsibility from his long-fingered hands. He looked from the expressive fingers to the inscrutable face, where smiling complacency was drawn smooth over a tortuous mind like a silk stocking over a scabby

129

leg. His own hands were laid in hard, knotted fists on the edge of the table.

"I shall issue muskets to the Deputies," he said.

Barras laughed condescendingly. "My dear man, they wouldn't know which end to load."

"Maybe. But if it should happen that tomorrow I am arrested for shedding the blood of the people, I do not intend to find myself alone on the bench of the accused. My meaning is clear—General Barras?"

"Oh, er—quite. Quite."

Barras stared at the door that still quivered from the violence of its shutting. He raised his hand and thoughtfully stroked his chin.

The clock of Saint-Roch at the end of the short, straight street struck four. The notes died away and there was no other sound, save when a man coughed and spat, or a horse jingled its bridle-rein. Yet through the silent darkness of the early morning you could sense them, like an acrid taint on the air. Forty thousand waiting men. Not individual men, but atoms welded together into a single force with only one life among them, one breath, one instinct. The mob. The darkness throbbed with the beating of its pulse—the life-pulse of a huge animal-thing, savage, powerful, dim-minded, held in check only by its jungle-fear of the trap.

There was no intelligence there, only instinct. Intelligence would have known that legal authority lay as helpless before that great strength as a tethered goat before a tiger.

Four o'clock. If the dawn came before the guns, the mob would see for itself that there was no trap. Nothing would be able to save the goat then—bleating with terror as it already was.

The guns. He listened. There was no sound from the distance save the far-off crowing of a cock. The dawn. Very soon now, and the beast would be able to see.

He had done everything that a man could do. He had set in his colored pins here, and here, and here. Save only the scarlet pins of the guns.

He listened. Silence. Then dim but vibrant, like the humming of a bee—

Behind him, a man began to whistle between his teeth. That would be Junot. Where he had come from, it was impossible to say. But there he was. He had a sort of homing-pigeon instinct for any trouble that held out the slightest hope of violence.

Quietly, without turning his head, he said, "Be silent, damn you."

Junot checked his whistling, then let out his breath in a soft "Ah!"

The hum grew louder. Metallic, harsh. A roaring, shattering thunder. Brief sparks driven from granite stones, long smooth gleams from polished bronze. The acrid tang of sweated horses, the sweetish smell of heated axles. The guns.

The dawn came with no sun, only an acid luminosity, slowly biting down through the darkness of the streets.

The mob was visible now, lying dark and clotted at the bottom of the rue Saint-Roch, and on the steps of the Church at its far end. But only its front ranks, its myriad-eyed head. The huge body of it lay out of sight beyond the angle of the rue Saint-Honoré. Under the strengthening light it began to stir, oozing forward a little—but heavily and sluggishly, like half-congealed lava.

The guns too caught the light, the threatening metallic teeth of the trap. The dark mass halted, and contracted a little on itself. It lay there watchful, uneasy, as though belly to ground measuring the distance.

"A target! A fair target!" muttered Junot behind him, and a gunner spat on the breech of his piece for luck.

A target dozens wide, hundreds deep. A blatantly easy target, and an atrociously difficult one. Had that been an enemy out there, one would have been grateful for his insanity, and blasted him out of the street. But this wasn't an enemy, save in the sense that a drunken man with a pistol in his hand is an enemy. This was some thousands of otherwise decent citizens, intoxicated with mob emotion. There need be no question of kill or be killed with a drunken man. A dash of cold water in the face, a whiff of pepper in the eyes, were enough to bring him to his senses. But forty thousand emotion-drunk men— One couldn't afford to make mistakes with a force like that.

No, a mob was different. Yet was it? After all, as a single man acts, so in general does man in the mass. A whiff of pepper. A whiff of grape-shot.

"Load with grape," he ordered.

The dark mass lay there, uneasy, watching, tense and wary. Hour after hour. The waiting was unbearable. Perhaps— But no. Once you have written your decisions clearly in your mind, never try to erase or alter. That only led to illegibility and confusion. He walked from gun to gun, verifying, adjusting, testing.

Noon. Junot brought him cold meat and bread on a plate, and a glass of wine. He had no consciousness of eating and drinking. Every sense was concentrated on the dark mass that lay out there, heavily motionless, save for a faint ebb and flow like the tremor along taut muscles. At any moment the flow might heave itself forward with the whole weight of its strength behind it. The time to turn your head, to glance over your shoulder, might be enough.

Three o'clock. A drizzle of rain set in. The dash of cold water. Parisians in the face of death were as single-minded as a swarm of bees—but a Parisian with cold water running down the back of his neck was as individual as a spoilt child. The mass thinned a little, as with the beginnings of disintegration.

The gunners took off their hats to protect their lighted matches. Cavalrymen spread the tails of their greatcoats over the rumps of their horses. The infantry pointed the muzzles of their muskets downwards, and shielded the locks between elbow and side.

Four o'clock. The rain had stopped. Not enough. The loosening particles of the dark mass hardened to solidity again—the solidity of ice over rising water, trembling and straining with the invisible power that thrust at it. The ice still held, but the slightest shock—a thrown stone, a single shot—

From a window in the rue Saint-Roch it came—a brief jet of fire, a sharp crack of sound. Another. A clattering rattle, the darting flames dimmed by smoke.

A gunner coughed, and slouched forward over his piece. A Guard shook his hand, spattering blood. A horse whickered at the sharp prick of pain, and clashed its bit.

The echo of the shots was drowned in a snarling roar of furious voices, a thunder of drumming feet as the mob broke free of uncertainty.

He drew his sword and stood with his eyes fixed on the forward-surging mass, estimating, judging the range, the speed of the target, the exact moment when force must be met by force and the silent threat of the guns give place to roaring action. There, just half-way down the street, where a jutting lantern broke the surface of the wall—up to that point the beast might still be cowed—beyond, and not even the guns could check it. There, where the lantern jutted out— He raised his sword over his head, then brought it sharply down.

"Fire!"

Five o'clock. Gunners lounged against their pieces, cavalrymen, bridles looped over their arms, walked their horses slowly up and down. Guards stamped their feet and flailed their arms to quicken their chilled blood. In the rain-sodden rue Saint-Roch was nothing but a drift of white mist, acrid to the nostrils and bitter in the mouth.

No need to stare down that street any more. No need to hold one's judgment as delicately balanced as a chemist's scales. The experiment was over. The whiff of grape-shot had succeeded, splitting the single mob-monster into its component atoms of forty thousand people. Angry people, frightened people, resentful people, but people. Not beasts.

"A horse," he threw over his shoulder to the attendant shadow at his heels that was Junot. The horse was there, and he mounted.

"The stirrups—" protested Junot, snatching at a leather. The stirrups were too long, but it didn't matter. He was an awkward horseman at any time. He pushed Junot's hand away with his knee, and turned his mount towards the rue Saint-Roch. Junot moved beside him, catching at the stirrup.

"But you can't— Not alone. Wait, let me—"

He touched the horse with the spur, and jerked free of the entanglement of Junot's anxiety. For Junot, an action was finished when his opponent ceased to resist. He couldn't see that the most difficult part came after. A man who experimented in authority must be willing to pay in his own person—to let himself be assassinated if necessary. Otherwise the experiment was incomplete.

He turned his horse up the rue Saint-Roch. There was a little blood on the paving-stones. Not much. Not like the reeking courtyards of '92. And the dead had been decently disposed of, the wounded were being cared for by military surgeons in the Tuileries.

The people were showing themselves again now, coming out of doorways and porches, from side turnings and from the shelter of the Church. They began to crowd the street, but moving in little eddies and cross-currents now, without cohesion—shouldering each other, pushing for place to stare with an almost detached curiosity at the blood-stains on the stones, and at the little pits the grape-shot had dug in the pillars of Saint-Roch. They had their women-folk with them now. Women in a crowd were both a danger and a safe-guard. You couldn't give them even the lightest whiff of grape, but they kept their men-folk separate and conscious of themselves as individuals.

He rode slowly up the street towards the Church—and because his was the only purposeful movement amid the uneasy shifting of the people, they began to follow after. At the Church, where the rue Saint-Honoré crossed the rue Saint-Roch, the great bulk of the crowd that had had no part in the brief drama was pressing forward, sullenly intent on seeing, at least, the empty stage. Their shifting mass filled the street, blocking the way. He reined in and sat quite still, watching them.

They drifted past, looking up at him, at first with the faint curiosity of indifference, then with a growing antagonism that sharpened their interest. Their onward flow checked, and began to swirl about him, circling in closer and closer. From them rose an indistinct murmur, half of shifting feet and half of angry breathing.

He sat quite still, watching.

Their circle narrowed and narrowed, until his horse shifted nervously under the push of their bodies. The threat of them rose in pitch, but it was still in their throats and not yet in their fists. Then a hand reached up and snatched at his belt—the hand of a market-woman, huge-bosomed, thick-shouldered, and solid-waisted. Her grip, strong as a man's, was at his belt, her great red face was pushed against his knee. Her fingers tautened in a downward jerk, and she flung the hoarse threat of her anger up at him.

"Down with the epaulettes! Down with the hired assassins of the people! Down!"

His stirrup was too long for him to brace himself against it, and at his belt was her gripping fist, with her great weight behind it, jerking and dragging him down. Down below were the granite cobblestones and iron-shod sabots gritting over them.

The impersonal threat of an enemy battery wasn't hard to face, because the death it sent wasn't directed against you as a man, but through you to the cause or idea beyond. But human violence snatching at a man in his person, in the very flesh and blood and bone of his body— There was something of insanity about that, and of all horrors, insanity was the most terrible. The taste of nausea rose bitter in his throat.

"Down with the jacks-in-office, who fattened on the hunger of the people!"

He sat very still, only his eyes moving, searching from face to face, gripping with his knees against the downward pull of the furious hand. He looked from stupid face to brutal face, from brutal face to angry face. Then at the face of a big laborer with a wide mouth and laughter wrinkles about his eyes. He stared straight at him, forcing the man's gaze with his own. Then he smiled.

"You," he said. "You over there, in the blue blouse. Judge between us. Which of us two is the fatter—this good lady or I?"

The man's eyes, uncomprehending at first, shifted from the whip-lash leanness above to the large-curved mass below. Then his eyes narrowed and his mouth widened. He chuckled. He threw back his head and guffawed. The laughter caught here and there through the crowd, like sun-sparks on a tossing sea. Then it ran together in a great shout of merriment.

Indignant with surprise, the woman breathed heavily and tightened her grip for a moment. Then she loosed her hand, and brought it down with a clacking slap on his thigh.

"Get along with you for a saucy brat!" she said.

It was six o'clock.

PART III
1796

*"Woman, torment, happiness, hope of my
life and of my soul, whom I worship, whom
I fear—"*

BONAPARTE TO JOSEPHINE

*"It was his first passion, and he felt
it with all the vigor of his nature. He was twenty-six, she more
than thirty-two."*

MARMONT

CHAPTER

≈ XVI ≈

January.

FRÉRON SPREAD HIS LONG, CLEVER FINGERS OUT ON THE TABLECLOTH
and looked at the ice on his plate. He quirked an eyebrow at it,
and smiled apologetically.

"I am sorry," he said clearly and distinctly, "but I cannot eat
this ice."

The hum of conversation about the table was checked. A
white-gloved hand on the end of a crimson and gold sleeve in-
serted itself over his shoulder, removed his plate, and replaced
it by another. He surveyed it with interest for a moment, then
shook his head and sighed.

"I am more than sorry," he said, "but I really cannot—"

Again the gold and crimson arm renewed the plate. Again he
looked at it, and spread out his hands.

"I am truly desolated, but I—"

Beside him Céleste turned in her chair, breathing heavily with
anxiety. "What's the matter? Got the colic again? I told you you
needed a dose." She looked from his face to his plate, frowned,
then brightened. "Oh, poor lamb, it hasn't got a spoon! Here,
take mine."

She sucked it and laid it beside his plate. He flicked it aside
with his forefinger, and glanced sideways at Barras at the head
of the table. Barras was vexed. There'd been a flaw in his impeccable hospitality, and he didn't like it. Didn't like the ripple
of laughter that followed, either. It offended his dignity—and
Barras had never learned that dignity was a quality bearable only
in women and kings.

"You and General Bonaparte," said Barras, tight-voiced, "seem
to be peculiarly gifted in the art of, er—inspiring mirth."

Barras hadn't got over that yet, even after three months. Damn' funny it had been, too. Barras rushing before the Convention to praise General Bonaparte for daring to take the responsibility of firing on the people, while at exactly the same moment General Bonaparte was collecting his own applause from the people themselves. Barras had been too quick for once to give somebody else the credit for the dirty work. Having given the credit, he had to give the reward as well. Damn' awkward, that, and annoying, too, being obliged to make a popular man Military Governor of Paris.

He looked at Barras, and smiled deprecatingly. "Don't grudge General Bonaparte and myself our little successes," he said.

He heard Theresia laugh—the hard, boisterous laugh she used when she wasn't amused. He couldn't see her because she was on his side of the table, with Céleste and Ouvrard between. Barras at the heard of the table had stopped smiling, and was looking haughty. He was very satisfactorily vexed. Conceited fool, he fancied himself in that grotesque outfit the Directors had chosen to wear.

Céleste said, "Get on with your ice. There's no sense in going out to lunch unless you eat the food."

He said, "How impeccable is your logic, my queen," and picked up the fresh spoon the red and gold arm had supplied. It was a good ice—maraschino, stuffed full of brandied cherries. He wondered if the four other Directors had maraschino ices presented by crimson and gold sleeves. He doubted it. The others had their fancy costumes and their apartments in the Luxembourg Palace like Barras, but they hadn't got a Theresia Tallien who in her turn had got multi-millionaire Ouvrard.

He looked about the table. He and Tallien were opposite each other, at the foot. Tallien was tolerated because he was still useful for fetching and carrying and opening doors—though not that of his lady's bed-chamber, one gathered. He was busy fishing out the cherries from his ice. He wasn't allowed to drink in public now, lest he have another of his fits, which would be annoying for everybody. So he was consoling himself by sucking the brandy out of his cherries and spitting the pulp onto his plate.

He himself was tolerated because of the article he would presently write for the *Orateur*—a touching account of this harmonious New Year's festival, this gathering together in amiable concord of the Army, Society, and Finance—the Court of His Majesty, Director Barras. Finance was hidden from him on the far side of Céleste's imposing bosom, but he could hear it being amused by Theresia's bawdy stories—the tittering laugh of the bourgeois whose natural prudery was being tickled with the feather of impropriety.

On the opposite side of the table the Army, in the shape of General Bonaparte, was seemingly at its devotions before the altar of Society, personified by Madame de Beauharnais, who was apparently on the point of tears. Tallien was still spitting out cherries, and there was really little else for him to do, since his view was completely cut off by the meager but determined back of General Bonaparte.

But he was forgetting the most touching element of all, that of the sacred French family, personified by Mademoiselle Hortense de Beauharnais—present, though for the time being invisible, between the converging forces of the Army and Society. Poor child, she couldn't be enjoying her first adult party very much, what with General Bonaparte's shoulder in her face and his elbow in her plate, while across her prostrate body, as it were, he paid public homage to her mother.

Barras was beginning to unbend again a little, as well he might, with Theresia on his left and Josephine on his right, both his hunting-bitches obediently bringing in their catch to lay at his feet. He wondered what would happen if some day one of them brought back a hungry wolf instead of a fat hare.

He glanced at General Bonaparte, who looked hungry enough, in all conscience. But was he anything else besides? Would he let himself be fattened? Military Governor of Paris, a tempting dish for a young man of twenty-six. He looked more closely. It was a fine head in its way, if you looked beyond the starved gauntness of it. You could see the resemblance, too. Pauline Bonaparte. Paulette. The same gray eyes, the same finely-cut bones, the same firmly-set mouth. It was curious, that—the resemblance between the bleak-faced, black-browed man and the radiant, laughing girl.

He hadn't thought of Pauline Bonaparte for months. She was worth thinking of, even if her brother should be content with the Governorship of Paris. Yes, worth thinking of. That would vex Barras, too. A brother-in-law would after all be in a better position than a second-hand mistress. And things had obviously not gone as far as that yet. No man—not even a hungry Corsican—flattened his nose against the pastry-cook's window when he'd had his dinner.

The pastry-cook herself was smiling at General Bonaparte—that new, close-lipped smile she imagined to be enigmatic, when everybody knew it was to hide her teeth that were beginning to decay. That was why she daren't put frozen sweets in her mouth, too.

He leaned forward across the table and inquired with polite concern,

"Madame de Beauharnais, do you also find yourself unable to eat your ice?"

She looked up, first at him, then at Céleste, who was audibly enjoying her second ice. She smiled, close-lipped.

"Old women," she said, "and school-girls can afford to take liberties with their figures. But when one is approaching twenty-eight—" She shrugged, and made a little grimace.

He sank back with a sigh of relief. "No necessity for martyr-dom, then—since you yourself, with every day that passes, are leaving that age further and further—" He waved his hand.

The blue eyes slowly filled with tears. Astonishing, how she could always manage that. A pity, though, to waste so useful an accomplishment on—

Barras said, coldly and firmly, "And how soon, my dear Fréron, may Marseilles hope to be, er—favored with your presence?"

He smiled amiably. "Oh, very soon now. Very soon." And that too, my dear friend—my favor in Marseilles—that'll irritate you most abominably.

Marseilles. He could remember the address now. Rue Paradis. Though there was little enough of Paradise about that sordid little alley-way and the basement lodging that was not only sordid too, but literally infested with Bonapartes—Bonapartes of every shape and size, sex and age, from a smutty-nosed school-boy to the dragon-faced mother herself. That of course was a drawback. Brother-in-law to General Bonaparte was one thing, brother-in-law to a tribe of Bonapartes was another. Still, one couldn't have anything for nothing. Probably the little General had done something about the sordid apartment—but unfortu-nately one could scarcely expect him to drown his surplus brothers and sisters, even in the best of causes.

Madame de Beauharnais was demonstrating for the benefit of

General Bonaparte the fact that she could blush at Theresia's conversation. A silly little woman, but damned clever for all that.

Decidedly, he would go to Marseilles very soon. In the meantime, it would be as well if General Bonaparte didn't flatten his nose on the pastry-cook's window too persistently. He coughed deprecatingly into his napkin.

"It is unfortunate," he said with an apologetic smile, "that Mademoiselle Hortense is unable to eat her ice."

Madame de Beauharnais frowned very slightly, then looked vaguely at her own half-melted ice. General Bonaparte started, scowled, and drew sharply back, as though he'd been caught improperly clad at an open window. Hortense emerged into view and attacked her ice, with the heavy breathing of a swimmer who has been too long submerged. General Bonaparte glared blackly for a moment at the interrupter of his meditations. Then he swept the whole table with fierce-eyed imperiousness, and spoke:

"Dysentery and body-lice," he announced firmly, "are the chief enemies of the modern army on active service."

Barras found the maraschino ice very chilling to the stomach. With every spoonful he said to himself, "Damn the little man!" and the chill in his stomach increased.

Was there no gratitude at all in human nature? Here he'd taken this insignificant little nobody, literally starving, out of the gutter, and made him Military Governor of Paris. And was he satisfied with his fine uniform, his pay, his rank? Not a bit of it. He actually wanted to govern the accursed city as well. Free bread for the poor, to be paid for by the State; work for the unemployed, to be paid for by the State; distribution of fuel, to be paid for by the State. Anybody'd think the State was a charitable institution. And he called himself an artillery officer! Would any self-respecting soldier bother with such unmilitary things? Poking his nose into accounts, too. Checking up army-contractors' tenders. Scrawling across them his impertinent "I will have's" and "I won't have's." An artillery officer, indeed! He was a Robespierre on horseback. Worse. He was a popular Robespierre. Damn the little man.

That's what made it so awkward. One couldn't get rid of him without starting another riot—and his artillery on the wrong side this time. And one had been so sure the people themselves would take care of that part of it—instead of which, they'd laughed. Laughed! That's what came of trusting to the good sense of the common people.

You couldn't even disgrace him, because those same imbeciles of people would object. So there was no way at all of getting rid of him. Unless of course Carnot had his way and promoted him to the Army of Italy. There again. If he had his army, you'd loose the small remains of authority you still could exercise over him—you wouldn't have any control at all. Nobody would have any control. Damn the little man! Damn Carnot, too.

There was Fréron being insolent again. Fréron would have to be sent on mission to Bordeaux as soon as possible. You couldn't just disgrace him either, because of his accursed newspaper. He'd begun to be insolent in that too—referring to Theresia as "Her Serene Highness." Very funny. He wouldn't find it so amusing when his absence in Marseilles caused his paper to deteriorate to such an extent that it had to cease publication altogether.

He wished Theresia hadn't felt it desirable to display the perfection of her bosom in a Hussar's tight-fitting tunic, or to pile up her hair in imitation of a bear-skin bonnet with a two-foot plume of cock's feathers towering above it. He disliked this aping of male fashions—it was unwomanly, vulgar, and without charm. Though probably Ouvrard admired it. A mouse-like, timid, little creature like that would be sure to. And that, after all, was what mattered.

Josephine now, in her little white fur jacket and what looked like a saucerful of Parma violets over her left ear— Though God alone knew what it had all cost, and probably even He had no idea who was going to pay for it. She had no pity on a man. She would unhesitatingly drink gold out of her lover's skull. Not that he had any intention of offering it in that receptable, nor in any other, if it could be avoided.

So far it had been avoided by the useful process of claims for compensation against the State—compensation for Alexander's horses, compensation for Alexander's wardrobe, compensation for Alexander's Paris house, compensation for property looted from Alexander's country château—and now, to console her for an enforced, er—partnership with Theresia, the Ferté-Beauharnais itself restored to her by the State. Decidedly Alexander was a better provider dead than alive—but even he couldn't be made to go on paying indefinitely. Still there was General Bonaparte, who seemed to have lost his head as effectively as General de Beauharnais.

General Bonaparte said, "Dysentery and body-lice—"

Damn the little man! Now if he weren't cut short, there'd be an interminable lecture on military diseases, their cause, effect, and cure. Who cared anyway of what disgusting maladies soldiers died, so long as they did die in sufficient quantities and get themselves crossed off the payroll. Not that one did pay them, of course—

"Very interesting and, er—informative, General Bonaparte. ... Shall we take coffee in the drawing-room?"

> *"This cannot go on, these Directors do not know how to do anything for the imagination of the people."*
> GENERAL BONAPARTE

CHAPTER

❧ XVII ❧

February.

THERESIA TALLIEN THREW OPEN HER CLOAK AND, LEANING BACK against the white marble mantel-shelf, stretched out her arm along it. Her cloak was of fur-lined wine-red velvet, and her bonnet with its enormous jockey's peak was of the same rich stuff.

Velvet was unprocurable in France—but for Ouvrard the financier, to whom bankers the world over and of every nationality paid homage, the picking up of a few meters of the finest Genoese weave was as simple an affair as the procuring of white bread by a politician like, say, Barras.

Barras. Poltician. Usurer of privilege and influence, complacent, incompetent, not even understanding the human values he juggled with. There was no tolerance in the appraisal of the great dark eyes she turned upon him.

"'A little Corsican soldier of no account—'" she quoted accusingly.

Barras, his elbows on the arms of his chair, pressed his finger-tips together and smiled up at her over them. "So he is, my dear—so he is." He stretched out his legs towards the blazing fire, and settled more comfortably in his chair. She tapped with her polished nails on the mantel-shelf and examined him with cold detachment.

He was looking old, she thought; though less with the age of his years than of his social class. He wasn't even a politician. An aristocrat. Member of a caste that had clung so long to the exquisite flower of its blooming that it had withered without fruit. That was it. He was decayed without ever having come to maturity.

She'd done what she could to give him new life, she'd played the sexless political intriguer for him, she'd played the harlot. She'd even been willing to play the devoted wife. He hadn't wanted any of those things. He'd already got what he wanted. He was Director Barras, the head of the State, with a fine apartment in the Luxembourg Palace, and opportunity to plunder public funds in security. An aristocrat, with only the ambition of an aristocrat—to maintain his little place apart in the world. To him, money was a strong wall between himself and outer darkness; to her, money was power—a vast ocean whose tide, uncontrollable yet predictable, was both master and servant of the world.

"Of no account," she repeated, "the Commander-in-Chief of the Army of Italy?"

He examined the curved perfection of his finger-nails, then let his hands fall to the arms of his chair. "The title is, I admit, er—impressive. But the reality, my dear Theresia, is far different. The Army of Italy—" He shrugged slightly. "The little man calls it an avalanche, but it's only last year's snow, rotting away to dirty slush. A rabble, a disintegrating rabble. Nothing more."

"Maybe. But you gave him a rabble once before to deal with, and—"

He waved a dismissing hand. "Unfortunate," he said, "but after all, the force of events that no one could have foreseen."

"I have never very much believed," she said slowly, "in the force of events, but a great deal in the power of a man who can direct them."

She visualized the man Bonaparte. She had sat nearly opposite him at Barras' luncheon of a month ago. Until then, she had thought of him as a rather grotesque young man for whom she had once obtained a voucher for a pair of new breeches, and who had shown his gratitude by making a nuisance of himself. During that lunch she had thought him naïve to the point of imbecility, with his moon-struck staring at Josephine. Then he had made his extraordinary contribution to the general conversation, and for a moment he had looked her straight in the face. The gaze of the pale gray eyes, deep-set under level dark brows, had been as expressionless and unwinking as the stare of a falcon. Yet under it she had become suddenly conscious of the impropriety of the military tunic used to display her woman's bosom. She had felt abashed. No ordinary man could abash Theresia Tallien. She wondered—

"You said yourself," she argued, "that the soldier was the greatest danger—"

"If I remember correctly," he interrupted, "I said, the victorious soldier. And that, I can assure you, General Bonaparte will not be."

"I wonder—"

"You need not wonder. I myself make no pretense of being an expert on military matters. But we sent his famous plan of campaign to Schèrer, who has been in command of the Army of Italy these twelve months past—and Schèrer sent it back, scribbled across it, 'Let the madman who conceived this come and execute it.' Even I could see that it was based not on the hard logic of strategy, but on a fanatical belief in his own ability to do the impossible."

"Fanatics sometimes do do the impossible."

"Sometimes, but not this time." He pulled himself up in his chair a little, and leaned forward on his elbows. "Listen to me, my dear. I have investigated the Army of Italy. Otherwise, I should never have allowed myself to be persuaded by Carnot that General Bonaparte was the, er—ideal commander for it. The Army of Italy has been neither paid nor supplied for these eighteen months past. It is at the moment dispersed to, er—live off the country. In other words, it has become a leaderless horde of vagabonds, beggars, and foot-pads, infesting the back doors and highways of the Mediterranean coast.

"It has neither horses nor guns nor ammunition. It hasn't even shoes to its feet. And naturally the Government isn't in a, er—position to supply it with any. On the other hand, the Austrians have in Italy eighty thousand of the world's finest professional soldiers, well-equipped and well-supplied. That means thirty thousand ragged conscripts against more than twice their number of trained veterans. The result is inevitable."

"Still— There was Wattignies."

"Wattignies! I'm sick of the name of that confounded battle. A lucky chance, an accident. Such things don't happen twice. And there at least the men themselves were enthusiastic. But these!" He spread out his hands and shrugged. "They've already been, er—blessed with more than one Commander-in-Chief of a relatively mild form of incompetence. Are they likely to rally to a man they've never even heard of, and who is quite obviously mad? Then what of the staff-officers—Augereau, Lannes, Masséna, La Harpe—men of mature age and wide experience? Are they going to be pleased to find themselves under the orders of an obscure Corsican nobody of twenty-six with only a street-brawl to his credit? Are they likely to coöperate, to be enthusiastic and helpful? No, no, my dear. He'll never even get his army down out of the Alps, let alone into Italy."

She ran her finger along the edge of the mantel-shelf, and frowned down at it. There was after all something in what he said. He might not have a wide intelligence, but he had a narrow cunning. The scales of chance would certainly not be weighted in General Bonaparte's favor. Yet she mistrusted chance. Chance was like a decimal-point, capable of changing values without altering figures. "Perhaps not," she said slowly. "Yet suppose—"

"Suppose! Suppose!" He flung himself back impatiently in his chair. "Well, for the sake of a futile argument, suppose he does get his army into Italy. What of it? Either he makes contact with the Austrians, and we are rid of him and his accursed army in the bargain—a, er—disaster for which, naturally, Carnot will be responsible—or he does not make contact. In which case the affair becomes nothing more than a military raid into a rich and flourishing country, of which the results will be no more and no less than they always are in such petty forays—a certain amount of loot and booty. And even you, my dear, must admit that any such, er—contribution would be more than welcome at the moment."

She nodded without answering and, leaning against the mantel-shelf, turned her head and stared out of the window. Slowly she turned back to him. "You forget, my friend," she said, "that England has important loans in Vienna—and therefore any attack on Austria will put English finance on the defensive. Your loot won't help you much then."

"I am not altogether a fool," he said, a little edge of irritation on his voice, "and I forget nothing. If by some miraculous chance the little man shows signs of, er—seriously irritating Austria, we can simply disown him as an adventurer."

She twisted about, her arms crossed on the mantel-shelf, staring down between them at the fire. An adventurer. The strange gray eyes, pale as flames in the sunlight. Adventurer. One who ventures. Not a man like Barras, who sat crouched, miser-like, over his little horde of power, but the true adventurer, the expender of power, the soldier. Military power was the only thing that was free of the power of money, since the soldier neither bought, nor sold, nor bartered. Only steel was stronger than gold—but only gold was untarnishable.

Still gazing down into the fire she said, *"You* can disown him, perhaps. The people won't. He's popular."

"Oh, popular—" he said, with an indifferent wave of his hand. "He will no longer be, once he's lost his campaign of Italy—and his army."

She kicked at the fire with the toe of her shoe. "Nevertheless, I think it would be safer if he lost his popularity before his campaign. There are ways." She turned about and faced him again, her elbow on the mantel-shelf. "There is such a thing as scandal."

He shook his head and smiled up at her tolerantly. "My dear, even I was capable of thinking of so elementary a device as that. The Secret Police have left no stone unturned, in the hopes of finding some, er—distressing revelation beneath. They found nothing but an oppressively virtuous widowed lady old enough to be his mother. And even there his intentions, though, er—quaint, were painfully honorable."

She laughed sharply. "He seems to have a weakness for middle-aged widows."

He frowned a little without answering. Now he was on his dignity. How childish even the most cynical of men could be when you touched their masculine vanity! After all she was only trying to help him, to protect his little horde of power—a negative power, yet still capable of producing the official signatures and seals that even multi-millionaires sometimes found useful. She moved forward and sat on the arm of his chair. Her voice was gentler when she spoke, and she fingered the lapel of his coat.

"Adventurer he may be," she said, "but the people believe in him. He has caught their imagination—and the imagination of the people is a dangerous thing. They love an adventurer. But you yourself said they were respectable at heart. And what would they think of a man who managed to worm himself into the good graces of another man's mistress—the mistress of the head of the State, and his benefactor. What would they think of him if he obtained her favors—and with them a high command to which neither his age nor his military record entitles him? What would they think of a man who did that—eh, Barras?"

He looked up at her silently for a moment, then laid his hand over hers. "I myself," he said, "have never permitted my conscience to, er—tyrannize over my intelligence. But I—even I could never have imagined so scabrous a plan as that. You are a remarkable woman, Theresia—truly remarkable." He bent his head, and kissed her lightly on the palm of her hand. Then, caressing her hand between his own, he frowned a little.

"Remains, however," he said, "to convince Josephine of the desirability of permitting—in fact, of insuring that her, er—virtue be assailed."

"There is a very certain method," she answered dryly, "of convincing Josephine of the desirability of anything."

"Yes," he said hesitatingly. "Yes—certain, but—damned expensive." He looked down at her hand, twisting a ring on her finger. "Still," he went on more firmly, "Josephine's bills. After all— Well, it would undoubtedly be the duty—and the pleasure, of my, er—successful rival to assume that responsibility as well. The fellow can scarcely do less, can he?"

His hands still caressed her own. And suddenly his touch was repellent, nauseating. Its soft smoothness seemed to be the flabby slime of decay, smearing and contaminating. She snatched her hand away, and jerked herself to her feet. She was as ready as he to barter her soul, but at least she demanded a worthy price. He asked no more for his than a receipted bill.

Aristocrat! Not even that. Not even the great vices of his kind were left in him. That handsome surface over nothingness was beginning to crack. A strong enemy was a lesser danger than a feeble ally. She moved away from him to the center table where she had left her muff and gloves. Her back to him, she began to gather them up, putting on her gloves, jerking them roughly into place.

"Use Josephine as a minnow to catch your pike if you can," she said coldly. "But I'm not live bait for any man. I catch my own fish." She fastened her cloak, pushed her hands into her muff and turned about, standing very erect and stiff, looking at him narrow-eyed.

He turned the mild surprise of his face towards her. "Of course, my dear, of course. I am sure no man would, er—presume— Still, if you would permit me the honor—if I might offer my humble escort as far as your door—" Both hands on the arms of his chair, he began slowly to draw himself up from its depths.

She passed behind him towards the door. "There is no need," she said indifferently. "Ouvrard is waiting in my carriage."

Still leaning forward in his chair, his eyebrows raised in sharp dismay, he turned to watch her as she crossed the floor. "In this bitter cold—you've kept—*Ouvrard* waiting an hour and more?"

With her hand on the doorknob, she looked back at him over her shoulder.

"It's not an hour, but a year, that I've kept him waiting."

> *"Bonaparte is in adoration before*
> *me as though I were a divinity."*
> JOSEPHINE

CHAPTER

❧ XVIII ❧

February.

SHE SAT STILL WHERE BARRAS HAD LEFT HER, ELBOW ON KNEE, CHIN on hand, staring at the scorched place on the carpet. There really wasn't very much time to—to consider General Bonaparte. In a week or so he'd know for himself he'd got—what was it?—his Army of Italy, and then of course it would be too late to do anything about it. So there wasn't much time. That was like Barras, of course. He always knew exactly what should be done, but when it came to how to do it he just walked away and didn't help at all.

There was the Directors' reception at the Luxembourg tonight, of course. General Bonaparte always went there, though one might wonder why, since he only stood about in corners glowering at people. Or talking too much and too loudly. Not that he hadn't his little social accomplishments, too. He could read the lines of the hand. A really useful and interesting thing to be able to do, that. She would have liked him to read hers. But she'd never asked him. She'd felt—peculiar about the idea of putting her hand in his. Not that his hands weren't clean. Quite nice hands really, surprising in a man of his class—small and delicate and well-tended. Still, she'd never asked him.

He was really quite good at it, too. The other night, when Theresia was dressed up as Diana, with a tunic right up above her knees, and a silver crescent in her hair, she'd pushed her hand in front of him, laughing in that outrageous fashion of hers. He hadn't even looked at it, but at the silver crescent in her hair, and said, "The days of mythology are over for you, Madame, and those of history just beginning." Theresia had been furious. But you couldn't make a mockery of a man in public and expect him to forget it. That was the sort of thing Theresia could never learn.

Hoche, too—all the six-foot two of swaggering complacency of him—holding out his big coarse hand. He'd looked like a barnyard rooster contemptuously facing a bantam cock. But the little man had held his ground. He'd glanced at Hoche's hand, then glared up at him, and said, "You will die very soon, General ... in your bed," and abruptly turned his back. Hoche hadn't liked it. Of course, nobody liked to be told they were going to die, not even comfortably in their own bed instead of messily on a battle-field. Yet it was the little man who'd looked the angrier of the two. She frowned a little. It would be—unfortunate, if he'd heard— Still, it didn't really matter. He'd only think what after all was the truth—that Hoche was a cowardly ruffian who wasn't ashamed to defame a woman to cover his own discomfiture. Yes, General Bonaparte was really quite good at fortune-telling, though she'd never asked him to tell her own. Not yet.

Lots of other women did. Not that they really took an intelligent interest in scientific things, but just because, last October, he'd fired off his cannon in the streets of Paris—which, after all, couldn't have been a very difficult thing to do. But some women were so silly, they'd run after any man who got himself talked about.

She herself had no necessity to run after him. None at all. She had only to look at him, quite casually, and then walk indifferently away. It would be amusing to do that to-night—to go late to the reception after everybody else had arrived, then just look at him, and take him away. Yes, amusing. Though after all, perhaps, a trifle obvious, a little crude. The sort of thing Theresia would do. Or try to do.

No. It would be far more—delicate, if both of them just stayed away from the reception altogether. Everybody would notice, but nobody could say anything, could they? Of course they would think—people have such unpleasant minds—but they couldn't really *say*— Yes, that would be much more subtle. And quite easy, really.

Of course there was her dress, that she'd had made specially for to-night. A pity to waste that on just one man—and one, too, who certainly didn't know the difference between mattress-ticking and mousseline-de-soie. Yet perhaps after all there'd be no need.

She got up and stood before the long cheval glass between the windows, studying herself. Her cream-colored lace negligée was really very attractive. It was close-fitting at the girdle, but around the hem it was meters, but literally meters wide—so that when she stood quite still it hung in long, deep flutings to her feet, but when she walked, its little train caught at the carpet, drawing it as closely back against the long, smooth curves of her thighs and hips as though she were moving against a strong wind. A really successful negligée. Still, it was made of lace, and lace was—well, transparent. It wouldn't do to—disturb the little man. Not too soon. No, it would have to be the dress. A pity.

First of all, though, General Bonaparte must be—must be made aware that he wasn't going to the reception at the Luxembourg tonight. She went to her dressing-table and opened a drawer. She had a pen somewhere— Yes, here it was. A bright vermillion-dyed quill. She didn't often write letters, but she was really quite good at it when she tried.

Paper— She opened another drawer. Bills. She half-closed it quickly, then pulled it out again. Once or twice she'd written notes to men on the backs of unpaid bills, and it had worked very well. Still, it would be ill-bred to do that unless you really knew the man—and actually she hardly knew General Bonaparte at all. She sorted through the bills. Here was one on a double sheet, the figures discreetly hidden on the second page. Six handkerchiefs, with point d'esprit lace, two thousand four hundred francs. Oh dear! And she couldn't really remember— The covering page, however, was blank, save for quite an impressive-looking crest at the top. She sharpened the crease with her finger-nail, then carefully slit off the upper sheet with her wooden complexion-knife.

She picked up her quill, and began to write.

> *"To die without being loved by you, to die without that certitude, is the torment of Hell, is the living, terrifying vision of total annihilation."*
>
> BONAPARTE TO JOSEPHINE

CHAPTER

February.

GENERAL BONAPARTE DESCENDED FROM HIS CARRIAGE AND MOUNTED the steps of his mansion in the rue Neuve des Capucines. There had been something of a thrill in that at first. His carriage, his mansion. The satisfaction had been brief. It was an official carriage, an official mansion, and he the official who temporarily made use of them. An official. A bureaucrat. A man who read police reports and wrote reports of his own. At twenty-six, a quill-pusher.

The door opened before he had time to knock on it. He went in, and a pair of hands relieved him of his gloves, hat, and overcoat. He hesitated a moment. The handsome new double-breasted overcoat with the gold-embroidered collar and the silk lining— The itch was still on him to make certain that it was properly disposed on its wooden frame that preserved the line of the shoulders. He was convinced that the lackey did nothing but carelessly hang it on a peg, so that the whole weight of it dragged down from the neck, ruining the set of the collar. But that, too. It was an official coat, uniform of the Military Governor of Paris.

Without turning his head to ascertain the fate of the coat he went upstairs to his office on the floor above. An office. A desk, and piles of dossiers, and ink and pens. On the wall, a map of Italy. The dusty, red road to Genoa, the pass in the

154

mountains above Savona— He jerked his eyes from it and went to the desk.

The day was already darkening, his man had drawn the curtains and lit the desk-lamp. A wasteful thing to do, that— when he might not have been home for an hour or more. He sat down at the desk and looked at the papers before him.

Police-report on the theaters of Paris. The theaters! Good God, and the red road to Genoa— The Opéra, the Vaudeville, the Louvois. Nothing to report. At Feydeau's Theater, "unseemly mirth." What sort of mirth did a police-officer consider to be unseemly? Ha! The patriotic song that must, by order of the Government, be sung every night on every stage. Not the great old songs of '89, the *Marseillaise,* the *Chant du Départ,* the *Sambre et Meuse,* but the new, hysterical rubbish, the Réveil, the Voix du Peuple. Feydeau had obeyed the order—only the song had been sung by a dwarf dressed in a costume which, the police gravely suspected, had been modeled on that of the Directors— and both it and the song had been greeted by the "unseemly mirth" of the audience. Unseemly was the right word, for it was stern indignation rather than frivolous laughter that the degraded caperings of the Directorate should inspire. Yet after all it was true that ridicule was more dangerous to men in position than any conspirators' plots. Especially in Paris.

Grain was coming into the city more abundantly now. There were still bread-queues, but they were orderly, and everybody had to present his own card. Though nobody had as yet seen Barras in a bread-queue, nor his table bare of white bread.

Something more energetic would have to be done about the four thousand children abandoned in the streets of Paris, pitiful result of the infamous five-minute divorce laws that had turned marriage into wholesale prostitution. The new morality as they called it, that permitted little children to be treated like unwanted kittens. Worse, for no one even took the trouble to drown them. He frowned, and pushed aside the reports.

He looked up at the map of Italy. The rose-red road along the coast— A strong body of cavalry sent full tilt down it, to make a feint towards Genoa. That would bring the Austrians eastwards to screen the city, drawing them away from the Sardinians to the west, and leaving a gap between them. Then your main body wheeling abruptly north from Savona, crossing the mountain-pass, thrusting itself into the gap—there, at Montenotte. If he—if one did that, it would be placing greatly weaker forces between the Austrian hammer and the Sardinian anvil. But it would also be flanking both enemies from, as it were, an interior position. With so small a force as the Army of Italy it would be useless to attempt the old method of feeling for both left and right flanks along an extended front, like a wrestler straining to wind both arms about his opponent's body. His own arms would be far too short for that. No. The thing was to gather your strength together into one small, hard, compact mass and drive it onto the enemy's weakest spot, like a clenched fist to the wind. He clenched his own fist, and looked at it.

Yes, the right fist, the main body, jabbed short and sharp into the unguarded midriff, then the left fist, the reserves, brought up in a wider sweep to the head, while it was still fuddled with surprise. There was no need for a small army to be intimidated by a great one, any more than for a small man—

Barras. Barras of course would go on opposing the plan, even though Carnot himself was beginning to be convinced. It wasn't fear of disaster that made him resist and criticize and sneer, but fear of success. And there would be success. Nothing could prevent it. Nothing but death on the battle-field—

He had often thought of death, thought of it as an ultimate door that couldn't be shut in any man's face, when at last he could no longer endure the nothingness of life. More than once it had taken courage not to push it open with his own hand. But not now. Now it was death itself that was nothingness and emptiness, frightening, terrible. For when one's soul has already found its own Heaven—elsewhere, then death of the body must mean extinction, utter and complete. Annihilation—

He stared at the map of Italy. The red road darkening under the long slow column of marching men, as red velvet darkens under a finger-tip dragging the wrong way of the pile. The rocky defile clashing with the metallic roar of gun-wheels as artillery passed where it was impossible that artillery could pass. On the crest of the mountains the dusty little town of Montenotte, the soft spot, the solar-plexus, where a small, hard fist driven resolutely home—

He smashed his fist down on the desk, and felt something strange beneath it. A little packet, that he hadn't noticed before. He picked it up, weighing it on the palm of his hand. A snuff-box probably, or even a watch, that some gaming-house proprietor thought was the price of a government official. Perhaps it was. But not of an artillery officer. He dropped it contemptuously, then picked it up again. He had never, since he was a child, been able to resist the temptation of a tied and sealed packet. The seals were like the closed covers of a book, and the itch to know what was inside was irresistible. He opened it. A letter, crested and mauve-tinted, folded about—

The skin of his cheeks puckered and tautened as the blood ebbed out of his face. It was— And he had struck it, struck it with his clenched fist! He had struck— He laid it down gently and withdrew his hand. Not moving, not touching, he stared. His hands were very cold, yet the blood scorched his cheekbones and roared like fire in his ears. It was not, of course, true. Such things didn't happen. He stretched out a finger, and touched. It was real.

A little plaque of ivory, so small you could hide it in the palm of your hand—yet so enormous it blotted out the world and everything in it. A little plaque of ivory, with all the glory of Heaven and earth reflected, concentrated, on it. All beauty and all happiness in miniature. A miniature of Josephine. Her smile—tender, yet a little mocking, with above it the grave intelligence of her quite indescribable blue eyes. Her little head, with its divine crown of small curls that her sweet simplicity abandoned to the unstudied charm of nature—little tendrils of innocence, frail as gossamer, yet able to twine about a man's heart so strongly that the blood was squeezed from it, and it cracked with the unendurable pain of its delight. Josephine—

She had sent— But why? For what purpose? There was a letter—there, unfolded before him. He stretched out his hand, hesitated, and drew it back. He knew what was in it. The reproof that her divine kindness wouldn't permit her to administer to his face. Who but she could have known how to soften the hurt of a rebuff by offering the consolation of the painted image to eyes forbidden henceforth to raise themselves to the unattainable original? Reproof—gentle, forbearing, but reproof. So much was certain.

He got up and walked about the room, his legs feeling strange and numb, as though he waded through icy water. He stopped before the map of Italy, and stared at it. The incredible blue of Josephine's eyes, darkening under the downward sweep of her lashes. The tender shadow between Josephine's breasts that no man might even dare to imagine— The certainty of defeat.

The uncertainty that was a torment worse than defeat. He went back to the desk, and picked up the letter.

Certitude. On that single sheet of tinted paper, in those brief lines, those few words—

"You do not come to see a friend who is fond of you, you have completely abandoned her. You are wrong, for she is attached to you.

"Come soon. I want to see you, and talk to you about yourself."

The paper in his hand quivered so that the writing on it blurred before eyes that stung as though salt had been rubbed into them. He laughed. He bit his lip and shook with laughter. He laid the note beside the miniature and looked at it, laughing with short, hard, indrawn breaths. He marched up and down the room. He rubbed at his eyes with the palms of his hands. He kicked at the fire, so that its blazing heart pitched forward onto the hearth. He snatched up a paper-knife, examined it intently, snapped it in half, and flung the pieces on the floor.

"Come soon. I want to see you. Come soon— Come soon—"

That of course was quite incredible, unbelievable, impossible. He rushed back to his desk. Miraculously, the little tinted sheet of paper was still there—and still more miraculously, the words on it hadn't disappeared.

"Come soon. Come soon."

The cramp of sudden panic knotted the muscles of his stomach. Soon. How long had—*it* been there? When was it that his stupid oaf of a servant had laid it there, tossed it probably with a careless, a sacrilegious hand, to lie, like a flower on a muck-heap, on a pile of police dossiers? Police dossiers! But it was he who was the oaf, the callous-souled barbarian, not to have sensed in every nerve of his body, every fiber of his soul, the instant he came into its presence. Oaf! With a jerk of the hand he swept the dossiers to the floor, and left *it* and the miniature alone on the polished wood altar of his desk.

"Come soon—"

He rushed out of the room and down the stairs, three steps at a time. He flung open the street door. Fool! One didn't hurl one's self into a lady's house hatless, coatless, and gloveless. He turned back. The coat— Why must servants have this mania for secreting things, why couldn't they leave a coat hung over a vestibule chair, where a man could get at it in a hurry.

He found the coat in a dressing-room beneath the stairs. Of

course, it had been put onto that complicated wooden thing, instead of hung, ready to hand, on the nearest hook. And buttoned all the way down. He tore the buttons from their holes, jerked the coat from its frame. He plunged his arms into the sleeves. He had forgotten to hold the cuffs with his fingers, and his under-sleeves rucked up and caught at his forearms. But it wasn't worth the delay of taking the overcoat off again. By pushing a little harder, he forced his arms through.

His hat at least was on a peg, ready to be snatched. Gloves— Not in the overcoat pockets. What imbeciles servants were, as though it mattered whether coat pockets bulged or not. The little dressing-table wedged in a corner— He jerked at its drawer, and it came right out and spilled its contents on the floor. He stirred at it with his foot. A scarf. A clothes-brush, handkerchiefs, a hair-brush and comb. A box of snuff, that had spilled out over everything else. No gloves.

He tugged at the bell-pull. He waited quite five seconds. Damn all servants! He snatched his hat onto his head, and flung out into the vestibule. After all, it wasn't gloves that she wanted to see. She— The Citizeness Beauharnais. Madame de Beauharnais. Madame the Viscountess de Beauharnais. Josephine— Josephine—Josephine—

He dashed out into the night, leaving the front door wide open behind him.

> *"None of her attractions were of Nature, but of art ... as perfected an art as was ever displayed by the courtesans of Greece and Rome."*
> BARRAS

CHAPTER

XX

February.

SHE GLANCED AT THE CLOCK, AND FROWNED A LITTLE. SHE SHIFTED the small blue porcelain bowl of snowdrops farther along the dressing-table. She picked up a little jeweled frame, and dropped it into a drawer. It was just as well it shouldn't be seen—and of course it would have been poor taste to send so valuable a present to a man. She'd broken the points of her nail-scissors getting the miniature out, which was a nuisance, good steel was so hard to come by these days.

She walked slowly up and down the room, watching herself sideways in the long cheval-glass. Undoubtedly, Mademoiselle Germonde had surpassed herself. It took genius these days to create a dress that was fashionable, yet at the same time had dignity. The little bodice was an inspiration. Bands of white satin only palm-wide, like pale hands modestly crossed, shielding as best they could a virginal bosom. The sleeves, of mousseline-de-soie, were enormous, yet almost invisible puffs of transparency like great bubbles slipping from the falling curve of her shoulders. The skirt, of mousseline-de-soie as well, fell away from the bodice like a receding wave, pouring down from the girdle to her feet, a diaphanous transparency, light as spray, white as foam, translucent as water.

Beneath it she wore garters of brilliants. When she moved, the stones shimmered half-seen through the filmy material, like sunsparks on misty water. Oh, there was nothing vulgar about it, like Theresia, who wore jeweled rings on her bare toes and showed her legs blatantly naked up to her thighs. Such poor taste. Foolish, too. Men's eyes get bored so much more quickly than their imaginations. Her own legs—just that shimmering, under-surface hint of graceful movement—

She looked down at the floating mists of her skirts, then lifted her head, listening. She'd heard no sound of a carriage, but that was certainly the front door, shut with a sharp bang, as Louise did to make certain it could be heard from upstairs.

She glanced about the room. Her carriage-cloak was well displayed, lying ready over the back of a chair. The day-bed was at the proper angle on one side of the hearth, so that firelight and candle-light from the mantel-shelf above would fall obliquely over the shoulder. Light directly in the face was so trying to the eyes. At the foot of the couch, not too coldly distant yet not too close, a small arm-chair was set.

She peered into the mirror, and gently shifted a curl away from her ear, so that the whole of its small, pale shell was visible. She had no need to hide her ears, as some poor women did. She picked up her white feather fan and slipped its ribbon over her wrist. She stood sideways to the door, took up the little blue bowl of snowdrops, held it between the palms of her hands, and let her head droop over it.

She heard the door open softly, she heard the faint jingle of a spur. She stood quite still looking down at the flowers and smiling softly to herself. She heard the sharp click of the closing door, and with a quick indrawing of breath, turned towards it. She pressed the blue bowl of white flowers to her white bosom, and opened enormous blue eyes over it.

"Oh," she breathed. "Oh, you—you startled me."

And really he was enough to startle anybody. His hat was crammed so low on his head that it almost met his dark brows. His hair straggled lank over his high collar, his coat was crookedly buttoned. He stood pressed back against the door, scowling forbiddingly and breathing heavily through thin, taut nostrils.

She set down her flowers, and dropped him a curtsy, grave, formal. But as she swept upright again, she tilted back her head and gave a little flutter of laughter.

"I believe you are more—startled than I, General." She laughed again. "You must be thinking my little household quite mad. But it's only poor Louise. She was my waiting-woman at Versailles, in the days when we Court ladies used to receive our friends at our toilette—and she cannot forget." She swayed again in a shallow dip. "You must forgive, General—"

He still stood pressed back against the door, glowering darkly from under his hat. Surely a peasant, without even the natural good manners of a—what was his name?—Captain Plessis.

"You forgive, General?" she said again.

The blood rushed up over his face so that, because of its dark weather-staining, it turned a dull copper color.

"I—forgive, Madame? It is you— I am importunate. But your letter, Madame. You wrote—I came— But I am untimely, I—" He hooked a forefinger into his black satin stock, and jerked at it.

"Not untimely," she said, "but in fact most timely. For in another five minutes I should have been on my way to the reception at the Luxembourg. You see I hadn't expected—hoped —you would be able to spare me a moment so soon—your time is so valuable, so taken up with serious matters."

Was the man glued to the door? What a funny little bourgeois he was! Decidedly it was just as well she hadn't kept on her negligée. She tried again.

"I had of course hoped to see you to-night at the Luxembourg."

She swept up her lashes for an instant, then lowered them again. "But one can't talk—not really talk—at a public reception, can one? . . . So boring, these State functions, don't you think?"

"I— Unless you are— That is—yes."

"Then suppose you come in? That will make talking easier, won't it?"

He turned copper-color again, pried himself loose from the door, and advanced a few paces.

"Your coat and hat. You will be more comfortable without them, won't you?"

He snatched at his hat, as though only then aware he had it on. With it in his hand, he made a complicated business of getting out of his coat. Then he stood, hat in one hand, coat in the other, glancing uneasily about him. A giggle rose in her throat. Did he expect her to have a man's coat-form in her bedroom? She took the things from him.

"Now sit down, General. It will be more—friendly, won't it?" She laid his hat and coat on her dressing-stool. Oh dear, he was going to sit in the rose-wood armchair with his sword on, and it would undoubtedly scratch the hand-polish— She hurried back to him.

"Your sword too, General. If you will permit a woman—"

She put her hands to his belt, fingering the buckles, bending her head over it. He stood rigid, staring before him. She looked up at him without raising her head. It wasn't very easy to look up at a man who was just one's own height.

"Your help, General. These things you soldiers wear—so hard for a woman's fingers—"

He looked down. Bending forward as she was, her bosom— His fingers came over hers, hard, crushing, hurting. How clumsy he was!

"How strong you are," she breathed.

She stood for a moment with his sword in her hand, stroking the plain steel scabbard with her palm. He hadn't taken time to change. Not even his dress-sword. Very slowly she swept up her lashes and looked at him. He hadn't even waited to shave. And he needed it. One wouldn't have imagined he had so heavy a beard. Not like Hoche's of course, little splinters of gold pushing through firm white flesh. He looked rather as though his jaw were made of steel, with the metal showing darkly through the taut-drawn skin that seemed to be its only covering. Not Hoche. No. She sighed.

162

She sank down gracefully on the day-bed, and leaned back against the cushions. The candle-light from the mantel-shelf behind and above her flooded softly over her shoulder, casting a dim shadow between her breasts that fluttered a little with the rise and fall of her breath. He stood quite still where he was, only one hand twisting and twisting at a button of his coat. The little giggle rose in her throat again. How long, if she just sat saying nothing— Decidedly uncouth, was General Bonaparte. She fingered her fan and looked up at him, slowly, and made a small, timid gesture with her hand.

"Won't you sit down, General? Standing there— You military men, a little—intimidating.... There. That's more—friendly, isn't it? Now we can talk, can't we?"

He sat stiffly on the edge of his chair. He jerked at his cravat. He said nothing.

"We can talk," she said, "for a little while. Then you can escort me to the Luxembourg—can't you?"

He caught at the arms of his chair, half rising.

"I— Now, if you wish, Madame."

How incredibly naïve he was! "Oh, no!" she protested. "Now that I have you to myself— And we haven't had our talk yet, have we? Unless you find it boring—a man like you, and a silly woman like me."

He sat back again, and rubbed his palms on his knees. "A woman like you, Madame," he said jerkily. "Like you— You don't know what you are—you don't know—" He looked at his hands, and gripped them together between his knees.

"It is what you are that matters," she said. "Tell me about yourself—all about yourself. Your life. Your ideas. Everything."

He stared at her blankly for a moment, then suddenly he smiled. It was really almost startling when he did that—when he stopped looking as though he hated everybody and expected them to hate him. It made him look quite—attractive. His mouth, when he wasn't being fierce, was curved and, well—gentle. And his teeth—quite absurd for a man, of course. She unfurled her fan and held it before her own mouth. It really wasn't fair, a man didn't need—

"If you are so—so gracious, Madame, as to be interested, I will tell you." He leaned forward in his chair, rested his forearms on his knees, fixed his eyes on her face, and told her.

Enough men had already told her things so that she was quite able, by the mere tones of their voices, to know when to be

163

incredulous, or startled, or admiring. He told her—leaning forward in his chair, staring at her.

She raised her fan to her mouth to hide a yawn. His words came as steadily as the ticking of a clock, a persistence of sound that you didn't really hear until it stopped. For he did stop—at last—with a final, slowing, tick or two.

"You see, Madame?"

She drew in a breath of tremulous emotion. "But how extraordinary! How really wonderful you are—so *different!* . . . And then, General?"

"Then Madame, there came October. They gave me my back-pay, and I was able at last to do my duty by my mother. I was able to send her sixty thousand francs."

Sixty thousand— She stared at him. He had had— Only last year, only four months ago he'd had—and he'd—

"You are a very—devoted son, General."

"Devoted? I am a son, and my mother is—my mother." He clenched his fist on his knee. "My mother, Madame, who in our own country has a right to call herself Countess—my mother who sacrificed everything for the Revolution—our house burned down, our property confiscated—has been obliged to live in a Marseilles slum, to wash other people's linen to buy food for her children, while men like Barras—politicians—muck in silk stockings—who have had nothing but profit from the Revolution—they live in palaces with their harlots who cover the nakedness of their shameless flesh only with diamonds! It's monstrous, Madame—monstrous!"

"Oh!" she said. She looked down at the shimmering highlights at her knee, and arranged the folds of her dress. She raised her eyes slowly. "But not everybody's like that. And you see, for a woman—alone—" She sighed tremulously. "A woman with two young—very young children— For their sakes, she has to—to make sacrifices. So you see—" She bit her lip, and made a small, helpless gesture with her hands.

He sat still farther forward, so that his knee almost touched the folds of her skirt. His face was strained, tense—his hands that he gripped together between his knees were shaking. A muscle jerked spasmodically beneath his cheekbone. He looked rather like a jack-in-the-box really, with the lid tightly shut down on him. Just by stretching out a finger one could release the catch, and then—

"You," he said, "you, in that refuse-heap—"

She slid out her feet a little, and lightly crossed her ankles. She'd been right to put on the silk stockings, in spite of what Louise had said. She might have a few—just a few brilliants on, but they weren't—what was it?—on her naked, shameless flesh. Besides, the thin film of silk made a soft highlight along the arched curve of her instep. His eyes followed her movement, and she could hear the knuckles of his clenched hands crack.

"You who are—"

"And you too, General," she interrupted quickly. "You are not a politician—but a soldier. A great soldier."

He stared at his clenched hands. "I," he said slowly. "I am a—a gendarme."

"Oh, no!" she protested. "A soldier—with your future before you. And think what you've already done, for Paris—so wonderful of you! The streets repaved, so that it's really a pleasure to drive again—and all those dreadful people gone, so that it's safe to go out at night, even for a women alone—like myself."

"All people are dreadful when they are hungry. I know.... Paris—" He stared somberly at his hands, then looked up. "If I were the master of Paris, I would make of her not only the loveliest city there is, or that has ever been—but the loveliest city there ever could be. I would make her a city fit for—for—" He half stretched out a hand towards her, then let it drop. "But it's Barras who's master here. And Barras would sell Paris, France itself, to pay for his horses, his dogs, and his women." He suddenly sat up very straight, a fist on each knee, and glared at her.

"Good God, Madame! Is that what the Declaration of the Rights of Man signifies?—the right of Barras and his kind to pawn the nation to the money-masters of the world? Was it for that that the men of France marched barefoot and in rags against the trained armies of Austria and Prussia?—was it for that that they watered the ground of Valmy, Wattignies, Fleurus with their blood, fertilized it with the rotting flesh of their bodies?—so that it might produce a poisonous toadstool crop of stock-jobbers and army-contractors? Was it for that?"

Glaring at her, his mouth twisted and bitter, as though she herself were one of his toadstools— What an odd young man he was! Afraid to come into a woman's bedroom, yet when he was there, behaving as though it were a—a political club! In a minute he'd be talking about dysentery and—

"Oh," she breathed, "how cleverly you explain things, so

that even I— But still, all that—that horror—battles, and the Revolution—it's all finished and done with now, isn't it?"

He struck his fist on the arm of his chair and scowled more blackly than ever.

"No, Madame, no! It is neither finished nor done with!" He sat in accusing silence for a moment, then, spreading out his thin, nervous hands, went on in the tone of voice that men use for explaining to women. "The Revolution, do you see, Madame, was a melting-down of the symbols of the past—feudalism, the divine right, privilege. All that was thrown into the melting-pot—not for destruction, but for reshaping. The process is finished now—the molten stuff purified, refined. It is beginning to cool—and it is being permitted to harden untempered and unshaped. And why, Madame? Why?"

How old-fashioned he was! He talked like the things they used to print in the papers in Robespierre's time. And banging on the arm of his chair like a—like a Jacobin. A delicate chair too, in the fragile style of the last reign. She looked at it anxiously.

"I'd never thought of the Revolution like that," she said. "But of course it's true. How intelligent you are! Tell me why it—it—"

"Because," he said fiercely, "this Government of Paris, this Directoire, hasn't the intelligence—the imagination—to create a mold worthy of the metal. Good metal, Madame, the metal of France—and being left to set into a shapeless mass of inertia and despair. But it cannot go on, Madame! It cannot go on.... Though I can see no way out, save that the nation should put itself into the hands of one strong man. But where—?" He shrugged and spread out his hands. "The people have lost interest in votes that are worth no more than paper *assignats*. The soldiers themselves no longer call themselves soldiers of France, but of Jourdan, Marceau, Hoche.... But it can't go on."

Her eyes intent on his, she swayed forward a little towards him, and the fluttering shadow between her breasts sank lower.

"And—the soldiers of Bonaparte?"

The knuckles of his clenched fist whitened. "The soldiers of Bonaparte—the soldiers of Italy. I could—I could—" He broke off and jerked up his chin, as though his collar were too tight.

Keeping her eyes on his she stretched out her hand very

166

slowly and laid it on his fist. She unclasped his fingers, laid her palm flat on his.

"You—could," she said softly.

She slid her finger-tips a little way up his wrist, and felt the tendons jerk and stiffen under her touch. His face was pewter-gray, stained with the dark tarnish of his growing beard. She began slowly to withdraw her hand, but his fingers closed about her wrist. He was on his feet, her hand crushed to his breast, bending over her—his hands that held hers shaking, the whole of him shaking—

"I can do nothing without you—you! I cannot understand how I ever existed without you. I do not exist—nothing exists but you!—and the rest of the world blotted out from my sight."

Just the touch of a finger. It was quite easy. She shrank back, pulling against his hands, unfurling her fan between them.

"Oh," she faltered. "You—frighten me. I think you forget—"

The dull copper-color flooded up over his face. He dropped her hands, and stood back.

"I— Your pardon, Madame. It is true I—forget. The soldiers of Bonaparte are the gendarmerie of Paris—and I—" He jerked up his chin and walked past her to the hearth. He stood with his back to her and kicked at the fire—and then, of course, set his ash-soiled boot down again on the white carpet. He laid his two fists on the edge of the mantel-shelf, and stared down between them at the fire.

"I am a barbarian—a savage. I have frightened you—you, whom I worship, respect, honor." He lifted his head and stared into the mirror before him.

From that angle, he could see her reflection in profile. She lowered her lashes until they lay in a long, pure curve against her cheeks—then slowly swept them up, turned her head a little, and looked up at him over her shoulder. The candle-light struck directly down into the brilliant blue of her eyes.

He stared into the mirror, and spoke in a whisper, as though to the reflected image so close to his mouth.

"You see, Madame—women have never been kind to me before —and I— You are gracious, patient, you let me talk, you listen to me. You are kind—and I forget myself. I will go now." He turned to face her, and made a stiff little jerk of a bow.

"I will go," he said again.

She tilted her head back a little on the slender stalk of her neck, and half stretched out her hand towards him palm up-wards.

"Is it your wish—to go?"

He was kneeling beside her, her offered hand pressed to his hot lips, to the harsh roughness of his cheek.

She was almost sure he was kneeling on her dress, and these fragile, hand-woven stuffs, the slightest jerk was enough— But you could scarcely ask a man to get up while you arranged your skirts, could you?

"My wish," he said brokenly. "Only to love you—only to make you happy. To do nothing to displease you. That is the whole of my destiny—the one goal of my life."

He was quite docile now, all the spring gone out of him. He could be put back in his box and the lid closed down on him at any time. Quite easily.

She touched his hair with her free hand, running her fingers lightly through it, and feeling him shiver and tremble against her knee. Yes, quite easily. With her palms against his cheeks she raised his head, looking down at him from beneath the shadows of her sweeping lashes. Very slowly she leaned her face, lower and lower, towards his—

> *"I live for Josephine. There is the history of my life."*
> **BONAPARTE**

CHAPTER

March.

THE ROOM WAS VERY DIM, BECAUSE SHE DIDN'T LIKE THE EARLY morning light. He moved about it very cautiously, because she didn't like to be wakened. Always he did that, left the curtains drawn and moved cautiously. Always he tried to do that to please her—leave her abandoned to the shadowy loveliness of her sleep. And always he failed.

Always the temptation was too great. Even now—even after all those other mornings—it was impossible to forego for so much as once the ecstasy of watching the first drawing up of those dark curtains of her lashes from the dawn-blue of her eyes. And time was getting so desperately short—

He leaned down over her dressing-table to arrange the folds of his cravat in her mirror—her mirror that was different to any other mirror, having a soul of its own, the invisible spirit of her reflected beauty. He looked at the little vanities spread out before him, small, adorable, feminine trifles, cased in ivory, silver, and crystal. The very sight of them was enough to twist a man's heart in his body. Little things. And he had only ten more days to look at them.

Only ten days more to move cautiously and in obscurity—

He wished it might be ten years, for the broad daylight of adventure had become garish. He wished it might be ten minutes, for the glory of achievement had a shrine now in which to hang its trophies.

Achievement. That's what marriage did for a man. Turned the flaring comet of adventure into the fixed star of a man's destiny. Marriage with Josephine. For he was married to Josephine, irrevocably, unchangeably, by every possible law of God and nature, of the soul and of the body. Beside them, the law of man seemed so trivial, so petty a thing—

She, whose feminine vanities were such little things, whose woman's generosity was so limitless, she had no understanding of mediocre, practical things—the little outward badges of possession that are a man's vanities, like the badges of rank upon his coat.

He would put on his coat—his coat with the badges of a Commander-in-Chief—and then he would go boldly to demand the insignia of his subordination—the legal proof of his bond of marriage with Josephine. He would go to the side of the wide bed, he would wake her with three kisses—on her brow, her eyes, her mouth. She would stir and pout and frown a little, pushing his face away with the heartbreakingly futile strength of her woman's violence—the little petulant rebuffs more sweetly intimate than any moment of passion could ever be.

Little gestures, little things. Only ten days more. He looked at the little things. He touched. Opened. A rose-red stuff, soft and powdery. He stirred it with his forefinger. Red and powdery as the dust of the road to Genoa. Ten days. Then the twelfth of March. On the twenty-seventh he could be in Nice. The twenty-seventh to the day. He knew every posting-station on the way, every kilometer that joined them, every hour of travel that separated them. The twenty-seventh of March. Then the second week of April— He looked at his forefinger, that was coated with reddish powder. There would be marching feet coated with dust like that, gun-barrels filmed with it, men's sweating faces caked with it. Thirty thousand of them. Marching against the combined armies of Austria and Sardinia. Thirty thousand—and, of course, himself.

Himself. That was all he was taking to the Army of Italy by way of reinforcement. But it was—adequate. It was equipped and armed at every point. Every detail had been inspected, tested, polished, set in its proper place. Except one. A little thing, but that was as necessary to his dignity of a man as a uniform was to his dignity of a soldier. Official recognition of his married state.

He looked at the ruddy dust on his finger, and wiped it off on the sleeve of his shirt. He put on his coat, his sash, his belt. He went boldly to the window. He hesitated—then with a brusk gesture, drew the curtains. The daylight, practical and gray, swept coldly in. He went to the bed and leaned over it, one hand on either side of her body, his face above hers. He stooped and kissed her brow, her eyes. He slipped his fingers beneath her neck, and kissed her mouth.

She stirred, sighed, frowned a little. She opened her eyes. She said, "Oh, are you still here? Oh, your hands are cold!" She pushed away his face, and stared over his shoulder at the bleak daylight of the window. She said, "You know I've told you— You know I don't like, I can't bear—"

He caught her protesting hand in his and, holding it, sat on the edge of the bed, facing her. Under the adorable discontent of her brows her lashes swept drowsily up and down, with the slow beat of a butterfly's wings.

"Incomparable Josephine! *Mio dolce amor!* Only ten days more, Josephine—only ten days more."

She yawned, and drew up the sheet to shield her face from the light.

"In ten days I shall have to abandon my adorable Josephine."

"Oh, yes," she said sleepily. "So you will—won't you?"

He smiled at her, and pulled the sheet down from her face.

"Ten days. And, Josephine, men who go into battle don't always come out alive. I am afraid of death, Josephine—afraid to die, unless I can take certainty with me—certainty utter, final, complete. The certainty of marriage with Josephine."

Her lashes flew sharply up, withdrawing their shadow from her eyes that were like—like—

"Marriage?" she said. "Why?"

He lifted her hand and kissed its palm. "My sweet innocent!" he said. "Because, though I know that we are bound to each other body and soul, heart and mind, it is necessary that other men should know it, too. It is necessary that we should be married in their eyes as well as in our own."

She stared at him for a moment, then snatched her hand from his and sat up very straight in the bed. "Oh, no!" she said. "I couldn't. You can't imagine—you can't expect— Oh, no!"

It was as though she'd repelled a kiss by striking him on the mouth—inexplicable, incomprehensible. He drew slowly back from her.

"What could I expect," he said, "save what I have a right to ask of you—and what could you expect of me, but that I should honor—respect, as well as love you? ...If you can have any other thought in your mind, then you are very unjust, Madame, and I—most unhappy."

She looked down at the sheet, and twitched at it with her fingers. "It is I who am unhappy," she said tremulously, "I who thought you would always be the same."

"But how—in what way have I changed?"

"Oh, not changed. You men never change. You take a woman's love for your pleasure—your profit—and when you've got what you want, you—you abandon her. And you—you think you can— pay by an offer of marriage flung at her—at me.... That's what you call your man's honor. And I—I who thought you loved me for myself alone."

He leaned towards her again, his hands on her knees. "I do not—understand. For whom then, for what, do you think I love you, if not for you—you, yourself—"

She lifted clear blue eyes and fixed them on him, unwavering.

"Why, but of course—for the protection of the Directors. To get your Army of Italy."

He sat quite still, looking at her. Her words were like a poisonous vapor between them, so that his mouth was bitter with its taste, scorched with its fumes, his eyes blinded by its density. And she at its heart, a dim pallor, vague, wavering, unreal—

He stretched out his hand and gripped it—there, where a ribbon had slipped leaving her shoulder bare. Her shoulder—smooth and round and polished as ivory—the ivory casing of her flesh in which she kept her petty vanity. Not even that—not even the weight of rose-red powder, not so much as the value of a pinch of dust— Empty even of vanity—

She stirred, and cried out a little. "Oh, you're hurting—"

His hand dropped. He stood up, and the blackness dropped away, leaving only a hard clarity behind it. A clarity so sharp, so intense, that it was impossible to tell whether the scarifying pain of it was of heat or of cold.

"You are pleased to debase, to degrade, Madame. I have no need of the protection of the Directors. Very soon they will be in need of mine. I have my sword by my side, and with it I shall go far. Alone. I have no need of the protection of—any one."

The hard, sharp whiteness of light, dissolving the soft whiteness of her flesh, so that only the blue of her eyes— Candid, innocent, pure. Pure as water. It wasn't possible that from the depths of those limpid pools should have come so foul a thing. Not possible. No. Pools of innocence, reflecting only the things about them—the vileness of men, their brutality and greed. Reflecting, and themselves remaining pure, pure as clear water—

As he looked, the clear water welled up, gently, softly, as though from the very springs of purity within her. Josephine—

He stooped over the low bed, raising her in his arms, feeling the softness of her hair against his mouth, the little shuddering breaths of her sobbing against his heart.

Josephine.... Woman—torment—happiness! What have you done to me? You drive me away with outrage, you poison my whole existence with a single word—yet with one tear you bring me back, and I fall again. A wish of yours and I deny my soul, my conscience. You have taken from me more than life, my very soul is in your body—and I, without pride, without willpower, at your feet. Josephine!—love me as your eyes—yourself—more than yourself, your thoughts, your mind, your life, your all. Love me as your soul—love me....

She picked up her hand-mirror from the bedside table and looked at herself. She put it down quickly. The crudity of this early morning light would be trying to any woman's face, making even dimples look like the beginning of wrinkles—the light and, of course, being obliged to cry before she'd had time to oil her lashes, so that they got all sodden and matted. You'd think a man would have more consideration, wouldn't you?

But then he had no manners, of course—literally none at all. She twisted her arm towards the light and examined it. Yes, by looking closely it was quite possible to see the marks. Never in her life, never— Not even poor Alexander. When he was angry, he just used to go away and write her a letter about it— quite abominable letters they were, though one wasn't absolutely obliged to read them. Not Hoche, either. He'd said that perfectly shameful thing, of course, but he'd never permitted himself to lay a finger on her. Not like that. And words couldn't make bruises—but perfectly enormous black bruises—on your white skin, could they? As for Barras, all he ever did was to say, "Quite, my soul's treasure—quite," and talk about something else.

But to make a scene—actually to make a scene! Never in all her life— Of course it was an experience, and experience was so broadening to the mind, wasn't it? Still, it had been a shock to her nerves, so that she probably wouldn't be able to see him again for days now. And what, after all, had she said, except what the whole of Paris was saying already? So unreasonable of him! Of course she was sorry if she'd upset him, one didn't want to hurt anybody's feelings. But it was his own fault, wasn't it?—jerking the curtains open like that before she'd had so much as an instant to look at her face, and then throwing that grotesque suggestion at her. Marriage! How funny he was!

She yawned and slipped down into the bed. And now if he was going to be difficult— But then of course he never thought about other people's feelings. He'd gone off now leaving the window-curtains still open. And her nail-polish— She could see it from here, spilled all over the top of the dressing-table. Her powdered coral that came from Italy, and that you couldn't get any more because of the war. Men didn't realize how inconvenient wars could be for women. Though Theresia of course had her Italian velvet. It didn't seem fair, did it? Still, if Bonaparte was going to invade Italy, he might be able to get her some, too. There was that about him, he did try to do the things you asked him to. He wasn't a bad little soul, really. Not bad at all.

As a lover, of course, he was impossible—but quite impossible. He took—things—so desperately seriously. So—so *unbalanced* of him! She herself was passionately—but passionately devoted to

173

her bath. But that didn't mean she wasn't able to think about anything else at all, did it?

As a husband— How could he possibly have imagined such a thing? Though of course little men often were very conceited. Why, he had no money to speak of—practically none at all, no house, no property—only what he called his "sword at his side," like an old-fashioned tragic actor. He had his salary, of course. Quite a good salary, really. Barras had told her. And it was true that if you had a man with a good salary, people were much less difficult about giving you credit. There was his mother to be thought of, too. Sixty thousand francs— A man like that, so bourgeois-minded, would be quite capable of putting his mother before his mistress. But his wife—

His wife— After all, if she hadn't been Alexander's wife, but actually his wife, Barras wouldn't have been able to do anything at all about it, would he? Not even Barras. And Bonaparte had said himself that men who went into battle didn't always come out of it alive. Barras thought it was almost certain that he wouldn't. Not that she wished the poor little man any harm— she was really quite fond of him in a way. But one had to think of one's self sometimes—and of course of one's children— She giggled. He'd be step-father to Eugène—and Eugène was—well, he was excessively tall for his age. It would be rather comic, wouldn't it?

He had only—how many?—ten days left. It wasn't really very long—and one had to be kind, hadn't one? If anything should happen to the poor little man, she'd never forgive herself if she'd refused him such a little thing—a formality, that took less time and trouble than hiring a new servant.

Ten days. Not even that. For nobody could expect a woman to take so grave a step as marriage without very careful consideration, could they? Besides, she simply hadn't a thing—but not a thing fit to wear even in the office of a District Mayor. One had to dress decently—one had to consider the dignity of a man who, after all, was a Commander-in-Chief. It was only fair.

Ten days. Say a week for really thinking things over quite seriously. That would leave him three days. Or perhaps two— But no. If you gave a thing at all, you should give generously. In the meantime, she'd have her house to herself again. It wouldn't be delicate for an engaged couple to be under the same roof together. And that would be an advantage too—she'd be able really to do something about her face. As it was, she was scarcely able to spend an hour without her complexion on. So bad for the skin. And sleep. Being wakened in that brutal fashion, before the day had even begun— Quite unbearable for a woman's nerves. Enough to make one really ill. But he should have his three days, of course. One had to be fair.

She yawned, and made the sheet into a little tent to shield her face from the light. She closed her eyes and burrowed her head into the pillow.

"Bonaparte is so funny!"
JOSEPHINE

CHAPTER

❦ XXII ❧

March.

GENERAL BONAPARTE LOOKED AT HIMSELF IN THE MIRROR. ROYAL-blue breeches, navy-blue coat with only a narrow edging of gold braid, black stock, black hat and gauntleted gloves. A little— somber. But those were the clothes his men had put on him, and that Junot said were correct. For he said—Junot said—that when one married a lady who wasn't—who'd been married before, one should dress discreetly. He would have liked to put on his dress uniform with its lavish display of gold embroidery on breast and sleeves, white breeches, and his hat with the cock's-feathers cockade.

He wanted of course to manœuvre—to behave correctly, but then he wanted so many things. He wanted to parade her through the streets so that every man in Paris would envy him, and he wanted to lock her up in a little room where no man except himself would ever be able to see her again. He wanted her to blaze like the sun, and be as secret as the moon—to be frank as the earth, and mysterious as the sea. He wanted to stay eternally at her feet, and he wanted to dash off instantly to gain glory for her. He wanted to think of her happy in her marriage to him, desolate at the approaching parting. He wanted—

He looked at the clock. A quarter-past eight. Another fifteen minutes. It was like waiting for an inspecting General when one was a Second Lieutenant. He was quite alone. His man had gone to take the last of his possessions to the rue Chantereine. Junot had gone to see to his own dressing. But he knew what he had to do. Junot had told him. He was to stay where he was without jerking at the bow of his sash or meddling with the buttons of his coat until exactly half-past eight. Then he was to go downstairs and get into the carriage that Junot had ordered to be there. Then he was to drive to Junot's lodging to pick him up, then to the Mairie, then— Then he would be able to leave behind him a private life as ordered and disciplined as the Army of Italy would be ordered and disciplined before he'd done with it.

He looked about him. It was the last evening he would spend in the Governor's mansion. Already his things were gone—his books, his clothes, his papers, his maps. His maps— His best, large-scale map of northern Italy with all his markings, his dotted lines, his calculations on it, still pinned to the wall. Trust a servant to forget the most important thing of all! That of course couldn't possibly be left where it was, not even until to-morrow, lest by some appalling chance something should happen to it in the night.

He picked at the flat-headed pins that held the lower corners, but with his gloved hands he couldn't get his finger-nails beneath them. He took off his gloves, and tossed them to the floor. He worked the pins loose and dropped them in his pocket. Pins like that were always useful to have about one. He stretched up to release the upper corners of the map, but couldn't reach. He scowled. It was—humiliating not to be quite so tall as other men. He flung his hat into a corner of the room, brought a chair, and stood on it.

He held the map in his hands, looking at it. If it was properly folded it went as flat as a letter and would go into a breast pocket so neatly that not even Junot would notice a bulge. But if it weren't properly folded, it turned into a sort of concertina that sprang up at you as soon as you took your hand off it. Junot was excellent at folding maps. Only he wasn't here.

He took it to the desk, and spread it out. The desk-top wasn't big enough, and the thing hung down over the edges, so that when you tried to fold it along the middle crease, the top and bottom sections turned back on themselves and resisted with an exasperating, limp obstinacy. It was extraordinary the number of points of resistance a map could have. Damn Junot! Why wasn't he—

He snatched it off the desk and spread it on the floor. He unhooked his sword and knelt down before it. Certainly the center fold creased the same way all the way down—through Trente, Rivoli, Mantua. Mantua. The Austrians would undoubtedly make desperate efforts to hold a city that, after he had beaten them in the west, would be the only great stronghold they had left in all Italy. That would require a siege; and to cover it, one would have to hold—

The shadow of the desk fell irritatingly across the map just where you wanted most to see. He got up and reached for the desk-lamp, then knelt down again, setting the lamp on the floor beside the map. Yes, one would have to hold Legnano, Verona, Peschiera. The Austrians would probably—the difficulties of the mountain-passes to the north being enormous—try to relieve the place by striking down through the Valley of the Adige, by way of Rivoli. Rivoli—

He shrugged himself out of his coat without getting up, and tossed it aside. He lay down on his stomach, leaned forward on his elbows, and with his forefinger traced the line of the Adige. Rivoli, Verona, Arcole....

Barras looked with distaste at the face of the Mayor of the Second Paris District. It was the face of a petty office-holder, a bourgeois, a salary-earner. It was moreover the face of a man who was quite obviously, though decorously and discreetly, asleep.

He, Paul Barras, Director and head of the State, was not accustomed to be kept waiting in the presence of even the most wakeful of minor city dignitaries. He was not accustomed to sitting on a hard wooden bench while he waited. He was not accustomed to sitting at all in grimy little offices of grimy little officials waiting for them to perform their grimy little ceremonies. And he was not accustomed—most decidedly not accustomed to doing any of those things because it suited the good pleasure of an upstart little Corsican nobody. Damn the little man! He almost regretted that he'd ever let him have his Army of Italy— and Josephine.

Josephine. He looked at her, where she sat beside him on the bench. Her expression showed just that degree of well-bred anguish you might see on the face of a lady of fashion who had already waited for an hour at the spice merchant's, and was beginning to be afraid she might after all have to go home without her promised pound of coffee.

She was dressed in gray taffetas, with gray squirrel muff and stole, and just the faintest hint of blush-rose beneath the brim of her bonnet and on her pretty mouth. All very simple and modest and demure, and costing— But that, thank God, was no longer any affair of his. From now on he would be able to admire in perfect comfort, without so much as a twinge of apprehension to spoil the pleasure. Or he should have been able to, if that confounded little—

He looked at his watch, he looked at the clock on the wall. Ten minutes to ten. Fifty minutes late while the whole of France, as it were, waited for him. If the arrangement hadn't been quite so perfect he, Barras, would have made a dignified exit at the end of five minutes. But it was perfect. What after all could be more admirable than to place your, er—secret agent in your opponent's camp, not only with his enthusiastic consent, but actually at his expense? The whole situation was as delightfully stimulating to a sophisticated imagination as fine champagne to a sophisticated palate—and requiring of course as sophisticated a sense of humor fully to appreciate it.

Tallien, for instance—sitting on the far side of Josephine, with his elbows on his knees, glowering at his hat that he dangled in his hands, sulking because he hadn't been allowed to celebrate the wedding in advance. Tallien had only been able to see the broader aspect of the comedy, the crude jest to be applauded by guffaws and lewd gestures.

As for Josephine— Josephine's appreciation of humor seldom rose above the level of the pun or the practical joke. She had seen nothing even vaguely amusing in asking him—*him*, Paul Barras, to be the principal witness at her wedding. Even he had been just a trifle shocked at the suggestion—and it was a very long time since he'd been shocked. No, she had done it quite seriously, because he was the only really important man she was in a position to ask.

And it was undoubtedly true that of all the signatures on the wedding certificates, his was the only one that would be remembered even ten years from now. Even to-day—General Bonaparte himself was known to the masses of Paris only as General October. He, Barras, had no idea what the initial N—or was it a V?—stood for. As for the others, the groom's witnesses— There was a silent, gray man who sat over there almost invisible in the gray shadows of his corner. The second was to be some vague soldier, Colonel of Dragoons and apparently highly inefficient aide-de-camp to General Bonaparte.

The clock ticked. The Mayor slept decorously on. The two tallow candles before him smoked and stank. The wedding-party sat in stagnant silence, its trickle of small-talk long since dried up. Neither a joke nor a glass of champagne can be left standing for—he pulled out his watch—exactly an hour, without losing its sparkle and zest. It became only a sour acidity to the palate. He, Paul Barras, was damned if he was going to be obliged to swallow it by an ill-mannered young savage who had the impudence to keep a Director of the Republic waiting—and his bride too, of course. He dropped his watch back into his pocket, and reached for his hat on the bench beside him. He was damned if he—

The door opened, and the bridegroom entered—or rather he flung himself into the room, with much of the ceremonial courtesy of a small pike entering a preserve of fat carp. He was either—it was difficult to tell which—towing behind him, or being pursued by, a tall young man who closed the door and stood before it as though on guard, smiling about him with the half-deprecating, half-complacent air of a conjurer who has at last succeeded in producing the lady's watch from his hat—after taking a dashed long time about it.

As for the bridegroom— One would have expected at least some outward sign of humility, of contrition. But not a bit of it. He stood there in the middle of the floor scowling about him as though he had stumbled by accident onto an enemy out-post, and was considering the quickest means of exterminating it. The outrageous insolence, the— It was an awkward situation, like having somebody else's servant rude to one in a public place.

All one could do was to maintain an attitude of dignified imperturbability.

He got up, and offered his hand. "At last. The happy and, er—impatient bridegroom."

Bonaparte staring at him, ignoring him, turning his back on him. Marching to the Mayor's desk, shaking the slumbering official by the shoulder. Marching back. Marching, as it were, on Josephine. Totally ignoring—

"Now, General, if you will be so good as to take the right hand of Madame de Beauharnais in your left, and lead her—"

Bonaparte snatching Josephine's left wrist with his right hand,

179

dragging her to the desk as though she were an unwilling conscript being haled to the recruiting office. Rapping on the edge of the desk with his knuckles, barking out, "Come, Citizen Mayor, we are waiting!" Waiting! The incredible effrontery, the—

Dignified imperturbability, Ah, well— He took up his stand with Tallien behind Josephine, while the gray anonymity and the military anonymity placed themselves behind Bonaparte. A personable young fellow, the military one. Josephine sliding a glance up at him over her shoulder— General Bonaparte would be well advised to refrain from using this particular aide-de-camp as messenger between Italy and Paris. Josephine turning her head a little in profile, sweeping her lashes down for his edification. Bonaparte conscious of his bride, apparently, only as something that had to be signed for, and with attention only for the civilian official before him who was slow in getting on with the irritating formality. A charming little tableau, like a Louis XV engraving.

The Mayor clearing his throat and taking up his pen. "Citizen —Citizeness—your names and baptismal names, if you please?"

"Bonaparte, Napoleon."

"Nap—?" The incredulity—the quite comprehensible incredulity—of the Mayor. The equally comprehensible annoyance of General Bonaparte, spelling out his name letter by letter in hard, staccato taps, as though he were driving in a nail with a hammer. Napoleon. A curious name. Very curious. One understood why he signed only with an N—

"Rose-Josephe de Beauharnais, née Tascher de la Pagerie." Josephine slipping in a particle or two, though not quite venturing a title.

"Your birthplaces?"

"Ajaccio, in Corsica."

"Trois-Islets, in Martinique."

"Your ages?"

"Twenty-eight!"—a little too promptly, too aggressively.

"Twenty-eight"—a more artistic note of regretful resignation. Twenty-eight. Interesting. Double falsification of an official document, in the presence, and for the confirmation, of the head of the State in person. An, er—unusual procedure—

"The signatures of the principles— Thank you. Of the witnesses— Thank you." The gray anonymity proving to be one Calmelet, of the tribe of lawyers. The military anonymity, Colonel Junot, Andoche.

180

"That will be all, Citizeness. That will be one gold louis, or two thousand, four hundred francs paper, Citizen General—"

Josephine married. Josephine definitely and legally in the possession of another man. The idea was gently shaded with melancholy, even a delicate tinge of regret— Though of course it would be only for three days.

Josephine surrounded by the witnesses and in quite charming confusion submitting to congratulatory salutations on cheek and brow. Bonaparte, with his back turned, counting out his money—

Colonel Junot, stooping his tall body to lay a respectful salute on the modestly lowered brow of his Commander's lady. The lady suddenly raising her head—a quite comprehensible nervous gesture, doubtless—so that the homage of the young man's lips fell full on her mouth—

Timidly alarmed "Oh!" of the lady.

Aggressively protective advance of the husband.

Retreat in abashed confusion of the gallant.

Quite charming. Exquisitely perfect little comedy, in three acts and three seconds.

The marriage of Josephine.

She blew out the dressing-table candles, and crossed to the bed. Her reading-lamp was alight by its side, her book laid ready on its turned-back sheet, Fortuné asleep in its middle. Fortuné! The precious lamb! She tickled his ear, kissed his nose, and pulled a face at him. His presence was Louise's recognition that General Bonaparte was no longer Madame's gentleman, but Madame's husband.

She got into bed, and Fortuné snuggled down beside her under the covers. She picked up her book. Her husband— She could hear him moving about, in the next room where she used to keep her old dresses, and that she'd had prepared for him. She'd had to throw away a lot of things that might have been useful sometime, but still he had a right to his own room that he could be alone in, hadn't he? He was her husband, after all, a man actually living in the house, wasn't he?

She'd really taken a great deal of trouble over the room. She'd had it done exactly like a soldier's tent, with drapery that hung flat against the walls and was gathered into a point in the middle of the ceiling—not that coarse canvas stuff of course, but toile de Jouy, a cream background with little red battle-scenes all over it. Quite delightfully amusing. She'd got a military camp-bed too, a real one, hard and narrow, as soldiers liked them. For seats she'd had some of those tall infantry drums stuffed with horse-hair and white leather cushions fitted into the heads. So diverting and original. For wardrobe she'd had a rack of muskets fastened to the wall, they'd be excellent for hanging clothes on. Nobody could say she hadn't gone to trouble—but quite enormous trouble to make him feel comfortable and at home in his own room.

She opened her book. Everybody ought to read, of course, it improved the mind. But it was quite impossible to find the time, even an instant, except sometimes in bed at night. She had only a chapter or two of this one left, she'd probably be able to finish it to-night. Such an interesting book—and instructive, too. History was so fascinating. The door opening— Oh, dear!

Without raising her eyes she could see him, over the top of her book. A red cashmere dressing-gown and black leather slippers, all very new and bright. He looked like somebody in a Molière play. She choked down a giggle, and kept her eyes on the book. He came to the side of the bed and stood there, very quietly. She went on reading.

"Josephine—"

She gave a little cry, and dropped her book. "Oh!—you frightened me!"

"I—frighten you? *Mio dolce amor!* My wife!" He leaned over her. "My wife," he said again.

Of course she was his wife, why did he have to keep on saying it? So irritating of him! He bent lower. Fortuné thrust a menacing, wrinkled black head out from under the covers and snarled in his face. He started back. Of course, Fortuné was a little startling sometimes if you didn't know he was there— though of course he didn't mean any harm, the little pet. She kissed Fortuné on the nose.

"Give me the little dog, Josephine, and I'll put him out."

Put Fortuné out?—put the poor little thing out in the middle of the night with nowhere to go? She curled her arm about him and drew him to her. "Oh, no!" she said. "You can't take Fortuné away from me—not Fortuné!"

"Not take anything away from you, ever, my Josephine. Just put the little dog somewhere else."

She tucked Fortuné's head beneath her chin, and looked up over the black, wrinkled mask. "Oh, but you can't! Don't you *see?*—Fortuné's the only thing I've had to love all these years—and now you—you want to take him away—"

"But, Josephine—a dog! One doesn't share one's bed with a dog."

How *selfish* men were! Getting everything they wanted—an army, or a—a wife, and then grudging even a little dog—a poor little helpless black pug-dog!

She turned her head away from him. "Oh, very well," she said. She picked up her book and opened it. "There are other beds in the house. You're welcome to any of them."

"Josephine!"

She turned a page. She could see him standing there, looking down at her, very still and quiet. She turned another page. He took off his dressing-gown and threw it over a chair. Very stiff and disapproving. She stifled a giggle. Men looked comic enough in their nightshirts anyway, without trying to be dignified. He put out the light.

Fortuné stirred against her side. Fortuné crouched. Fortuné charged, and delivered a slashing attack. General Bonaparte said, "Damn the filthy little beast!"

Fortuné— He'd always been a jealous little soul, and so brave—not a bit afraid, not even in the dark. She did hope he wouldn't be hurt— But no, he hadn't screamed, and he always screamed if he was so much as touched. He was so highly strung— He executed a successful retreat across her knees, and installed himself snarling in triumph on the far side of the bed.

General Bonaparte said, "Filthy little beast!" again. She pressed her hand against her mouth. How funny—how quite indescribably funny it must have looked! How unutterably comic when you pictured—

She lay and quaked with suppressed laughter in the arms of the Commander-in-Chief of the Army of Italy.

PART IV
1796-1797

"Think of me, write to me, love me. Be often with your lover in your dreams, and know that there is but one thing that he fears—to be no longer loved of his Josephine."

BONAPARTE TO JOSEPHINE

"The little bougre frightened me."
AUGEREAU

CHAPTER

❧ XXIII ❧

April.

GENERAL BONAPARTE WAS NO LONGER A MAN IN A DARKENED ROOM, searching stumblingly for a way out. He was a man on a mountain-top, following a steep, straight, narrow path that led directly to his goal.

The path, trampled through the deep snow, ended up there at the crest of the mountain, at the wooden hut where the gentlemen of the Staff of the Army of Italy had installed their Headquarters. As a Headquarters it would serve the purpose well enough. And he would see to it that the gentlemen of the Staff did too. They had not seen fit to come down from their lofty perch to meet him in Nice. They would come down soon enough now.

The dry snow squeaked and slithered beneath his tread. The bitter air stabbed at his lungs, but he clenched his teeth against the cough. He wore neither overcoat nor gloves. The men of the Army of Italy had no overcoats or gloves. They had no shoes either, most of them, nor yet rations or pay. He himself was bringing them none of those things. He was bringing them nothing but confidence. That was to say, himself.

He had confidence. He was confidence. He had proved it. He had gone to the bankers of Nice and demanded money, offering no other security than his name. They had never heard his name. They had looked shocked. But they'd loaned the money. Oh, not vast sums, but enough to supplement the fifteen thousand francs that Barras had had the cynical effrontery to label with the pompous title of "war-chest."

He had gone to the Commander of the coastal defenses and demanded guns, on no other authority than his own. The Commander had looked shocked too, and said it was quite impossible without written authority from Paris. But he had given the guns. Only a few, yet sufficient to dignify by the name of artillery.

As for horses, the gentlemen on their perches up there would supply those. The gentlemen would go on foot, as he himself would go on foot. Those who wished to ride must look to the Austrians to mount them.

Confidence. Down below in the valley he had a wagon labeled "Army treasury," empty—but surrounded day and night by a strong-armed guard. He had a train of ammunition-wagons loaded for the most part with stones. He had Quartermaster's supply-wagons heaped with forage. No soldier would betray his natural pride by demanding an overcoat while his Commander-in-Chief went without. Not, that is, if he imagined he could have one for the asking.

But all that was more by way of initial assurance than of final confidence—a sort of drum-beating to draw the soldiers of the Army of Italy together. When they were gathered, they should be given true confidence. Not the superficial excitement of imposed enthusiasm, but the profounder emotion of confidence in themselves. They should be told bluntly that a Government which owed them everything, could or would give them nothing. That the thing which was to be done must be done by themselves, with no help at all save their own sweat and blood. And that, since the effort and the toil would be theirs, theirs too would be the honor and the glory—and theirs only. Soldiers have a natural dignity that responds more readily to the simple dignity of truth than to the bombast of tawdry heroics.

The soldiers of the Army of Italy. There were a few of them scattered over the icy slope of the mountain, men with dirty sheep-skins tied over their ragged uniforms, with rags or sacking bound about their feet. Little groups of them huddled under improvised shelters of pine-branches, individuals crouched over smoky fires of rotting pine-cones in the open. The detachment considered necessary, doubtless, for the serving and provisioning of the gentlemen on their perch above. None of them displayed curiosity in their new Commander-in-Chief by so much as a turned head or raised eyelid. Why should they? They had already seen Dumberion, Kellerman, Schèrer pass that way, and nothing had been changed in the futile misery of their existence.

But it would be changed now. He would lead them out of the dark prison of their despair as he had been led out of his. He would set them in as narrow and straight a path towards as certain a goal as he himself was following. He would give them that sense of fulfilment, that sureness of purpose, that certainty of direction, which is to an army what marriage is to a man. Marriage. Josephine—woman—wife—star of destiny—

Something blocked his path. A man, though more like some strange hairy beast with his great body clumsy in sheepskin wrappings, his head shaggy with a tangle of beard and unkempt hair, and the red snow-dazzle staining his eyes. Coming straight down the narrow path, with the indifferent yet inexorable advance of an ox. A soldier. If one could call soldier a man whose sense of discipline had slipped back through time to an age when the authority of greater physical bulk and strength shouldered the lesser strength masterfully out of its path.

When it was a matter of disputing the right of way with a man who was a foot taller than yourself, who stood on higher ground, and who was no longer a soldier, you couldn't force respect for your rank merely by the epaulettes on your shoulders. But you could jerk up your chin high enough to look him in the eyes, look him in his sullen, bloodshot eyes until they shifted and dropped, until his oncoming march slackened, wavered, slouched out of the path. Until his cold-blackened hand rose in a clumsy, half-forgotten gesture of salute, and he stood aside to let you pass.

Confidence. He went straight on and up, to the door of the hut on the edge of the wind-swept crest. The perch of the gentlemen of the Staff. He thrust open the door and went in.

They were seated there about the rough boards of their council-table. Seven of them. Three on either side, one at the head. Three unknown to him, four familiar by name and reputation. All sat in rigid silence, their arms folded stiffly across their breasts, their hats set firmly on their heads. He walked to the foot of the table, laid the tips of his fingers on its surface, and looked at the men before him.

"Well, gentlemen?"

They stared straight before them, unspeaking, unmoving, bitter resentment in their averted faces, hard obstinacy in the set of their shoulders.

Masséna, middle-aged, a peasant, with a peasant's strong endurance and suspicious reserve in his hard jaw and cold eyes. A difficult man, but useful.

Lannes, younger, a bourgeois, with the quick red of frank hot temper on his cheek-bones, and honest indignation on his generous mouth. A man worth winning.

Sérurier, aristocrat, professional soldier with forty years of service to his credit. Narrowed eyes and sneering mouth. Hurt dignity shielding behind contemptuous indifference. A proud man, and so reliable at bottom.

Three others. All mature men, capable, experienced, intelligent. Yet lacking something, or they wouldn't still be sitting here on their perch. Confidence.

At the head of the table, facing him squarely, Augereau. Risen from the ranks of the old Royal Army. A man with a hot-blooded murder on his record, though probably not on his conscience. A great brawny hulk, all bone and muscle, but with a strong, intelligent head on his massive shoulders. Augereau, Second-in-Command of the Army of Italy—sitting now in the place of the Commander-in-Chief, that should have been unoccupied.

Yet sitting was too light a word for so weighty a gesture. Rather he had taken up his position there, had unhesitatingly seized the advantage of the terrain. He had drawn about him by way of support the anger, the resentment, the jealousy of his subordinates. He himself was too large a man for such petty emotions as those to fill. There was nothing in him but a huge determination—a determination not to be ousted from the place he held.

Magnificent fighter, superb leader of men. Yet there was about him something of the ox-like soldier of the narrow path. As the soldier relied on strength of body to get his way, so his superior relied on strength of will. A man who relies on violence of any kind to dominate others confesses to spiritual weakness—to a lack of utter confidence in himself.

Coldly aggressive, Augereau sat firmly in his place, staring at him with hard-eyed defiance down the length of the table, while he, standing erect at its foot, his finger-tips posed lightly on its surface, looked back. He looked steadily, yet almost indifferently, without anger or challenge, only with the certain knowledge that in the end Augereau's gaze would hesitate, waver, turn aside.

Augereau stared unwinking. The gold fringe of his epaulettes vibrated under the flexing of his vast shoulders. His square-tipped fingers dug into the biceps of his folded arms. He stared. His eyelids quivered. His teeth unlocked, and bit at his lip. His hands slid from his arms, and clenched on the edge of the table. He looked down at them. His shoulders stooped forward a little over them. Then, with a slow thrust of his arms against them, he drove himself upright. Rising to the full measure of his great height, he took off his hat and, bareheaded, moved back from the head of the table.

Like the soldier on the mountain-path, Augereau gave place where there was room for one only to pass. As for the others....

After the granite wall of Augereau's resistance, theirs was so much cobweb to be brushed aside. He looked briefly from face to face, and one by one they rose, pulled off their hats, made way. He took off his own hat then, and tossed it onto the middle of the table. He walked deliberately to its head, and sat in the place of the Commander-in-Chief.

"Well, gentlemen?"

Augereau scraped with his feet, then brought his heels together. "Orders have been issued—"

"Wait!" He flattened his hand on the table, and looked up at the great bulk towering over him. "Let it first be understood," he said, "that one man and one man only issues orders to the Army of Italy. Myself."

> *"Without you, without you, I can be of no use here. My soul is suffocated in this exile, I cannot coldly calculate my victories."*
>
> BONAPARTE TO JOSEPHINE

CHAPTER

XXIV

June.

WAITING FOR HIS GUESTS TO ARRIVE FROM PARIS, BARRAS STROLLED on the terrace and looked out over his domain of Grosbois. It was a fine property. He had acquired it for a mere handful of *assignats.* The château and grounds did, of course, cost a good deal of money to keep up. But then, at the moment, he had a good deal of money. Something over a million francs in sound Italian gold coin, safely deposited in a London bank. In his own name, naturally, for security.

He had made no mistake about the Italian campaign. But

then he seldom, if ever, did make mistakes. It had all turned out exactly as he had prophesied to Theresia that it would—an armed foray into the King of Sardinia's rich territory of the Piedmont, and a fat war indemnity to end the business. For ended it undoubtedly was. Even Bonaparte could scarcely be mad enough to expect a repetition of the astounding good luck that had permitted him to catch the Sardinians unsupported by their Austrian ally.

Of course, the little man had exceeded even his previous capacity for insolence by concluding an armistice with the King of Sardinia without the authority, or even the knowledge, of the Directorate. One had felt strongly inclined to disavow him then and there, save that the almost superstitious veneration with which the people of Paris insisted on regarding him made such a move inadvisable for the time being. And, of course, there had been the matter of the indemnity, which one would have been obliged to disavow at the same time.

Then, too, his own popularity had been augmented now that he had permitted it to be generally known that it was he himself who had insisted on nominating General Bonaparte in the face of Carnot's opposition. And above all, there was the million in gold in the London bank. Gold in the bank was like seed in the ground. It grew of itself—while with a little expert care, it could be made to yield fruit in season and out. The expert—Ouvrard. . . .

Theresia had really done very well with Ouvrard. Very well indeed. He looked at his watch. They would be here very soon now. Yes, she had been right to keep him dangling, to give him the novelty of wanting without having. But to-night— Well, it so happened that the two finest guest-chambers of the château were side by side—and naturally one gave one's friends—one's good friends—the best one had, didn't one?

They had talked about art—pictures, the theater, books—and then about the recently terminated Italian campaign. Now for a little they were silent, he and Theresia and Ouvrard. He glanced to the right at Ouvrard's face—so nondescript a face that one had continually to look at it to remember what it was like. One might call it either delicate or weak—secret or vacant—supremely confident, or merely indifferent. The face of Ouvrard the multimillionaire nevertheless.

"A most excellent brandy, my dear Barras," said Ouvrard.

"Ha, yes. You were saying, the Italian campaign.... On what grounds do you maintain that it is indeed terminated?"

"On the grounds, naturally, that Bonaparte is a paid servant of the Republic, and as such will do as he is told."

"Yet your paid servant behaved in somewhat masterful fashion, if I am not mistaken, in his dealings with the King of Sardinia."

On the other side of the table, Theresia laughed. "I would have liked to see that," she said. "The dignified plenipotentiaries of the King of Sardinia waiting to receive the equally dignified plenipotentiaries of the Republic of France—and having come in to them an insignificant little officer of twenty-six, who offered only his own soldiers lining the street by way of Letters of Credit. Yes, I would have liked to see that."

"And I very decidedly would not," Barras said testily. "Nor will any one else have the opportunity of seeing it again. Ever." It was incredible how even the most intelligent of women could be attracted by lawlessness in any male.

"There was nothing in the least admirable in the whole affair," he went on. "By the most incredible good luck he managed to beat the Sardinians—by the use of a cheap trick contrary to every known law of strategy, he succeeded in misleading the Austrians. But even his outrageous conceit can scarcely persuade him he can do the same thing again. No, you may depend on it—he will be content with his little Sardinian triumph. He won't throw it away for the certainty of defeat at the hands of the Austrians."

Ouvrard again savored his brandy, again smiled his appreciation. "Then," he said, "one is at a loss to understand for what purpose General Bonaparte is demanding reinforcements, munitions, supplies."

It was possible that Theresia had, after all, gone just a shade too far with Ouvrard. Amatory, er—revelations were one thing, political, quite another. "General Bonaparte," he said, "has no purpose whatsoever save to harass and annoy certain, er—members of the Government. In any case, he has already had the last sweepings of a completely empty Treasury—fifteen thousand francs, to be exact. He can scarcely hope for more."

Ouvrard set his glass down with precise care. "Yet, my dear Barras—he has, has he not, certain grounds for believing that the Treasury is no longer completely empty. And—ill-mannered as we know him to be—it is just possible that he might take it into his head to make public inquiry into the complete absence of funds that he himself has so recently supplied."

Ouvrard might be a clever enough financier, but he had no understanding of the subtleties of, er—administration. "In that case, my dear Ouvrard, we shall be obliged to reveal—though regretfully, of course—that it is Carnot who, jealous of the brilliant success of his young subordinate, is responsible for withholding supplies from him. A disclosure that will, unfortunately, go a long way towards destroying his popularity and may, in fact, er—oblige us to remove him from office."

"Quite," said Ouvrard. "But for the moment, Carnot is still in office—and he is not, I believe, either a timid or a reticent man. It seems to me, therefore, that it would be advisable to supply General Bonaparte with the material he demands. No, no"—raising a small, blunt-fingered hand—"I do not suggest interfering with the undoubtedly admirable—disposition you have already made of the Italian gold. To the contrary. I myself, in my capacity of Army Contractor, am in a position to supply the goods—and I am moreover prepared to lend you—that is, the Government—the necessary funds for their purchase."

"An excellent arrangement. Most excellent. Save for the small matter of the use to which General Bonaparte may put the material you so, er—generously propose to supply to him."

Ouvrard smiled. "Even General Bonaparte," he said, "will, I fancy, have difficulty in constructing many bricks with the straw he will receive. Still, I agree that the matter requires watching. One might, perhaps, introduce some reliable and conscientious individual into his councils."

Barras nodded. "The idea had already occurred to me—to the Government. Realizing the, er—excessive strain of sole command for one of his delicate physique, we proposed to send him a second General officer to, er—share the burden of it with him, and relieve him of unnecessary fatigue. By way of gratitude for our consideration, Bonaparte at once resigned, on the plea that one bad General was better than two good ones. Naturally, we ourselves would not have dreamed of standing in the way of his, er—well-earned repose save that, public opinion being what it unfortunately is, we felt constrained—" He spread out his hands and shrugged.

Theresia bit through a nut-kernel with a small, sharp click of her teeth. "Send Josephine," she said.

He smiled, and raised amused eyebrows at her. "Josephine? My dear child, love-struck though Bonaparte may be, even he would hardly be fool enough to imagine her intelligence to be, er—robust enough to be entrusted with his secret plans for the future."

"Rubbish! Any man thinks any woman intelligent, provided she knows how to flatter him. And even she's clever enough for that."

"Possibly. But you know as well as I that she won't go to him. You know she's been using every artifice she can possibly imagine to avoid it, telling him she's ill, even that she's pregnant. She won't go."

Theresia laughed sharply. "Will she not? Then he'll come back to Paris to fetch her."

"He—"

"Oh, yes. That's one of his secret plans for the future he's already confided to her. She's in a panic already."

Bonaparte in Paris! That would be awkward—damned awkward.

"Anyway," Theresia went on, putting her elbows on the table and resting her chin on her fists, "it's time you got her out of Paris—with the people running after her whenever she shows herself and shouting 'Our Lady of Victory!' after her. And she making sure, believe me, that they have ample opportunity. 'Our Lady of Victory,' indeed!—that addlebrained little simpleton."

Barras smiled to himself. So the practical-minded Theresia wasn't entirely without feminine weakness, after all. The Lady of July didn't like seeing a Lady of Victory raised to her own level—perhaps even above it. Still, there was good sense in what she said. Josephine was after all married to the man, bore his name—and the less one heard of that name on the streets of Paris, the better. Yes, there was something in it—

"And surely," said Ouvrard gently, "the hero who has won the laurel-crown deserves to be rewarded with that of myrtle as well, does he not?"

July.

She blinked back her tears, swallowed down her sobs. She couldn't even cry properly, because Louise had already taken her dressing-case with all her complexion things in it downstairs. In a few minutes she too would have to go down— It was like "going out" from the Carmes prison. It was really almost more than she could bear, that sort of horror all over again. It just showed how naturally cruel men were—protesting in every letter how much he loved her, then dragging her away from Paris, from everything that made life worth living, just because—so he said—his own life was a "perpetual nightmare" without her. So—so *bourgeois* of him. Selfish, too. She hadn't written pages and pages —but literally hundreds of pages of reproaches because he stayed away from her in Italy, had she? Then why should he do it just because she wanted to stay away from him in Paris? So unfair—

She turned her head and listened, rushed to the window. Yes, *it* was there. The—the tumbril. There was an escort of Hussars, too. Twenty of them. Everybody in the streets would notice that, and wonder. If she sat well forward in her seat, they'd see who it was—their Lady of Victory, who was leaving them. They'd wave to her, kiss their hands, shout, "Our Lady of Victory!"—for the last time. The last time. She dabbed at her eyes with her hand-kerchief. In a very few minutes now— She looked about her lovely room, that was dismally hideous now with dust-sheets over everything but the long cheval-glass. She didn't want an Italian palace, she wanted only her own little world in the heart of Paris, and to be left in peace to enjoy it. That's all she wanted —it wasn't really much to ask of a man, was it, just that he leave you alone to be happy? He'd got what he wanted, hadn't he, his Army of Italy? Then why couldn't he let her be happy too, now that she'd got what she wanted?

Theresia and Ouvrard—she and Barras—Barras, too. It just showed you couldn't trust any man—not a single one. Looking at her with that smug expression on his face, saying, "My soul's treasure, it's quite obvious, isn't it, that a woman's place is with her, er—husband?" He didn't say that to Theresia, did he? Oh, no! But then of course Theresia'd got a multimillionaire, and she'd only got a funny little Corsican soldier that nobody liked. It wasn't her fault, was it? Anybody'd think she'd actually *wanted* to marry the man—

"The gentlemen are waiting, Madame."

There was Louise, in her traveling hat and coat. Though of course she wasn't just Louise now, but Mademoiselle Louise. It was more—more dignified, wasn't it, to travel with a companion than just a maid.

The gentlemen. Not even they would be amusing—not really amusing. Junot of course was all right to look at, but that's as far as it went. He was so *unintelligent,* behaving to her as though she were a—a holy relic; with enormous respect, but not any interest—not real interest. As for Joseph—well, he was Bonaparte's brother, wasn't he? So he wasn't any use at all. There was General Murat, of course. He might be— Bonaparte had always sent Junot before to fetch her to Italy, but this time he'd sent the Murat man as well.

She wondered what Murat— She turned again to her mirror, but Louise had put a dust-sheet over that too, now. Tears pricked at her eyes. Her mirror—the last, the very last spark of Paris was quenched. She picked up her reticule. Still, for another half-hour she could pretend she was just going for a drive through Paris with three young men—though one of them was only brother Joseph, of course. She sighed. . . .

> *"My heart alone is capable of loving as I love."*
> BONAPARTE

CHAPTER

❧ XXV ❧

July.

DESPITE THE FIERCE JULY SUN OUTSIDE, THE ROOM FELT DAMP AND chill, as Italian palaces practically always did. Though of course all palaces were dreary places, except the ones with Kings and Courts in them. But a palace—an Italian palace with Bonaparte in it—

Anyway, it was quite impossible to be comfortable sitting at table with a man who either bolted his food without looking at it, or didn't eat it at all, and who got up at odd moments and fidgeted about the room, opening things, looking into things, touching, fingering, and then kissing her on the back of the neck when she wasn't expecting it, so that her whole skin crinkled with irritation.

To-day, because he was leaving that afternoon for his new Headquarters at Brescia, they were lunching alone together, though usually they had their meals in the big dining-room with the other officers of the Staff. At first she'd thought that would be amusing, because Bonaparte, who was so odd about that sort of thing, wouldn't let the poor young men bring their women into the palace, so that she was the only one at table. But it wasn't amusing at all, because they all just sat there waiting for Bonaparte to say something first, and as he always either said nothing at all, or else so much that nobody else had a chance to say anything, why, she might just as well not have been there at all. It was quite incomprehensible, all these young men— Not that they were very interesting, the officers of the staff—not even Murat, when you actually saw him properly, in spite of his uniform. He was really only a sort of ruffianly peasant, coarsely handsome as that sort of man sometimes was. He'd taken a quite common woman from the Milan Opera for mistress. Such a vulgarly obvious thing—

Bonaparte speared a peach from the fruit-dish with his fork. She did wish he wouldn't do that sort of thing—

"I shall leave General Leclerc here," he said, "to see to my supplies. He'll take care of you, too."

His supplies first, of course. And she didn't want to be taken care of by General Leclerc—dull, pedantic, stiff— Oh, an aristocrat of course, but not the Versailles kind of aristocrat, the provincial kind that talked about the honor of their name and had literally dozens of children to uphold it. A solemn young man, who thought he looked like Bonaparte. It was quite extraordinary, really, the number of people who tried to look like Bonaparte. Anybody'd think he was something unusual, instead of just—

She said, "Yes, of course," to whatever it was Bonaparte was saying, and giggled, thinking of General Leclerc's aide-de-camp— what was his name? Oh yes, Captain Charles—thinking of Captain Charles imitating General Leclerc imitating Bonaparte. She hadn't laughed—not really laughed so much since she last saw Desirée. So extraordinarily clever and amusing a young man. After Bonaparte's quite depressing intensity, he made her feel her own natural self again. So young a man too, only a boy really— But she supposed she ought to listen to Bonaparte, because of Barras—

"So you see, *mio dolce amor*," he was saying, looking up from the peach he still held on his fork but was peeling with his fingers. "You see, I feel now that I can do other things than make war."

Well, there was nothing extraordinary in that. Most people could, couldn't they?

"Like—well, the secret clause I insisted on in my Armistice terms with the Sardinians, permitting me to cross the Po at

Valenza"—he scraped peach-skin off his fingers on the edge of his plate. "Naturally, it remained secret just long enough for a Sardinian courier to carry the good news to the Austrians. So that while they, trusting their ally, massed before Valenza to stop me, I, trusting nobody but myself, crossed the river at Piacenza, and they found me suddenly at their backs. But the cream of the joke is," and he grinned like a school-boy, "that the Austrians think the Sardinians betrayed them, whereas they were only trying to betray me. You see, my Josephine?"

Oh yes, she saw. But it didn't seem any cleverer than recommending one dressmaker to all your friends, and then going to another yourself.

"Oh," she said, "but how clever, how extraordinary of you! And now?"

"Now," he said, "I must find a way of crossing the Adige too, and preventing the Austrians from relieving Mantua by the river valley. And it won't be easy. An unfordable river and I, naturally, without a pontoon to my name, thanks to those stinking vultures of Army Contractors. Army Contractors!" He smashed his fist down on the table, the peach leaped from his fork, bounced off his plate, and came to rest on the embroidered table-cloth—and peach-juice *stained* so— Now he'd made her forget the name of the river, and she was sure Barras would be interested.

He pushed back his chair with a nerve-racking scrape, and began to pace about the room—picking things up, putting them down again upside down or in the wrong places, until your very scalp pricked with irritation. If only he wouldn't *fidget* so—

"Army Contractors!" he said again. "Robespierre threw them into the gutter where they belong—but Barras's picked them up again." He smashed his fist into the palm of his hand. "I tell you, he's selling the armies to them—selling the armies of France like so many cast-off garments. But it won't stop me—it won't stop me. I'll have the Austrians out of Mantua like that!" He snatched a handful of roses from a vase and threw them on the floor. Her lovely roses, that it had taken her hours—literally hours, to arrange. She didn't go about throwing his precious maps on the floor, did she? He kicked the roses aside, and went on tramping up and down.

"And then," he said, "I shall drive them north, drive them to the frontier. There I shall link up with Hoche or Moreau and the Army of the Rhine, and then— Then I will make peace. I will make my own peace in Vienna, with the Emperor Francis himself. What do you think of that—eh, my Josephine?"

She thought, naturally, that he was quite mad. Talking about Vienna as though it were some wretched little Italian village, and the Emperor as if he were just a—a person. It just showed how uncouth he was. As though an Emperor—a real Emperor—would ever dream even of deigning to receive—

"Oh," she said, "but I don't think Barras would like that. I'm quite sure he wouldn't."

He swung about to face her, and stood glaring, feet apart, hands on hips.

"Barras?" he said. "What's Barras got to do with it? This is my war—*my* war." He snatched up a pear from the table and twirled it by the stem between his finger and thumb. "That's what I'll do to Barras—when the pear's ripe." He shrugged and tossed it into the empty fireplace. Italian servants being what they were, it would probably stay there until it rotted, and there'd be flies and a smell—

He was standing behind her now, rubbing his hands along the back of the chair so that the polished wood squeaked beneath his palms, setting her teeth on edge.

"I shall have to be starting very soon—for Brescia," he said.

"So you will," she said. "Won't you?" Not of course that she minded his going to Brescia if he wanted to, she wasn't the jealous kind of wife who interfered in her husband's pleasure, but it was just a little odd, wasn't it? After all, she'd spent over three weeks on the road traveling practically night and day to get to him, and now, after only five days, he was quite ready to leave her and go somewhere else.

"Josephine," he said, "my mother was a soldier's wife. I was conceived in a military camp. I went through my first battle in my mother's womb."

"How—how nice for you," she said. She did wish he wouldn't be so *indelicate* in his speech. Of course it wasn't really his fault, it was only because he had no breeding—none at all. But at times it was quite embarrassing.

"You wrote me not long ago from Paris that you were pregnant," he said. "And I thought—a son of my own—"

What if she had? Everybody made mistakes, didn't they? If only he didn't take every little thing so *seriously*—

"And now you've got a son of your own, haven't you?" she said. "You've got Eugène."

He took his hand away and said, "Ah, Eugène—" in a flat sort of voice, as though Eugène weren't a son anybody could be proud of—

"And," she said, "there are your own young brothers and sisters. You have to be a father to them, don't you? You're responsible for them—you have to bring them up, provide for them—"

He said "I—" then broke off, frowning, and stood quite still for a moment.

"My sisters— What kind of a man is Fréron?"

She stared at him. He was so—so inconsequential, even in his mind. He couldn't concentrate on anything, not anything at all, for more than a minute at a time. And Fréron, who'd been in Marseilles for weeks now, where he couldn't annoy anybody.

"Fréron? Why, he—he does things for Barras. He writes things, he—"

"It's not his writing that interests me, but the man himself. He wants to marry my sister. Paulette. She thinks she's in love with him. She's only a young girl, not much older than Hortense, and he's— What is he?" He scowled at the top of the sugar-castor, and tried to bend it with his thumbs.

Fréron, marry? How comic! But why shouldn't he, if he wanted to? After all, that old harridan of his couldn't be frightfully amusing. "Not much older than Hortense...." Fréron smiling at her across the luncheon table, saying, "You who are leaving that age further and further behind...." And poor Céleste, who must be at least— How cruel, how ungrateful men were! Céleste, who'd been faithful to him for more years than one could remember. How horrible, how unfair—

"Oh, no!" she said. "No, you mustn't let him. Not a young girl like that! Why, he has two daughters of his own old enough to marry."

"Ah? And his wife. Dead, divorced?"

"Oh, not a wife! Men like Fréron don't, do they?—unless they're too old to—to— No, it's that stout, elderly woman who sat next him at Barras' luncheon. So devoted to him—"

He said, "Ha!" He picked up the nut-crackers, and with them managed to flatten the top of the sugar-castor. He examined it minutely, and tossed it into the fruit bowl. "So much for Fréron," he said. She did hope he wouldn't hurt poor Fréron's feelings, one didn't want to be unkind to anybody—but it was only fair to poor Céleste, wasn't it?

He dropped the nut-crackers and turned to look at the clock

on the mantel-shelf. "And I must go now. My carriage is probably waiting already." He turned towards her. "The last day, *mio dolce amor.*"

"Yes, so it is, isn't it?" If he had to go to Brescia, why didn't he go? Even—even Fréron would have known when he wasn't wanted, and have gone away. But then of course Fréron was a gentleman, after all.

He came closer to her. "You will write me by every courier? I—I cannot exist, otherwise."

"Yes. Yes, of course." Oh, why couldn't he *go!* Tears of exasperation rose in her eyes.

He took her hands in his and kissed them. "Tears," he said. "My adorable love! Your tears increase the torture of separation— yet to think there were no tears for me would be the torment of Hell, unending. My only Josephine!"

She felt laughter in her throat, sharp and hard as a dry crust. What did he want, then? A sort of—of gargoyle, grinning and spouting water at the same time? He was so—so *contrary.* Oh, dear! And now he was going to be—funny. He always was when his eyes went like that, opaque yet brilliant, like very pale fire-opals.

His arms were about her shoulders, her knees, he was lifting her against his breast, carrying her— Hoche, lifting her up out of the shadowy darkness of the prison corridor— You wouldn't think he was so strong. Not strong like Hoche. Hoche's strength was like the ground you walk on, firm and solid and calm. His was like—like a Martinique tornado.

Love shouldn't be like that. Love should be gay and bright and amusing—not this somber, fierce, imprisoning thing, snatching, frightening—

"Josephine! If I could draw you into myself. If I could tear off your little shoes, your pretty fripperies, and draw you—you, yourself—into my heart, into my very being!"

Oh, no—no! Love shouldn't be like that. Not like that at all. Besides, the harsh metallic embroidery of his coat was rasping her skin, its heavy bronze buttons were driving into her flesh. She pushed against him with her two hands.

"No," she said. "No. Put me down. You're—you're hurting me."

"But first—three kisses. On your hair—your eyes—your mouth. . . . Ah, Josephine. Josephine!"

*"Würmser shall pay me dearly for
these tears!"*

BONAPARTE

CHAPTER

❧ **XXVI** ❧

August.

SHE TURNED HER BACK TO HIM TO BE HOOKED UP. SHE COULD FEEL
the shaking of his fingers against her skin—not the sort of
trembling shudder she could always make him do when she tried,
but the nervous twitching of hurry and anxiety. He was clumsy
enough as it was with things like hooks and eyes, without getting
in a state about it. She swayed a little farther back towards him.
One might be able to gain ten minutes by doing that, and even
ten minutes might be just enough.

"If," he said, "you had sort of string things sewn on instead
of hooks and eyes, you could bring them round your waist to the
front, and do them up for yourself, couldn't you?"

She leaned against him and let herself go limp, so that he was
obliged to hold her to support her weight, and her head sank
back on his shoulder, so that her hair brushed against his cheek.
She raised her lashes slowly and looked up at him.

"But," she said very softly, "I don't want to do it up—myself."

He kissed her on the mouth, though not the slow, lingering
kiss that always irritated her so—a hard, abrupt kiss that hurt her
lips against her teeth. He held her, but only by her shoulders,
and with hands in which there was still that tremor of urgency.
How exasperatingly contrary he was! When she wanted him to
go, nothing could induce him to hurry—but now that she wanted
him to stay, he was in a perfect fever to get away. He was pushing
her from him—but actually pushing—

"Come, my Josephine, come! We still have time—but only
just. You must come!"

She twisted about in his arms and buried her face against his
coat. "No," she said, "no! Bonaparte—I'm afraid."

"My soul," he said, "you must show a brave face to the world—
to the army. My mother—"

She struck at his chest with her fists. "Oh! I know—I know! But I'm not your mother. I'm your wife—your wife. And I'm afraid!"

He held her away from him. "Do you think I'd let them touch a hair of my Josephine's head, unless they cut me in pieces first?"

Yes, but if they did cut him in pieces, what good— It was so *illogical* of him. "But," she said, "we've been happy here together—just we two, alone—haven't we?"

He snatched her to him again for an instant. "Ah, happy," he said. "Happy! Whatever happens now, we'll always be able to say, 'For so many days, we were happy!' Remember, my Josephine—whatever happens."

He pushed her from him once more. He snatched up her cloak and threw it about her shoulders. He stood and fidgeted while she tied on her bonnet—after all, she couldn't show herself with her bonnet on crooked, could she?—he seized her wrist and dragged her to the door—out on the landing—down the stairs. She might of course fall and hurt herself—he couldn't possibly just go on and leave her there with a broken leg or something, could he? Still, at the rate they were going, she might really hurt herself.

She was down the stairs, out of the front door, into the carriage, he flinging himself in after. Almost before he had settled himself beside her, she saw the driver's whip uncoil like a striking snake over the horses' backs, and they were off through the still sleeping streets of Brescia. Behind them clashed and clattered Junot's troop of fifty Becheney Hussars, the only French soldiers left in the town since the Staff had moved up to Verona the week before.

She closed her eyes and leaned back in her seat. They were definitely away now, and nothing could stop them any more, nothing, except— She shuddered. What were fifty Hussars against a whole Austrian army? And Bonaparte quite insane as he was— She was frightened. She had never been so terrified in her life, not even in the Carmes. They were away from Brescia now, on the open road, driving east as though a deadly danger were at their heels—and that was just the insane part of it. They weren't running away from danger, but towards it—towards it, and she was shut up here with Bonaparte who was quite mad, and she not able to stop him or to get out—to get out—

She looked over her shoulder through the little back window of the carriage, and saw the fifty Hussars in their scarlet and blue streaming out behind, like the bravely colored tail of a kite. Veiled by the dust of their riding, she could still see the towers and spires of Brescia— Brescia where in another day—another half day—she would have been safe.

She wished she'd never come to Brescia—she wished she'd never left Milan—left Paris. She wished she'd never married Bonaparte. She wished she'd never promised Barras— "Keep him in Brescia for ten days." That was all. It had seemed easy enough. Even then she wouldn't have done it, only Barras promised that if she did, the war would be over, and she'd be able to come back to Paris again. Only ten days. And she'd so nearly done it. So very nearly.

Ten days. By then, Barras said, a new Austrian army under a man with the quite extraordinary name of Würmser would have come down from the north, pushing between Bonaparte at Brescia and the French army at Verona. And without his army he couldn't besiege Mantua, could he?—and then of course everything would be over, and everybody satisfied. The Austrians would have Mantua, she could have Paris, Barras would have whatever it was he wanted, and Bonaparte—well, he'd have had his ten days alone with her, wouldn't he?

For she'd done that for him. Still exhausted—but utterly exhausted by her trip from Paris, she'd set off again, without any thought but giving him pleasure. She'd packed up her prettiest dresses, she'd left Milan and come alone, but quite alone, without even Louise, to join him at his Headquarters at Brescia, that was half-way to Verona. And she'd been kind to him—kinder than she'd ever been to any man in her life, for ten—no, nine whole days. You'd think a man—a man who said he loved her—would have been grateful, wouldn't you? But not Bonaparte. Oh, no. It only needed that dusty, dirty soldier who'd brought him a message from Augereau at Verona this morning to make him forget—but completely forget all about her. Or at least to make him drag her out of bed before dawn, when he knew quite well that it always upset her to get up before noon, and fling her, but literally fling her, into the middle of this horrible danger. She shuddered, and clutched her cloak about her.

"Cold, *mio dolce amor?* But it'll be warm enough soon—too warm, perhaps." He gave that sudden grin of his, that made him look quite stupidly young, like a gawky school-boy. He put his arm about her, but she pulled away.

"All my dresses, Bonaparte—my best dresses, left behind—"

"Never mind. You shall have the pick of the Mantua shops—once I've taken the place. And that won't be long."

Undoubtedly, he was quite mad. Take Mantua, with the new Austrian army— Besides, how could he imagine any woman—any decent woman, could possibly buy a dress anywhere, but anywhere in the world, except in Paris? And now she'd probably never see Paris again. Never. Not Paris, nor her lovely room, nor even poor Fortuné left behind in Milan, all alone. Perhaps he at least would care when she—

She hadn't been afraid in Brescia. It had felt like being on a high cliff, waiting for the stream of the Austrian army to flow safely by at her feet. But this—this insane dash across the very path of the oncoming flood— At any moment now it might come lapping over the low hills to the north, come seeping out of the woods below them, come sweeping across the road, this very road, *this* road, and she caught in the middle of it— She hadn't been able to stop him, not by being kind to him, or letting him hook up her dress, not even by leaning back against his shoulder and letting herself go limp. He'd just pushed her away—actually *pushed* her, as though she were no more than his—his kept woman.

He touched her on the arm. "Look," he said, leaning across her and pointing out of the window. "Lake Garda."

She didn't want to see Lake Garda, or any other Italian lake—not ever again, not as long as she lived. But she looked. It was a lake, just water stretching away to the left as far as you could see. But at least it was water, and even Austrians couldn't—

"Look," he said again. He snatched a map from the pocket inside the door, spread it out on his knee, and pointed with a pencil. "You see," he said, "it's a sort of triangle, standing on its apex—Brescia to the west, Verona to the east and Mantua, the apex, at the south. Here, just where we are now, halfway between Brescia and Verona, Lake Garda. The Austrians are coming down it in two columns, one by the eastern bank under Würmser, the other by the western, under Quasdanovich. In two columns, do you see, my Josephine—two columns. And that's where Würmser makes his mistake. It'll be another twenty-four—thirty hours, before they can join forces, and by that time—" He waved his pencil at her, his eyes dark and brilliant with excitement. Oh, it was all right for him, he was a soldier—and soldiers didn't mind being—being cut into pieces. But she—

"Of course," he went on, frowning, "I shall have to raise the siege of Mantua—for the time being."

Raise— Oh, there was no possible doubt that he was quite raving mad. All this fuss and bother, this quite horrible danger—and he was going to raise the siege anyway.

"But," she said, "then why—"

"Oh, I know what you're going to say," he interrupted, looking superior and triumphant. "The Staff'll say it, too. Mantua'll be provisioned again, I shall lose a hundred and forty siege-guns—all I've got. But you see, my Josephine—if I let the two Austrian columns join they'll be sixty thousand against my thirty-five. They'll overwhelm me and I'll not get ten thousand men alive out of Italy. You see?"

But of course she saw. That's just what she did see. They'd never get out of Italy alive. Never.

"So I must concentrate everything I've got at Verona, and leave Mantua open. Würmser'll think me in full retreat. He'll think it safe to push straight on south to occupy Mantua—instead of waiting to link up with Quasdanovich, as he should. In the meantime, I shall be in the east, in Verona, with my army—and as soon as Würmser has passed, I shall turn back and catch Quasdanovich before he too can reach Mantua. I shall catch him perhaps here, at the foot of the lake— By then Würmser'll have seen his mistake, but it'll be too late. I shall crush Würmser, too, as he comes north again to support Quasdanovich." He laughed, his teeth very white against the sun-darkened skin of his face. "You see, I'm not greedy. I'm willing to take two bites at my cherry. And when I've swallowed it, why then—then I shall find my guns again. Inside Mantua."

He put his pencil away. "All that," he said, "and only a day and a night to do it in. You see now, my Josephine, why I mustn't—I must not—be cut off from my army at Verona. But I'll get there in time, don't be afraid. I'll do it. Already we've passed the head of Quasdanovich's division—in a very little while—in an hour—we'll have passed Würmser's too."

He tried to refold his map, crumpled it, and threw it on the floor. He beat on his knees with his fists, and sat staring straight in front of him. The muscles of his face tautened so that the bones showed through, hard and sharp. He looked suddenly like an embalmed Egyptian head she'd once seen—the head of a man who was young, yet old beyond counting.

"The eyes of all the kings of Europe are on me," he said, "waiting for me to fail. But I will not. I will not!"

It was then that it happened. All along the dark edge of the wood little white puffs, quite round and soft, and half-transparent, like heads of dandelion seed—and, like dandelion seed when you blew it, drifting gently, lightly, slowly dissipating—

The carriage crashed to a halt with a rending shock, as though all the wheels had broken at once. It pitched her forward heavily, and so violently that she was thrown to the opposite seat. Glass shattered about her, horses clashed with their hoofs, men shouted. Bonaparte dragged her up, propped her back in her own corner without looking at her, tore the door open, hurled himself out, the glass of the broken window crunching beneath his feet.

Clutching at her throat that seemed to have closed so that she couldn't breathe, she stared out of the window. She saw the little filmy puffs of white again. She heard Junot's voice, not as it usually was, hesitating and stumbling, but clear and hard and brittle, the words breaking short like cracking ice. She saw a stream of blue and scarlet pour past like an unfurling ribbon as the line of Becheney Hussars heaved sinuously over the ditch and swept in a long thin stream across the flat of the field.

She saw one of them lurch sideways as they rose to the ditch, make a grotesque, doll-like gesture with his raised sword-arm, and slide with a curious, unnatural slowness down out of his saddle. Perhaps a broken stirrup leather— But it wasn't that. She knew it wasn't that. It was—it was the thing that made the white puffs, that had broken the window, that— The man fell, and because his grip was still tight on the rein, his lurching horse dragged him forward a little on his face. Then he lay quite still, only his hand moving horribly, like the flopping of a landed fish, because of the horse's jerking on the bridle-rein. His hand, moving like that by itself, and all the rest of him still, still as—

She screamed, and flung herself face downwards on the seat. She beat on the cushion with her fists, pressed it against her mouth, and bit at it with her teeth. She clasped her hands over her ears to shut out the fearful sounds—men's voices, ugly and male as she had never heard them before, horses' hoofs thundering like a hundred lunatic drums, a sharp, brittle sound like the snapping of dried sticks, and a shrill little whining note that rushed straight at her like an angry hornet—

She jerked her head up and looked. Her view was blocked.

Bonaparte was standing on the step of the carriage, with his shoulders pressed back against the empty window. He was standing between her and that horrible little whining thing. But it wasn't any use. He wasn't—wasn't *thick* enough. He wasn't any good—no good at all. She buried her face in the cushions again and wept. . . .

She felt a hand on her wrist, pulling at it. She screamed and screamed again. She thought of men like Murat—great brawny ruffians, more like triumphant beasts than men, snatching, devouring— The ugly fact wasn't in the least like the romantic picture had been. She screamed again.

"Josephine! Josephine!"

She looked up, and checked her screaming. It was only Bonaparte after all. She let out her breath in a shuddering gasp. Her ecstasy of fear burst like a soap-bubble, leaving only a little damp spot of misery behind. It was all his fault, of course—though as yet she wasn't quite sure what it was that was his fault.

She let him draw her out of the carriage. She stood trembling in the dust of the road. She saw the carriage-horses—the two leaders were down, one on its side with its legs stuck out stiff and straight like the legs of a child's rocking-horse, the other in a queer, unnatural attitude, its legs doubled under it, its long neck stretched out grotesquely on the ground before it. The four others were on their feet, but turned every which way, milling about, tossing their heads, kicking, while the coachman and the two postillions caught at their heads and snatched at tangled harness. As she watched, one of the postillions approached the kneeling horse, drew out his pistol, and shot it through the head—but shot it, just like that, as casually as though he were only cracking his whip. She shuddered and looked away.

Over the flat meadow-land she saw the blue and scarlet Hussars come slowly trotting back from the edge of the wood where there were no more puffs of musket-smoke, only here and there thin, vaporous drifts, like shreds of gauze caught in the trees.

Bonaparte put his arm about her shoulders. "You see, my soul's treasure," he said gently, "there's no danger. It was only a patrol, miles ahead of the main body. They're gone now. They didn't stop to fight, as they would have done if they'd had support anywhere near." He laughed. "No, they didn't stop to fight, once they saw Junot—a good soldier, Junot, when he's got the enemy in plain sight, and not just on a map. But they're gone—so you see there's no danger. None whatever."

She saw one of the Hussars dismount and bend over the fallen man, who still lay face-down in the ditch. She saw him turn him over, lift up his head, lay it back again.

"Oh," she gasped. "The man—the soldier—" She lowered her face into her hands and sobbed.

Bonaparte pressed her face to his shoulder. "Never mind the man," he said. "He's not suffering. He's quite dead."

She pulled away and stared at him, the tears streaming down her face. How incredibly stupid he was! Of course the man was dead. That was just it. It was the soldier who was dead, but it might just as well have been— And it would have been his fault— Bonaparte's fault—

He held her hands tightly pressed against his chest. "You are too tender-hearted, *mio dolce amor,*" he said. "But don't cry for him. Soldiers expect it, you know." Then suddenly he scowled. "But, by God!" he said. "I will make Würmser pay me dearly for those tears! And you shall see me do it! From Verona— you shall see me!"

She pulled at her hands, and tore them away from him. "Oh, no!" she sobbed, "I don't want to see anything—not anything at all!"

She ran back to the carriage, and stumbled into it. She saw him following. She clutched at the door and slammed it shut. She snatched at the handle and clung to it desperately. He put his hands on the edge of the glassless door and leaned in. "But, my Josephine—there's no more danger. And in a little while we'll be at Verona—"

She struck at his hands with her fists. "No, I won't go to Verona! I won't! I won't!"

He leaned farther into the carriage, his eyes very clear and pale in the darkness of his face. "Josephine," he said, "my mother—"

She pushed his face away with her hands. "I'm not your mother! I don't want to be your mother! I want to go away— to go away!"

He drew back. He was neither laughing nor scowling now. He had the expressionless, old-young face of the Egyptian head. "Very well," he said. "You're not yourself. You're upset. The heat—"

She shrank back in the corner, shaking in every bone and muscle, her teeth chattering. She heard him speak to Junot, to the coachman. She heard Junot shouting orders. She felt the carriage sway as the coachman climbed to the box again, felt it lurch as it was backed into the ditch, swung about, jerked back to the road again. She saw the two dead horses that had been cut from the traces and dragged to the roadside. Then the Hussars closed in on either side, and she saw nothing but their blue and scarlet, and the sweat-blackened flanks of their horses.

They went back the way they had come, back past the horrible little wood. But the Hussars were there now, two deep, their bodies and their horses between her and it. She looked back through the little rear window, and saw Bonaparte standing in the middle of the road looking after her. Behind him were a dozen or so Hussars, beside him Junot, holding the dead man's horse by the bridle. Bonaparte stood quite still, staring after the carriage. Then dust curled up in a heavy fog from the road, and hid him from view.

She leaned back limp and exhausted in the corner. How quite unbelievably callous he was! "You're upset—the heat—" He drove her straight into the very heart of an enormous enemy army, he forced her to sit in the carriage in the middle—the very middle of a perfectly horrible battle, then he made her get out on a road heaped—but literally heaped with dead men and horses—and he talked about being upset by the heat! How funny—how comic he was! She laughed. She laughed until she hiccupped. She hiccupped until she cried. She lay face downwards on the cushions of the seat and sobbed until she slept.

The carriage rolled and rocked its way southward. Always southward—away from the Austrians. Through Villafranca, almost beneath the walls of Mantua itself, on through Ferrara, Modena. She no longer counted the hours, she scarcely noticed the difference between night and day. Sometimes they paused to change horses. Sometimes food and wine were passed to her through the broken window of the carriage. Once—twice—she lay fully clothed for a few hours on the bed at an Inn, because the Captain who led the Hussars said his men could do no more. Though why great strong men should be tired, when she, who was only a woman—

At Bologna they swung east towards Lucca, towards Leghorn, the coast, the sea. Escape from Italy—from the Austrians—from Bonaparte.

Always before the smell of port towns had nauseated her. But not now. Leghorn smelled of fish, of salt, of tar, of ships—of the sea. She must get on, to the port, where the ships were, and safety. But it wasn't easy to get on, through the streets of Leghorn. Never before had she seen a town populated as this one was— every street literally choked with people, men and women talking, shouting, waving their hands. Italians of course were apt to behave like that—but it wasn't often that one saw so many of them all doing it at the same time. So many that the carriage could hardly move forward—was brought to a stop.

She stared anxiously out of the window. A man in the crowd saw her—pointed—shouted something—started forward. The whole crowd began to point, to shout, to move forward, hemming the carriage in closer and closer. The man who had first pointed thrust his head in at the window and shouted again, right in her face, his eyes starting from his head with some sort of emotion. She couldn't understand what he said, save for the name, over and over again, "Buonaparti! Buonaparti!" in the queer way Italians said it. She couldn't even hear what else he said, for at that moment every bell in Leghorn began to clash and clamor, a terrifying paroxysm of sound. Bells only rang like that for very important happenings, like kings or catastrophes—disasters— The tocsin! She understood then, and terror was about her again like a choking fog.

The Austrians were at her heels, at the gates of the city. They would plunder and burn and kill— It was Bonaparte's fault, and she was his wife— That's what they were shouting at her for. She was Bonaparte's wife, and everything was his fault. They were more dangerous than the Austrians, these people. They would drag her out of the carriage, tear her to pieces, kill—

The Hussars—they weren't even making an effort to ride the mob down, to get to her, save her. They were just sitting there on their horses, little brilliant-colored islands above the black-clad sea of people. Thinking of their own safety of course, not caring if she were trampled to death before their very eyes— She shut her own eyes, and crouched back in her corner. Outside the bells clashed, and the people shouted. "Buonaparti!"

Bells ringing. A drum beating. The calling of a name. Beauharnais—Bonaparte. And she was his wife— She was shut up—imprisoned—and she couldn't get out—she couldn't get out until they came and opened the door, and then— She was his wife—his wife—

She heard the door opening. She pressed her hands over her eyes so as not to see, whimpering a little, because her throat was

too tight-closed to let the scream come through. Beauharnais—
Bonaparte—and you couldn't escape twice, you couldn't—

"General Leclerc's compliments, Madame—"

Leclerc—Leclerc—General Leclerc. A little blond man who
thought he looked like— She let her fingers slip down from her
eyes to her cheeks, and stared over them. A sky-blue tunic, laced
and buttoned with gold, broad shoulders still broader for the
scarlet, gold-fringed epaulettes. Above, a bold young face set with
impudent black eyes and crowned with dark hair so glossy and
so tightly curled it might have been a cluster of black grapes.

"Oh," she gasped. "Oh, Charles! I mean, Captain Charles!
Oh—"

He smiled, showing small, white, pointed teeth. "General Leclerc's compliments, Madame—and I am entrusted with the
honor of escorting you back to Milan. . . . Madame permits?"

His plumed hat in one hand, the other on the edge of the door,
one foot on the carriage-step, he stood waiting permission to
mount.

"Oh, but of course, Captain Charles. Oh, but you don't know
how glad—" She caught at him with both hands, pulling so that
he half stumbled against her knees, and for a moment his face
was close against hers. He smelled of warm, clean young flesh and
orange-flower water, with just a little masculine prick of snuff—

"Your pardon, Madame," he said, "if beauty can pardon the
clumsy brute that I am." His face was still very close to hers, his
hands supporting himself on the back cushion on either side of
her head. Then he laughed, righted himself, and sat beside her.
The carriage was no longer a dark cell with death waiting outside, it was a dim little boudoir with life and youth come into it.
The vitality of his self-assurance jerked fear out of her like a
cork from a champagne bottle, and inside she felt the bright little
bubbles of happiness and laughter rising gaily to the surface.

The bells were still ringing, but it was no longer a wild cascade
of brazen sound—the notes were ordered and regular now, like
steady rain after a torrential cloudburst.

"The bells," she said. "What—?"

He tossed his hat onto the opposite seat, and turned half-facing
her. He wasn't a large man, but very virile, very muscular. No
taller than Bonaparte, but quite twice as thick, though very well
made, not in the least clumsy or—

"The bells, Madame, and the acclamations, are in honor of
Castiglioni."

A little shadow of disappointment came over her. She'd begun to hope that perhaps, after all, being his wife— "Who," she said, "is Cas— Cas—"

He laughed again. "Castiglioni, Madame, is a what, not a who. It is the place where the second of two Austrian Generals with quite unpronounceable names met and were defeated by a French General—"

She laughed too, and swept up her lashes at him. "With an equally unpronounceable name—eh, Captain Charles?"

"By this time tomorrow, Madame, the whole of Europe will be able to pronounce it—or will be trying to learn how. The people of Leghorn know it already, don't they? Show them your face, Madame, and you will hear if they do not—show them the face of the goddess who, after all, was the divine inspiration that led the mortal hero to victory."

How quite delightfully he said things! It was so much more— more exclusive to be a Goddess of Victory than just a Lady— Show your face— She hadn't thought of her face for hours—but literally for days. It must be quite impossibly spoiled—

"Oh!" she said, "my face!" She brought her little silver-framed mirror out of her reticule and looked at herself. Her complexion was quite gone, of course—but the pallor of her natural skin wasn't unbecoming. Especially when it went with eyes enormous with fatigue, languorous with relief, and delicately smudged about with the faint blue shadow of tears. The effect was quite new, but not in the least unsuccessful.

Captain Charles took the mirror from her. His hands were warm and smooth, gentle in touch, but very assured in gesture. Quite masterful hands, really—

"Why consult shallow glass on so deep a subject?" he said. "If you want to see the true reflection of your face, look into the eyes of any man out there in the street." He leaned a little closer—so close that she could see the faint down on his young unshaven upper lip, see his thick lashes quiver with the intensity of his gaze.

"Or look into mine, Madame—"

CHAPTER

❧ XXVII ❧

September.

SHE SAID, "BUT HOW QUITE CHARMING, GENERAL LECLERC—AND
how clever of you to have arranged it all! The little boats—the
music—everything!"

"If you are pleased, Madame, then I am more than satisfied."

She was pleased. It was going to be quite delightful, really.
She had never wanted to see an Italian lake again, but now she
was glad she'd come. She'd only done it actually to please poor
General Leclerc, who tried so hard to entertain her, and had gone
to so much trouble over the picnic that she couldn't bear to
disappoint him. Which just showed that it paid to be unselfish,
for at first she'd had no idea, but no idea at all, that Charles was
going to be there too. He was always so quite extraordinarily
entertaining—

General Leclerc said, "If Madame will give me her hand—"

He took it and helped her into the little boat—rather like a
Venetian gondola it was, long and narrow, with a man at the
back to pole it along. As she stepped in, the boat rocked. She
gave a little scream and clutched at General Leclerc. But he only
steadied her with respectful care, and helped her to her seat, a
low cushioned arm-chair with its back to the man with the pole.
General Leclerc sat on the cross-seat opposite her. Then Charles
helped Louise—Mademoiselle Louise—to get in, and sat with her
on the seat behind Leclerc. He looked at her over the General's
shoulder, and pulled one of those delightfully comic grimaces he
did so well. She giggled, and General Leclerc smiled politely
at her.

During the whole of August it had been quite too abominably
hot to do anything at all but sit in the coolest place in the Ser-
belloni Palace and play cards or talk. She'd seldom met a more

entertaining talker than Captain Charles, because he acted as secretary to General Leclerc and read all his letters. She'd never in her life laughed so much as when he'd told her about the— the misfortune Murat had caught from his precious Madame Rugat. One was sorry for poor Murat of course, but if he would choose common women like that— And Charles had been so quite divinely clever in his mimicry of the swaggering assurance of Murat's amorous advance, and the outraged fury of his retreat when he discovered the consequences— Charles was so absolutely devastatingly comic.

"Will you have your parasol, Madame, against the glare of the sun on the water?"

"Oh, thank you. How kind—how thoughtful you are, General."

And she had been out in the cool of the evening, of course, driving with Charles on the Corso of Milan, and to eat ices with him at Trentini's. And when the Opera reopened on the first of September she'd been there once or twice, too—always with Captain Charles, now she came to think of it. That was another reason for going on a picnic with General Leclerc. One didn't want the poor man to imagine one didn't enjoy his company. Besides, people were so quick to gossip about the least little thing, weren't they?

Of course, Charles was there today, too. But she was actually *with* General Leclerc, and nothing could be more respectable than a party with General Leclerc. She looked about at the party. They were all embarked now, in half a dozen of the gondola-things. The one in front carried musicians and the luncheon-baskets, the ones behind an assortment of young officers on leave, or convalescing from wounds, or belonging to General Leclerc's staff. They had their young women with them, and it was all very gay.

"—a military genius of the first rank," General Leclerc was saying. "First the Piedmont, and now Lombardy. Montenotte, Mondovi, Lodi, and a dozen others. Quasdanovich and Würmser defeated at Lonato and Castiglioni, and now a third Austrian Army under Davidovich practically annihilated at Roverito. Quite incredible, is it not, Madame?—and he barely twenty-seven."

"Twenty-nine," she said. "Oh, quite incredible. Quite."

She supposed Bonaparte really was doing very well in his war— only it was difficult to see what he got *out* of it, since all the money was sent to Bar—to the Government.

216

"—and now he's forced Würmser to take refuge inside Mantua itself, where his army will soon eat up the supplies the raising of the siege allowed to enter the city. Brilliant strategy. Brilliant."

"Yes," she said, "isn't it?" If he only knew how quite inconceivably tired she was of the brilliance of General Bonaparte. That was one thing about Charles. He seemed to be literally the only person in the whole of Milan who didn't talk incessantly—but incessantly, about General Bonaparte. She couldn't see what people could *find* so interesting— She looked at General Leclerc. That too was incomprehensible—not only that he should *want* to look like Bonaparte, but that he should actually believe he did—he with his soft blue eyes, pink and white complexion, and blond hair. Yes, that's what he liked to be called. The blond Bonaparte.

He was acting his part now—jerking at his cuff, pulling at his stock, shifting in his seat, frowning—which didn't make him look in the least intense, but just as though he'd picked up a flea somewhere. She looked at Charles over his shoulder. Charles scowled back at her, and jerked at his cuff. She bit her lip and said, "Oh, I quite agree with you, General Leclerc."

Charles leaned over the side of the boat, dabbling in the water. He pulled some water-lily buds for Louise. From a lily-pad, he negligently gathered up a bright green frog, and held it prisoner in his hand. He drew Louise's attention to a distant flight of birds, and adroitly let his captive drop into General Leclerc's coat-pocket.

Josephine too gazed at the birds, and she too trailed her hand in the water. She withdrew it, looked down at her dripping fingers, then up at General Leclerc. "Your handkerchief, if you would be so kind, General—"

He made haste to plunge his hand into his coat-pocket, and even greater haste to withdraw it. He stared incredulously at what he held in it—then, with a gesture of repulsion, let it fall to the bottom of the boat. With it he let fall a word that gentlemen do not utter in the presence of ladies—most certainly not in the presence of their commanding officer's lady.

The lady frowned reprovingly, first at him, then at the object of his displeasure. It stared back at her with topaz-yellow eyes, and made a tentative hop towards her. She hastily drew back her skirts.

"General Leclerc," she said coldly, "be good enough to—to restrain your pet."

General Leclerc flushed a deep pink—not at all like Bonaparte, who went copper-color when he was upset. He snatched up the small green creature and, before she could stop him, hurled it as far as he could into the lake. "Oh," she said, "you shouldn't have done that! I had no intention—I didn't want to deprive you of your—your little friend. Truly, I didn't."

General Leclerc said nothing, but wiped his hands fastidiously on the handkerchief he had at last found in his pocket. She smiled at him.

"A frog!" she said brightly. "So—so *original* of you, General! Though personally I should have thought a dog—or for the pocket, perhaps even a white mouse— But then I don't doubt that frogs have their little intelligences too, like the rest of us." She looked quickly at Charles over her shoulder.

General Leclerc threw his handkerchief after the frog. "Madame is quite right," he said stiffly. "The intelligence of a frog is quite on a level with that of—some of the rest of us."

Oh dear, now he was annoyed. He'd gone all prickly and stiff, forgetting even to jerk at his cuff. That was the trouble with these very young and very efficient men. They had no sense of humor—none at all. Still, one didn't want to hurt the poor man's feelings, and it was his party, after all. Besides, these serious young men—nobody could be so spiteful as they when their vanity was hurt, and there was no telling what he might write to—to other people.

She leaned back, lowered her chin, and swept up her lashes at him. "Oh," she said, "I do so agree with you—people are so shallow-minded, aren't they? That's what I find so—so *interesting* about you—the depth, the—the breadth, of your intelligence. So *unusual*. Mantua, and—and the other things Bonaparte's done. You've made even me understand. So fascinating. But you, too, General—the things you do. You're too modest. After all, they're just as important as—as shooting muskets and marching about, aren't they? And without you, General Bonaparte's armies wouldn't have anything to shoot with or any shoes to march in, would they? So you see— Tell me everything about it, General—but everything. So passionately interesting—"

He told her. She folded her hands in her lap, opened her eyes very wide, and fixed them on his. General Leclerc wasn't stiff any more. He wasn't even remembering to look intense. He was just being natural, which after all was only a young man of twenty-six talking about himself. Though how he imagined anybody could be *interested*....

General Leclerc was quite easy really, though of course incredibly dull. Still, she went on being kind to him, poor lad, all through the rest of the boat-ride, and all through the picnic-lunch afterwards. They had it on the splendid lawn that unrolled its green length all the way from the little white château above to the blue lake below. She let him carry up the arm-chair from the boat for her, and settle her cushions about her. She let him serve her himself, and sit at her feet keeping the mosquitoes away from her ankles with her fan. She was quite delightful to him. She even prevented Charles from putting a grass-snake in his pocket, and he put it down a girl's back instead. Charles was so original—

All the other young men and women sat about the lawn on cushions, and were waited on by the musicians in their quaint Italian costumes. Very charming they all looked, the women in their delicate flower-colored dresses, the men in the sterner finery of their uniforms. They looked quite like a group of Marie-Antoinette's young couriers at the Petit Trianon—and she in her arm-chair enthroned above them all, exactly like the Queen herself. More than Queen.... She hadn't thought about that since she married Bonaparte, because of course it was too absurd— Yet, when she came to consider it, Charles had called her Goddess of Victory, and a Goddess was more than a Queen, wasn't she? Charles—

The musicians were playing again, and Charles was showing an Italian girl how to do the new dance, the waltz, that was all the rage in Paris. The girl was shrieking in her Italian French, "Oh, Cappitaing Carlos! Your hand! Oh, you not-ti, not-ti man!" Still, she seemed to be enjoying it.

Ball-room dances were really a little out of place in a garden, in the open air. Besides, General Leclerc didn't approve, you could tell by his face. She sat up and clapped her hands. "Let's do something really amusing," she cried. "Something quite silly and childish. Play games. Blind-man's-buff. Oh, General Leclerc, let's!"

General Leclerc smiled with quite fatherly condescension. He thought blind-man's-buff would be a most charming pastime, and good, too, for the digestion. He got up, and helped her to her feet. She said, "Then give me your— No, I mean, Charles! Charles! Give me your handkerchief!"

219

She blindfolded a young Italian, and turned her around. The girl staggered and blundered about like a blind duck in a barnyard. Almost at once she caught another girl, and hadn't even the wit to guess wrong, so there was no amusement whatever to be had out of the forfeit. The second girl caught Leclerc, but that was only because he was too dignified to get out of the way. She made him kneel down and kiss her hand. No originality—but none at all.

General Leclerc played very earnestly and very conscientiously —you could tell he even had his eyes shut behind his bandage. He banged straight into Charles who, as soon as he was touched, gave a shrill squeal and cried in a high falsetto, "Oh, General Leclerc, your hand! Oh, you not-ti, not-ti man!"

Everybody laughed of course, and General Leclerc turned crimson, then jerked at his cuff quite ferociously and said, "Captain Charles!" He tore off his bandage, and snapped, "You forfeit, Sir, your next twenty-four-hour leave."

Oh, but how unkind! And poor Charles who hadn't done anything at all—at least, only such a very little thing. But of course he had no sense of humor at all, only an exaggerated sense of his own dignity. That was the trouble with these serious-minded, conscientious young men. But he shouldn't be conscientious again, she would see to it that he wasn't, spoiling everybody's pleasure.

"Give me the handkerchief, General," she said, "and I will blindfold Captain Charles." She did it properly—but really properly, as it had to be done, unless you only wanted to play a silly child's game with nothing really amusing about it at all. She turned him about, and pushed him off.

He ran hesitatingly, his hands gropingly outstretched before him and his head thrown back, exactly like a real blind man. He was such a clever mimic— Louise of course had to put herself directly in his way, and naturally he was obliged to catch her. Not that it really mattered, because he guessed wrong without any difficulty at all. He caught one Italian girl, then another, but had no luck with his guessing. She turned away to smile at General Leclerc.

She glanced over her shoulder, and there was Charles with his groping hand literally not six inches from her shoulder. She shrieked, and ran. But really ran. Not like the Italian girls with their ungainly tottering on short legs and high heels, but with all the graceful elegance of long limbs moving in the effortless speed of her flight. She heard Charles running after her. Really running, too.

She slipped between and about the other players, and he came after, unerringly. She dodged about the last couple of players, and there was only the wide stretch of lawn, sweeping up empty before her as far as the château. She laughed out loud, and ran. She slipped around a close hedge of clipped yew and stood, panting and laughing, just behind it. Charles, being blindfolded, would naturally see nothing at all, and go running on and past—

Charles dashed around the end of the hedge. He came so abruptly that she hadn't time to start aside, and he collided with her before he could stop. He nearly swept her off her feet— would have, if he hadn't at once thrown his arms about her to save her. He just stood quite still for a moment, holding her close, and she could feel the thudding of his heart beneath her own. They had both been running quite fast, of course— Then he slid one hand up her shoulder and neck, until he touched the curls at the back of her head.

"Ha!" he cried. "The little curls—the little, divine curls! I have caught the Goddess herself."

The hand at her waist still hold her pressed to him. With the other he tore the handkerchief from his eyes and tossed it away.

"I am right, am I not?—the Goddess of Victory in person."

His hand, warm and firm on the bare skin of her upper arm, the bold black eyes that were so male and so experienced, the clear, unshaven skin that was so incredibly, so touchingly young—

"The forfeit—eh, Madame?"

His red lips, parted over teeth that were small and white and sharp as a puppy's—

"Eh—Josephine? . . . Josephine!"

CHAPTER

❧ XXVIII ❦

November.

THE SOLID WORLD HAD RETURNED TO ITS BEGINNINGS, A CLOUDY nebula, and he himself was only a dim consciousness at its heart. There was nothing but mist, blinding, choking, annihilating. It rose sourly from the putrefaction of long-drowned land—it lay sluggish over the stagnation of rotting water—it dribbled sullenly from the powder-fouled muzzles of impotent guns. It oozed up darkly from the sweat-quenched fires of energy, bitter with the taint of exhaustion.

There was nothing left in existence that had shape or color or substance, nothing but the gray obscurity that wavered and drifted, he, too, wavering and drifting with it. A nebula, with no central meaning about which to gravitate, solidify, take form. Nothing that was tangible—nothing, save one small object, one atom of purpose in a purposeless void. A thing so small it could be grasped in a man's hand. It could be stared at, until vision gradually slid into focus again, steadied and cleared. The small, compact matrix of an unformed world, reflecting light like a star. He looked up from it at the big man standing beside him.

"Augereau," he said, "have you seen my wife's portrait?"

Augereau said, "Yes." Then, after a hesitating pause, "And you, General Bonaparte—have you seen the bridge of Arcola?"

He too said, "Yes," and was silent. He closed his fingers over the little portrait, and felt it smooth and firm and solid against the palm of his hand. He looked towards the bridge of Arcola. It was clearly visible now. All day a tepidly murky November sky had sucked vapor from sedgy river banks and sodden marshlands that summer heat no longer dried, and winter frost had not yet hardened. But now a cold dry wind swept down from the northern mountains, freshening the air of its miasmic vapors and men's bodies of the sticky irk of their sweat. The Adige, lying gray and smooth as steel in the oozy mud of its bed and the water-sodden marshes of its banks, gave dim reflection of the stained white walls of the little town beyond and of the stone piers and wooden planks of the bridge above—a sordid, crumbling little town, a frail and crumbling little bridge. The town and the bridge of Arcola.

"It cannot be done," said Augereau. "And when I say a thing cannot be done—" He shrugged and spat into the water-filled ditch at his feet. "You cannot ford the river, because of the marshes—and you cannot force thirty thousand French troops across a bridge only six feet wide, in the face of fifty thousand Austrians."

"Croats."

"Croats or Chinamen, it makes no difference—"

"It makes every difference."

"Nevertheless, there are fifty thousand of them. God knows where they get them all from! We've had Beaulieu, Würmser, Quasdanovich, Davidovich—and now we've got Alvinzi with another army. God knows how—"

"Because the Armies of the Rhine have been thrown back into Alsace, freeing men for Italy. We shall never make junction with the Armies of the Rhine now. I shall be obliged to enter Austria alone."

"Enter Austria— Where Moreau, Pichegru, Hoche, Bernadotte have failed, how can even you expect—"

"The Army of Italy shall march on Austrian soil though every other army of France has been thrown back." He unclasped his fingers and looked at the smooth, firm heart of reality in his palm. It gathered the diffused light of the sun on its polished surface, and flashed it back, concentrated, intensified. Like a star.

"With nothing but these narrow dykes by way of solid ground to move on, we cannot deploy our artillery."

"They cannot deploy their cavalry."

"The thing's impossible. Blow the bridge before they do, and try elsewhere."

"Neither they nor I will blow the bridge. We both need it. But they shall not have it. They shall not relieve Mantua. I will not raise the siege again. It no longer suits my purpose. I will cross the Adige by the bridge of Arcola. I will cut Alvinzi's lines in his rear, at Caldiero. I will force him to retreat north on Vicenza—on Bassano."

"This is the third day—the third effort, and we have failed. Failed."

"We have not failed. We have only so far not succeeded."

"You cannot ask men to do the impossible. And it is impossible. I led the last attack myself—and I know."

"You led it yourself. Yes."

Augereau swayed his great bulk back and forth uneasily, so that the mud oozed and squelched about his feet. "The men are exhausted—discouraged—without heart. And you yourself.... You cannot do the impossible, either. For three days and nights you haven't slept—you haven't rested. You haven't even been off your feet. You'll destroy the army—and yourself with it."

"Nothing can destroy me." He clenched his fingers for an instant about the little round portrait, then slid it into his breast pocket. He looked down at the feet that had carried him for three days and nights. He hadn't been conscious of them before. He was now. He was conscious vividly, intensely, acutely, of everything, tangible and intangible, about him; of the enormous vitality of Augereau's body and the anxious doubt in his mind; of the aching fatigue of his own body and the serene confidence in his own mind. He was conscious of the sallow sky overhead and the rotting ground underfoot. And as though he stared through a magnifying-glass he was conscious, with a sharply detailed clarity, of the bridge of Arcola.

From the dyke on which he stood, he looked down on it. He could see its solid stone piers, darkly ringed at their base with slime and waterweed. He could see the wooden planks of its floor, and a dangling span of its hand-rail, snapped where the weight of fighting bodies had thrust against it.

He looked up and down the flow of the Adige. Upstream, the first houses of Arcola rose abruptly from the water itself. Every window, he knew, hid a Croat marksman eager for a target. A few hundred yards downstream, where the river shallowed over slimy mud-flats, bedraggled willows on either bank made a thin and tattered screen to the open water between. He jerked his chin towards them.

"There—where the willows make cover—we could put men across on their flank, without being seen."

Augereau glanced at him sideways, shifted uneasily, and spat. "Perhaps a dozen," he said. "You might get a dozen across. But what you can expect to do—"

"I shall not need even so many.... Junot!"

Junot, from where he stood with the other aides-de-camp on the crest of the next dyke, scrambled down into the water-filled ditch below and clawed his way up the slithering mud of the opposite bank.

"Your orders, General?"

"Get me ten trumpeters, Junot—cavalry trumpeters."

Junot saluted with grimy fingers, and slid back into the ditch. Augereau squelched with his feet, frowned at them, glanced sideways, bit at his lip. Then he jerked up his head. "General Bonaparte, you are in command here, but—"

"Yes. I am in command here."

He watched the ten men file away along the ditch. Watched them reach the willow-screen, disappear behind it. Watched them flounder, bent double, through the shallows over the mud-flats, and disappear again behind the willows on the further bank. Then he too moved, following the crest of the dyke to where it sloped down to the level of the road. He turned left along it, towards the head of the bridge. He sent an anxious and reluctant Augereau back to the main body, and himself went on alone.

Behind him on the road he heard the advance guard coming up. They came steadily and unhesitatingly, but there was no enthusiasm, no spirit in their tread. Augereau was right. But it didn't matter. Before him he saw the Croat soldiers settle their hats on their heads, shift their muskets in their hands, take firmer grip of the ground with their feet. That too didn't matter.

His own men breasted the slight rise leading to the bridge. He waited still an instant longer, then drew his sword and flashed it up above his head. From the willow-copse down-stream and on the far side, the thin shrilling of bugles rang out. Cavalry bugles. The charge—the notes jerked and broken as cavalry calls are by the lurch and thrust of galloping horses. He turned his head, and shouted to the oncoming infantry.

"Look! They're taken in the flank—their flank's turned! Forward! The bridge, the bridge! Charge!"

He snatched the tri-colored banner from the standard-bearer, and set foot on the bridge of Arcola.

The mist was there again. He opened his eyes and stared at it. It raced up acridly pungent from blazing pine-logs—was sucked in sourish eddies from water-soaked garments—curled, bittersweet, from hot red wine in a little pewter kettle. It dribbled rankly from the smoke-fouled bowl of a short clay pipe.

There was nothing about him but a gray obscurity that wavered and drifted—yet he at its center was unwaveringly conscious of himself as a hard core of reality, about which all things gravitated and took perfect shape. There was the shape of Alvinzi—outwitted at Arcola, outmanœuvered at Caldiero. There was the shape of the Austrian's lines of communication torn apart, of his whole army in disordered retreat on Vicenza; the shape of Masséna's cavalry storming at his heels to see that he didn't tarry on the way.

He lay quite still, conscious too of the warmth and shelter of the Inn of Arcola, of the bruised fatigue of a body that it was no longer necessary to hold upright, of the pulsing ache of feet it was no longer essential to stand upon, conscious of—

"Augereau, that filthy pipe of yours again—"

Augereau grunted, jerked his shoulders away from the mantel-shelf, tossed his clay pipe into the fire, and spat after it. "So," he said, "you've come back to your senses at last."

"I was never out of them." He let his body relax still more slackly against the cushions of his chair, and drew closer the warmth of the blanket that covered him. He stretched his feet still farther towards the heat of the fire, and flexed his toes in the shabby comfort of the felt slippers that shod them. He looked at Augereau's feet that were still firmly planted on the ground, at his legs that were as strongly erect as tree-trunks, at his body that was as untiring as rock, and scowled. He looked at Augereau's face that was a hard mask of satisfaction spattered with mud and stained with unshaven beard, and gave his sudden smile.

"I said I'd do it—I said I'd cross the Adige by the bridge of Arcola, and I did it. Eh, Augereau?"

Augereau looked down at him, and rasped at his stubble-roughened chin with a blackened thumbnail.

"The Adige, yes. As for the bridge—" He shrugged his wide shoulders. "The first Austrian you met on it tossed you off into the river to get at somebody his own size. And there you would have stuck, belly up in the mud like a stranded fish, save for Junot, who ruined his only pair of breeches getting you out. Poor devil, he's afraid to take them off to dry them, lest they shrink—" He jerked his head sideways, to where Junot lay on a bench against the wall, fully dressed and sound asleep. He turned back again, with his hard peasant's face that would admit laughter only at the corners of the eyes.

"Your charges have spirit, General Bonaparte, but they're a trifle lacking in weight. And they're hefty fellows, these Austrians—"

"Croats."

Augereau shrugged. "Croats, if you like. Though of what importance the breed—"

"The utmost importance." He sat forward a little, with his elbows on the arms of the chair, and coughed with the movement. "That's your trouble, Augereau. No imagination. You only see the bodies of the enemy, not their minds. The Austrians are a sophisticated people. They'd never have believed in the fairytale of my phantom cavalry. But the Croats are primitive. They believe in magic and spells and devils. They'll face any danger—except the imaginary one."

Augereau shrugged. "Austrians or Croats—they'll all of them believe in a devil now—a Corsican devil. They won't need much imagination for that."

"Imagination." He leaned still farther forward. "It's imagination that wins battles, Augereau—and loses them. Imagination governs the world." He propped his chin on his fist, and for a moment stared into the fire. Then he looked up and smiled. "Three nights ago, we stole out of Verona by the Milan Gate, silently and in darkness. To-night we shall march in to the beating of drums and by the light of torches. . . . And the three days between have written our names in history. Imagine that, Augereau."

Augereau looked down his long, acquisitive peasant's nose. "Maybe. But to-night'll write your name on your tombstone if you ride to Verona now, worn out as you are, and in clothes still reeking wet—"

"Ha! My clothes—" He clutched the arms of his chair, and pulled himself to his feet. He coughed rackingly. Brilliant white sparks floated and circled before his eyes, and he stared at them until they dissolved. Then he dropped his blanket and began to draw on his clothes, that had been spread before the fire to dry, but that were still clammy with steamy moisture and stained with green marsh slime.

"We must be in Verona to-night," he said. "Masséna hasn't enough men to harry Alvinzi for more than a few hours, until the panic's worn off. We must pick up reinforcements at Verona. Then you, Augereau, will march on Dolce to prevent Davidovich from coming up, while I continue the pursuit of Alvinzi until he's where I want him—on the other side of the Brenta. Then I shall be able to rest. In a week—in ten days from now, I shall be in Milan. I shall be—well, in Milan."

"I see," said Augereau gravely. He held his commanding officer's coat for him, and settled it on his shoulders. "The pockets are probably still full of water," he said.

The pockets— He thrust his hand into the left breast-pocket. Nothing. He felt on the other side. Nothing. He dug into his coat-pockets. His fingers shook so that he could scarcely force them into the corners of the damp lining. A wet handkerchief. A packet of sodden letters. Nothing else. It was lost. It had been stamped into the mud of the river, shattered against the stones of its banks. Lost. An evil omen. Better a lost battle than lost luck. The waistcoat pocket— Something round and smooth. He breathed deeply, and drew it out. His snuff-box. He hurled it into the fire. It must be in the breast-pocket, after all. *Must* be. . . .

Augereau watched, the little crinkles deepening at the corners of his eyes. "It's on the mantel-shelf," he said, "where we put it for safety."

He snatched it up and held it to the firelight. Yes, it was safe. The water hadn't damaged it.

"Ah! Then you've seen it—my wife's portrait, Augereau?"

"Yes." The smile spread almost to the corners of his mouth. "But I don't mind seeing it again."

"My wife—*my* wife." He held the little portrait closer to the fire, so that its curved surface caught and reflected back the leaping flames, while it glowed and sparkled like a star. A bright red star. He held it on the palm of his hand, polishing its water-dimmed surface with the ball of his thumb. He frowned. The glass was, after all, cracked. A broken portrait meant broken faith— He stood rigid and unbreathing for a moment, feeling the tiny, thin edge of broken crystal beneath his thumb, feeling the desolation of exhaustion suddenly press down on his shoulders until his knees shook under its weight. Then he jerked his thumb away, hardened his shoulders. He wasn't after all a superstitious Croat. And it was he who lacked faith, who was unworthy, to allow the vaguest shadow of doubt to cross even the outer edges of his consciousness. He hid the miniature with his fingers, not surrendering it to Augereau's outstretched palm.

"No," he said. "For after all, no living artist could possibly do her justice. You see, Augereau, it's not so much the beauty of her eyes, her mouth, her nose, her hair. It's—it's herself. It's the way she turns her head—the way she speaks. The way she moves, or is still. There is charm—grace—in everything she does, or is. Everything. Even her faults. She is graceful in walking and sitting, graceful in lying down and getting up—in dressing and undressing, in— You've no idea, Augereau. You can't imagine."

"No," said Augereau dryly.

"She's—she's incomparable. And to think that in ten days— in ten days—" He stared before him into the fire.

Augereau pulled his shoulders away from the mantel-shelf. "In ten days you'll be in the tavern of Arcola, if you don't get your boots on.... Junot!—Junot, what have you done with the General's boots?"

His boots. He looked down at the shapeless felt slippers that were perhaps the property of a tender-footed inn-keeper. He sighed. Boots were, after all, a necessity. He sat while a blear-eyed and sodden Junot fetched the boots from in front of the fire and knelt before him, cautiously, because breeches shouldn't be strained at the knee while still damp.

The boots were on. He stood up, and stamped wincing feet yet farther into the sticky discomfort of heated but undried leather. He tightened his belt, hooked on his sword. He jerked at his cuff, fumbled with the buttons of his coat. He plunged his hand into his breast-pocket.

"Junot—have I ever shown you the portrait of my wife?"

"Josephine, you are an inexplicable monster—and I love you more every day."

BONAPARTE

CHAPTER

ᷤ XXIX ᷤ

November.

HE PULLED AT HIS CUFF, AND LOOKED AT HER BLACKLY FROM beneath the dark hair that straggled over his forehead. She, from her couch, looked back at him and giggled. He frowned savagely, and twitched his head sideways.

"It's no laughing matter, Madame," he said coldly. "And I—" he slapped at his chest— "I am not accustomed to being mocked at." He stared at her unwinkingly, then clasped his hands behind his back, thrust out his chin, and began to stride jerkily up and down the room. She giggled again. He stopped abruptly before her, folded his arms across his chest, and glowered down at her.

"Let it be understood, Madame," he said harshly, "that there is one man and one man only who gives orders here. Myself."

She leaned her head back against the cushions, and laughed aloud. She laughed until she felt weak, until she had to blink the tears back from her eyes.

"Oh, Charles!" she cried brokenly. "Oh, you mustn't—you shouldn't—!"

He laughed too, brushed the dangling hair back from his forehead, sat on the edge of the couch, and caressed her bare ankles with his firm, warm hand. "Nevertheless, my love," he said, "I mean it. You must do as I say. You must go back."

She pouted and looked down. "But I can't bear it, Charles. Truly, I can't. You remember yourself, the last time—the bells of Milan rang for five days and nights without stopping—absolutely without stopping for a single instant, and my nerves— Then all those people, Charles—everybody in Milan, going on and on, just like the bells. Quite exhausting. Anybody'd think nobody'd ever won a battle before—so silly of them, because one side or the other has to, hasn't it? I quite literally couldn't bear it all over again. And last time I could at least get a little rest and quiet by going to bed—but now, with Bonaparte there—"

He bent down and kissed her ankle. "I know, I know, my love. With him there, I shall be torn, devoured, tortured by jealousy. But one can't think only of one's self, can one? One has to think of other things. Of other people, and what they'll think. Public opinion. Public opinion, my love, doesn't understand real passion—only cheap sentiment. Public opinion would point the finger at you and say, 'Ha! The faithless wife, who isn't there when the conquering hero comes exhausted from the battle to lay his weary head on her bosom—'"

"But Charles! Can't you see? That's just what I don't want—"

"Naturally not, my love. Who would? But it must be done, nevertheless. The duty of a loyal and devoted wife—"

"But I have been loyal and—and devoted. I've been celebrating the victory here in Genoa, haven't I? Nobody can possibly say I haven't. Nobody could possibly think—"

"It's possible General Bonaparte can think. What was it Leclerc wrote? Where's the letter? ... 'Madame. General Bonaparte has been unconscious for five hours, and the doctors will not answer for the outcome unless you return at once—' You see, Josephine?"

She frowned. Of course she was sorry for poor Bonaparte if he wasn't well, but what she could possibly do— Anyway, he'd probably just gone to sleep. He did sometimes, just like that, without any reason at all. "Leclerc's an old woman—you know he is, Charles. He's just imagining things—"

"No, Josephine. Leclerc's an old woman perhaps, but he's not a fool. Neither are the doctors. And a man doesn't faint just because he comes home and his wife's out. There's more to it than that. If he ever suspects—if he ever thinks he has reason to suspect— He's not a man of the world, Josephine. He's a Corsican —a barbarian. And we can neither of us afford—"

She sat up a little, and looked at him anxiously. "But he can't possibly, Charles. We've been so—so— I mean, I haven't given him the least possible reason to suspect— I'm even staying with the Governor of Genoa and his wife, aren't I?—so dreadfully respectable. And receiving nobody in private—but literally nobody, unless they're there too. I don't see what more he can expect—" She smiled at him. "And it's not my fault, is it, if Louise has—admirers in secret?" She giggled. "The Governor's good lady even warned me, very discreetly, that Louise might not be quite—respectable. People have such suspicious minds, haven't they?" She smiled, then her mouth trembled. "And, oh, Charles— we have been happy, just we two together—haven't we?"

He slid a little higher up the couch, caught her hands in his, and kissed them. "Of course we have, my love. And we want to be happy again, don't we? So—"

She sighed tremulously, and looked down. "I suppose so." She swept up her lashes at him. "You *do* love me, Charles?"

He took her in his arms, and kissed her on the mouth, hotly, bruisingly, until she went limp against his chest. Then he held her away from him, and looked down into her face.

"You won't forget, Josephine?"

"How could I ever—ever forget, Charles?"

"No, of course not. But I mean about the Bodin Company."

"Oh yes, yes. Bodin—"

"You have only to tell him Henri Bodin is an old friend of yours, who's fallen on hard times. And I can assure you, the

Bodin Company's military supplies are no worse than anybody else's—though it's not the least use my telling Leclerc so. But Bonaparte—he doesn't mind your asking favors for your friends who are in distress?"

"Oh, no. No. He likes it. He thinks it's—it's womanly of me."

"Good." He kissed her again, and got up. "Don't forget the name. Bodin."

She watched him go out by the door leading to the little room behind her own, that was Louise's. She heard them speak, and laugh a little. Then heard their steps, ostentatiously stealthy, creeping down the marble corridor outside. She wrapped her dressing-gown about her, and ran to the window. From between the curtains she could see the garden of the Governor's mansion, every correct and respectable detail clear in the brilliant moonlight.

She heard the faint slither of bolts cautiously withdrawn, the sharp clink of a chain incautiously dropped. She heard them whispering and laughing softly together in the shadow of the porte-cochère. Then she saw them come out into the carriage-drive and stand facing each other, he holding her hands pressed to his breast, she looking up at him, her face as sharp-cut as a cameo in the stark light of the moon. Quite a pretty girl really, Louise, though of course an ordinary enough type—Charles put his arms about her, drew her close, and kissed her on the mouth.

She giggled as she watched, wondering who else in that respectable house was watching the little comedy. Charles was so clever. Whoever might be watching would be certain—but absolutely certain that he and Louise— She did hope though that Louise wouldn't be getting ideas. So disappointing for her.

She turned back into the room and sighed. She supposed Charles was right, he was so intelligent about that sort of thing. Look at the way he'd got Leclerc to send him to Genoa to receive something or other that was coming by sea for the army, and then gone about the whole day complaining that it was always he who was sent on tiresome errands. So clever and amusing of him! Oh yes, he was right of course—he always was. But she'd been so happy these five days past in Genoa, happier than she'd ever been since—yes, since that day with Desirée at Croissy, when Barras— Poor Desirée, she'd really try to go to see her when she got back to Paris. Paris— She'd never really be quite absolutely happy until she did get back to Paris. You'd think Bonaparte would realize that. He probably did. But he had no consideration for other people. None at all.

Coming back to Milan like that too, without a word of warning. Or practically not. Anyway, when he wrote she'd already made up her mind to come to Genoa, his letter had only made her leave Milan a few days earlier. He couldn't expect her to alter all her plans just because he chose to come rushing back to Milan in the very middle of his war, could he? So *irresponsible* of him!

She sat on the couch, and stretched out her feet towards the fire. Besides, there were the people of Genoa to be considered. They'd been so pleased, so flattered, to have her come to their celebrations for the victory of—of—well, the bridge thing. Bonaparte of course didn't understand that it was literally the duty of people in their position to show consideration for the feelings of the lower classes.

That was what she'd done, really—her duty. And they'd appreciated it, the people. Running after her carriage in the streets, standing up on their seats at the theater just to catch a glimpse of her. Theresia had never been so popular—not even begun to be. That of course was what Bonaparte didn't understand—the importance of social success. But then, poor soul, how could he?—with the manners he had. It was really almost more than one could bear, sometimes. Still, Charles was right, of course— She sighed, and climbed into the bed. She blew out the candle and lay down. Still, of course, if he really *was* ill— "Five hours unconscious—" She frowned, and stirred uneasily. Unconscious. Suppose he should go on and on being unconscious. Suppose he should— She opened her eyes wide and stared into the darkness.

What would she do if he—? What *could* she do, down here all alone in Italy? There would be Leclerc and Junot and Augereau and Murat and all the rest of them, looking at her accusingly, as though it were her fault. So unfair of them, as though she could possibly help—

Actually of course they were jealous of her, because she could make Bonaparte do things, and they couldn't. They were all the same—Leclerc with his nasty-minded suspicions, Junot who looked at her as if she might put poison in his precious Bonaparte's wine. They were all jealous of her, they all hated her, and she'd be left all alone with them, and nobody, nobody at all—

There was Charles, of course. But he, poor lad, hadn't any money, not any at all. He never would have either, unless Bonaparte did something about the Bodin person—and he couldn't do anything for anybody, not possibly, could he, if he— It was so *unreasonable* of him. Running about the country when he wasn't well, instead of staying quietly wherever he was until he was better, like any sensible person would. And now he was probably dead, and she with nobody— Oh dear, what could she do—what could she *do?* A tear trickled from the corner of her eye, and fell with a little plop onto the pillow.

It really was unfair of him. He wasn't at all ill, not in the very least. Of course his eyes were sunken and he coughed, but then they always were and he always did, so that it didn't really count. Actually, he looked unusually well. He even had a good high color on his cheek-bones, and his eyes were particularly clear and bright. She could see them, staring at her in the mirror over her shoulder.

He really was the most irritating man it was possible to imagine. After she'd sat up the whole night crying because she thought he was dead, after she'd nearly killed herself to get to Milan in time, even leaving Louise behind in Genoa to pack her things, he just stood behind her and stared at her in the mirror. He knew perfectly well how it got on her nerves. And he wasn't even ill, only in a bad temper. You could always tell, because he didn't stick his fingers into her pomade pots, or smear his hands with her rouge, or spill her powder. He just stood there and stared, without the slightest consideration for her nerves. And not doing anything—not anything at all, just—

He suddenly gripped her by the shoulders, jerked her from her dressing-stool, and stood her upright before him. His fingers dug into her flesh, and he was shaking her—or practically, because his hands were shaking, and she—

"Josephine! You're incomprehensible—inexplicable! Are you a woman at all, or a soulless monster? You turn my life into a perpetual nightmare. My unhappiness is past my endurance to bear. While you—you amuse yourself with your caprices—your whims. Your caprices," he said again, between his teeth. "A caprice gave you to me—a caprice takes you away. I was a fool— a credulous fool—ever to expect your love to equal mine. But I had a right not to expect—this."

Charles had been right. He knew. Fear jerked at her nerves so that her skin puckered and her throat closed. She was afraid of his eyes that looked strange and blind, pale as water in the dark pits of their sockets—afraid of his hands that shook, and yet were hard and strong as metal. A savage, Charles had said, a barbarian, capable of—

"You're—you're hurting me," she whispered.

"I—hurt you?" He gave a bitter, rasping laugh, but dropped his hands from her shoulders. "You're not capable of being hurt—not capable of any feeling at all. Not even hate. . . . No, you don't even hate me."

She wrung her hands together, and forced herself to look at his eyes, that were so frightening. "Hate you? Why— But you know I—I love you. Bonaparte—?"

"Love?" He laughed again, a sound like parchment torn across and across. "Love? I come straight from the battle-field itself—I abandon everything—I ride without pause to Milan only to see you. I rush to our apartment to take you in my arms, and you—you are not there! You know I am coming—you know I have only three days. And you go. You run after your pleasures—your galas—your balls—your receptions, that flatter your vanity! Love—" He raised both his hands clenched into tight fists, then let them fall and clasped them behind his back.

"Love—" he said again, his unwinking eyes fixed on hers. Then he jerked his shoulders, turned away, and began to pace up and down the room.

She breathed deeply, and shut her eyes for a moment. It was all right, then. He didn't know. He was only a little upset, a little disappointed. So childish— After all, she wasn't an army-corps, was she, to be marched and counter-marched at his orders? She gave a shuddering little sigh, and the tears rose softly to her eyes.

"But," she said gently, "I've come back—haven't I?"

He stared blackly at her over his shoulder. "It's a pity you should have incommoded yourself. It was not my intention to interfere with your amusements. I am not worth it. The happiness or unhappiness of a man you do not love has no right to a place in your thoughts. You would be wrong to bother your head about him."

Why *must* he go on and on like that! She'd come, hadn't she? So exasperating— Striding about the room, pulling at his cuff, jerking his chin sideways to glower at her. So exactly the way Charles— She pressed her handkerchief to her mouth.

"I—I'm sorry," she said tremulously.

He planted himself stiff-legged in front of the fire, and stared at her bleakly across the room.

"Do not reproach yourself," he said. "It is my own fault if

235

I cannot even interest you. It is not enough that I lived only through your life, took pleasure only in your happiness. It was not enough that my victories were so many offerings to be laid at your feet—that I devoted all my ambitions, my thoughts, the interests of my life, to you—you! That I loved you fiercely, and alone. Be happy—be happy. Happiness was made for you. I was wrong ever to expect you to sacrifice one moment of it for me."

She put her handkerchief to her eyes, and sobbed gently. "Bonaparte! How can you be so unkind—so cruel—so unfair!" She lowered her handkerchief to her lips, and looked at him over it. "Do you think I've been happy—without you? Do you think I haven't made sacrifices—for you?" She moved towards him a little, her trailing gown flowing out behind her, and dragging back from the long, pure line of her thighs.

"I went to Genoa—yes. For the celebrations in honor of your victory. You had won a battle—but, don't you see?—there are other things to be won, too. The people— Wherever I went, Bonaparte, they shouted your name—*your* name. They fought to get near me—to see me—to touch me. No, not me. Your wife. Don't you see, Bonaparte? Your wife." She gave a little sob. "I— I was only trying to help. To do something for your career—your glory—your reputation—"

She was so close to him now that she could hear the little dry, rasping sound of his breathing. She stretched out her hands to him, almost touching his breast. He didn't look at them—didn't move. Only the short, hard sound of his breathing. Then his lips twisted in an ugly smile that showed his teeth.

"My reputation?" he said bitterly. "You don't even respect your own. You don't even hold it above the reach of the pretty little gentlemen you permit to follow you about—to make you conspicuous—the object of common gossip." The dark copper-color flooded up over his face, and he clenched his jaws so that the muscles quivered. "My God! If I had my way, I'd exterminate that race of insolent coxcombs!"

Apprehension rushed back, checking her breath, making her eyelids quiver. But what—how much—? Bonaparte had said, "little gentlemen," not "gentleman." She let out her breath in a long, tremulous sigh.

She looked at him. She met his eyes with the limpid candor of her own. Then gradually they opened wider and wider, strained and troubled with incredulous horror. She withdrew her hands in a slow gesture of protesting dismay. Slowly she stepped back from him in shocked retreat.

"Bonaparte!" she breathed. "You don't mean—you can't imagine— It's not possible that you think— Oh, I can't even say it!"

She covered her eyes with her hands, and stumbling blindly, flung herself down on the couch. She buried her face in the cushions and sobbed.

She heard no sound but her own weeping. What was he doing? Was he watching her, looking at her?—at the ruddy-brown curls on the white skin of her nape, at the polished curve of her shoulder that had freed itself from her gown? Was he still standing hard and angry before the fire? Had he just gone off and left her, desolate, unhappy, and quite alone? She sobbed wildly and brokenly. What was he doing? She couldn't very well sit up and look.

She felt his hand on her hair. She shrank away from him, and buried her head deeper in the cushions. "No," she sobbed, "don't touch me! Don't! I can't bear—"

"Josephine!"

She felt his arms about her, lifting her. She struggled against him with little futile flutterings of her hands. He raised her from the couch, sat down and, with his arms about her shoulders, held her pressed against his breast. Not saying anything or doing anything. Just holding her.

Held like that her back was twisted, her neck ached, her side was cramped, the fringe of his epaulette caught at her hair. She was quite horribly uncomfortable. She pressed her cheek against his coat, closed her eyes, and gave a long, quavering sigh.

He had been—difficult. Much more difficult than usual. Quite exhausting. But he was all right now. Or was he? He still sat completely motionless. She let her head go slack against his arm, and looked up at him. The hot copper-color had ebbed away from his face, and he was quite pale and ordinary-looking again. His pupils had darkened and spread, so that his eyes were almost lost in the heavy shadows of his brows. Men—men like Junot and Murat—thought his face was hard and cruel, only of course they called it austere and determined. But then men never really saw other men's faces as women did, did they? His mouth was very firm and close-lipped, but its lines were wide, curved, tender. The shape of his jaw was hard and aggressive, but the bones were fine and light, almost delicate. And at the point of the chin, there was a faint shadow that, if he had a little more flesh, would be a cleft. With a man who had a face like that, it was best to be quite frank—quite utterly frank and truthful. Otherwise they might imagine—things. She smiled up at him.

"Bonaparte—you haven't stopped loving me?"

"It is no longer in my power to stop, *mio dolce amor.*" He bent his head and kissed her hair. "And sometimes it robs me of my reason—deprives me of my senses. Sometimes I think I would give you a lover myself, if it would bring you the slightest pleasure. But I know I would not. I know I would tear out his heart with my naked hands."

She laughed softly. "Oh, Bonaparte, how quite absurd you are! To let such a thing torment you! It's my poor little Captain Charles—isn't it? My cavalier servants! But I couldn't live without him—I quite literally couldn't exist. Running my errands for me, carrying my packages, opening my carriage door— All sorts of little things. Besides, it's the custom of the country. You, who are a sort of Italian, ought to know—"

He frowned sharply, and his mouth thinned. Oh dear, now he was going to be awkward again. And her back— She should have been tactful with him, instead of quite honest and truthful. It never paid to be really absolutely truthful—

"I am not a sort of Italian," he said coldly. "I am a Frenchman. I am of Corsican race and French nationality. Never forget that, Josephine!"

How funny he was! What a quite extraordinary thing to get upset about. So petty of him, when she'd thought—

"Ah, Josephine!" He suddenly tightened his arms about her, so that she was horribly uncomfortable and could scarcely breathe. "I am not an Italian or a Frenchman or a Corsican. I am not even a reasoning human being. I am one thing and one thing only. The lover of Josephine."

> *"The Directory cannot govern, and
> must therefore either conspire,
> obey, or plot."*
>
> DIPLOMATIC CORRESPONDENCE,
> ¹797

CHAPTER

September.

GENERAL AUGEREAU HAD PUT ON HIS BEST MANNERS AND HIS BEST
garments in honor of the occasion. He held his chicken-bone
with his thumb and forefinger only, while he rent off the last
shreds of flesh with his teeth. He wiped away the surplus grease
about his mouth with the back of his hand, so as not to soil
the fine linen napkin during the ceremonial gesture of its use.
He had graced his huge brown hands with an imposing display
of richly-jewelled rings. He had supplied elegance to his shabby
uniform by lavish cascades of lace at throat and wrists. He had
supplemented the natural odor of his person by a judicious
sprinkling of attar of roses. He attended to his dental hygiene
not with a broad thumb-nail, but with a gold tooth-pick.

Barras stared at his wineglass until he judged the distressing
exhibition of refinement to be over, then glanced up with an
engaging smile.

"Naturally, General Augereau," he said, "I am more than
honored to receive you at my table. But as a matter of, er—simple
curiosity, why has General Bonaparte not seen fit to answer my—
that is, the Government's summons to Paris in person?"

Augereau considered his tooth-pick. "The General has bigger
fish to fry, very likely—for the moment."

Barras raised his eyebrows. Fish—? "You refer to, er—his Imperial Majesty of Austria?"

Augereau planted his elbows on the table, and shrugged.
"Royal carp or mud-eels—they smell much the same once they're
in the pan. Eh, Director Barras?"

Barras looked at him sharply. With these simple men of the
people, it was difficult sometimes to know whether they were

239

being insolent, or merely—simple. His face was simple enough—simple as the face of a building-brick. But the small gray-green eyes had the malicious sharpness of two fragments of bottle-glass stuck into it. Still, after all, only a semi-illiterate peasant.

"And your General Bonaparte—what does he think he's going to do in Italy? Make himself King?"

Augereau helpfully pushed his plate towards the lackey who was changing the courses, and laid his big hands on the table before him, appreciatively eying his rings. "A King? No. He's much too well brought up a young man for that. He knows his manners, does General Bonaparte." He twisted a ruby on his little finger to show the stone to better advantage. "Besides—Italy doesn't suit his health. He's been ailing lately."

"I am distressed to hear it—though I hadn't marked any slackening of his, er—energy. He was, however, well enough, I trust, to give you full instructions before you left Italy?"

"Yes." Augereau moved his hands to make room for the savoury that was placed before him. "He told me to take my orders from you."

Barras frowned down at his plate. Of what value was military support that only placed a loaded weapon in your hand and told you to use it for yourself? Of what service was a military authority that left the responsibility on your own shoulders? He had humbled himself and his dignity to the extent of appealing to General Bonaparte for help, and instead of rushing to support the head of the State as it was his simple duty to do, he had flung him this grotesque ruffian of an Augereau, as he might have tossed a copper coin to a whining beggar. It was insufferable, intolerable, not to be borne. Yet was the man only a copper coin after all? He looked at him narrowly.

He was poking with his well-scraped finger-nail at the small, white, perfectly shaped Paris mushrooms before him. He looked up and met the eyes watching him from across the table. "Ha!" he said, pushing away his plate. "If you knew how those city-grown mushrooms were fertilized, you wouldn't eat 'em. Field mushrooms, now. Nothing worse than a little wholesome cow-dung."

Barras winced, and pushed his own plate away. Damn the man! If only he was as full of information on the subject of Bonaparte as he was on that of mushrooms— He, Barras, had been particularly fond of Paris mushrooms, and now he'd never be able to eat them again. Nor field mushrooms either, for that matter.

"But your wine's sound enough," said Augereau, pushing forward his glass. Barras filled it with some reluctance. He regretted now having produced his 1774 Burgundy. If it were true that wine brought out the truth, then either Augereau had no truth in him, or it was very firmly battened down. For more than an hour now, wine—1774 Burgundy—had been poured steadily into that great vat of a man, and so far nothing had come to the surface but bubbles. And even they— It was impossible to tell whether they were innocent surface-foam, or whether they oozed up from some muddy depth of secret iniquity.

"Now, this business of yours," said Augereau. From his pocket he produced a blackened clay pipe, which he proceeded to fill from a greasy leather pouch. Barras watched him with some apprehension, doubtful of the duty of a host towards a guest who proposed to smoke tobacco in his dining-room. He had seen pipes in operation in taverns and cheap dance-halls, but he had no idea how one went about setting them on fire. Doubtless a candle-lighter would serve. He rose, took one from the mantel-shelf, and lit it at the wood fire that tempered the first chill of September. With a courteous gesture he held it over the bowl of the pipe. Augereau plucked it from his fingers, and flung it in the fire.

"Man," he said, "never light a pipe with a taper. You get wax on the tobacco." He produced a briquet, and made his own conflagration. Then he swung about in his chair, straddled it with his great thighs and, with his arms folded across its back, puffed contentedly at his pipe.

"Bonaparte can't abide my pipe," he said placidly. "I daren't smoke it in his presence."

Barras removed himself as far as possible from the evil-smelling fog, and stood leaning against the mantel-shelf. "I am happy to find that I have one taste, at least, in common with General Bonaparte," he said stiffly. The man had the effrontery to smoke his filthy contraption in his presence, in the presence of Director Barras, the head of—

"Tobacco," said Augereau, spitting accurately into the fire, "is good for smoking out wasps' nests. And I understand that's your trouble. Wasps' nests to be smoked out."

Barras looked down at the fire, then sideways at the sharp, gray-green eyes fixed on his. He stirred his feet a little uneasily.

"You are certain General Bonaparte gave you no definite instructions?"

"He gave me very definite instructions. To take my orders from you."

Barras sighed. "Very well," he said. "There are two, er—wasps' nests. The Upper and the Lower Houses. They are both a mass of poisonous insects. Royalist Deputies. And unless they are, er—smoked out promptly, they'll sting the Republic to death. It is their intention to dispossess all purchasers of national property, to re-impose the subsidies and the salt-tax, to revise the trial of Louis XVI, massacre all the so-called regicides, and send every revolutionary to the galleys. And then to set the Bourbons back on their throne again. I—that is, the Government, the loyal section of the Government, cannot permit this atrocious, this anti-Republican, anti-Revolutionary plot to materialize. I—you, General Augereau, must use force to destroy it, before it uses force to destroy us."

Augereau wiped his mouth on the back of his hand. "Your orders to me then, Director Barras, are that I kill Royalist Deputies for you?"

Barras frowned. "You are, er—blunt, General Augereau."

Augereau shrugged. "I am a blunt man. I am a Republican, and it seems to me better to kill Royalists than to be killed by them."

"So am I—so are all of us Republicans," said Barras. "But not Terrorists. There must be no return to Jacobin methods. They represent as great a danger as the Royalists. There must be no massacre, General Augereau. A simple rounding up of the, er—undesirable Deputies—by surprise in the Chambers, as many as possible. The others where and when you can catch them. But no massacre, I beg of you."

"As you like," said Augereau.

"But those who resist arrest you are, of course, at liberty to, er—deal with. You understand, General Augereau?"

"Oh, I understand, Director Barras." He looked up, the firelight making hard, bright points of his eyes. "Have to save the plums from the wasps, eh?—and the pears too, now they're so nearly ripe."

Now what the devil did the man mean by that? Probably nothing at all. Possibly that he himself wouldn't be averse to a plum or two. Undoubtedly, with his peasant's virtues of patience, courage, and endurance, he had the peasant's faults of rapacity, cunning, and avarice. And a man's vices, after all, were often more useful than his virtues.

He took an easier pose against the mantel-shelf, leaning his elbow on it, and smiling down ingratiatingly at the big man. "There is no doubt," he said, "that General Bonaparte has done great things. Very great things. Still—he wasn't alone in Italy, was he, General Augereau? And it does sometimes happen that a leader is credited not only with what he has done himself, but what his subordinates have done, too. You, General Augereau— you are an older man than he, possibly a wiser, certainly a vastly more experienced. You are a strong man, a capable soldier and a brave one."

Augereau nodded his head. "So I am," he said. "So I am."

Barras took snuff, very deliberately, and slowly returned the box to his pocket. "You tell me, General Augereau, that General Bonaparte is not well. It would seem advisable, therefore, to look to the future, would it not? In the, er—unhappy event of General Bonaparte being obliged—solely for reasons of health, naturally— to relinquish his command, it would be to the advantage of—everybody concerned, that his place should be promptly and satisfactorily filled. You agree with me, General Augereau?"

Augereau took his pipe out of his mouth and wiped his lips on the back of his hand. "You mean," he said, "would I like you to throw General Bonaparte out of his place and give it to me?" He looked down at his pipe, then up at Barras. "Yes. There's nothing would please me more. Only the thing's impossible. A pity."

"Impossible? I—the Government has power to remove officers—"

"You can remove General Bonaparte from the Army, granted— but you can't remove the Army from him." He puffed at his pipe for a moment, staring at the fire. "You see, Director Barras, the Army's fallen in love with him."

Barras tapped impatiently on the mantel-shelf with his finger-tips. "You are pleased to be, er—humorous, General Augereau."

"Humorous? Not a bit of it. There's nothing in the world that's more like a pretty and head-strong wench than an army. Yes, it's an unaccountable, female thing—shy and bold, willing and unwilling, hot and cold. Any strong man can force it to obey. But if it mistrusts him, it'll go sulky on him, heavy in the hand. If it respects him, it'll do everything possible for him. But it's only when it falls in love that it'll do the impossible."

243

Barras smiled, and spread out deprecating hands. "Oh, the impossible—"

"Yes, the impossible. With the Army of Italy, Bonaparte's routed five times his weight in Austrians. With it, he's cleared northern Italy—he's forced the lines of the Po, the Adige, the Piave, the Tagliamento, the Isonzo. He's marched into Austria, to within a few miles of Vienna—as far as it suited his purpose to go. With it at his back, he's dictated his terms to your Imperial Majesty of Austria himself. And it'll do more for him than that, the Army—when he asks it to. Eh, Director Barras?" The fine, shrewd lines deepened at the corners of his eyes, and he heaved himself up from his chair. "Take my advice, Director Barras. Don't try to take General Bonaparte away from the Army— unless you're a better lover than he is. . . . Another glass of your most excellent wine to your very good health, Director Barras."

He filled his glass and stood, enormous and overpowering, able to look down even on the tall man that was Barras. "He's a little man, Director Barras—but he's bigger than the two of us put together. You know what he said to the plenipotentiaries of His Majesty of Austria? He took a porcelain vase from the council-table, and held it as I hold this glass—and he said, 'I hold your Empire in my hands—and I can smash it like—'"

The glass fell from his hands, and smashed on the marble hearth. He looked down at the fragments, and the corners of his mouth twitched. "Tchah! That was clumsy of me. But then, I'm a clumsy man."

He tightened his belt that he had loosened for the purpose of dining, and flicked a crumb from his lace jabot. "I'm sorry about your glass, Director Barras."

Barras flung open the long windows to clear the atmosphere of its over-emphatic reminder of General Augereau's presence. He folded his arms on the hand-rail and leaned out, breathing in the air that swept softly over the calm beauty of the Luxembourg gardens—September air, sweet with the perfume of ripe fruit, bitter with the tang of gardeners' bonfires. A lovely month, September. A month when, as that incredible ruffian of an Augereau had very truly reminded him, the pears were so nearly ripe for the picking.

So very nearly ripe. The people had eaten their fill of the green fruit of Democracy, and they were sick of it—so sick that they were beginning to yearn even after the rotting windfalls of

244

the Bourbon tree. But he, Barras, would save them from that. He would provide wholesome food for their nourishment.

Theresia was right. The time for naïve experiments in Government—Constitutions, elections, assemblies—was over. The moment had come for one strong man to brush aside the confused ideals of the people, and—why cavil at a word?—dictate a clear policy to the nation. He had already made a good beginning. He had effectively destroyed the Constitution by ordering the arrest of some fifty Deputies in office, for the sole crime of their political opinions. The rest would follow in due course.

In two days now, before dawn. In two days, the fourth of September. September. He frowned a little, and shifted his fingers on the hand-rail. The September massacres. Tallien of the September massacres. Barras of— But there would be no bloodshed. Or so little. Those who resist arrest— Carnot would never permit himself to be touched by the loot-decked hands of an Augereau. A pity, of course. Carnot was no Royalist, he was only pig-headed, narrow-minded, unenlightened, holding that the people had a right to elect Royalist Deputies if they liked, and the Deputies had a right to express their opinions. That it was illegal to stop them by force of arms. As though legal quibbles could be allowed to stand in the way when the fate of the nation was in the balance! And they should not be allowed to. In two days he would brush them aside. And then— But gradually, not brutally, the new law should take its place. The law of one strong man.

He straightened his shoulders, raised his head, and stared before him into the waning September day. The sun was setting now, and its reddening light turned the mist of bonfire-smoke to a shining haze of gold.

One strong man. After that, one would be able to deal with those so-called popular leaders—what were left of them. General Bonaparte, when next he had the impertinence to offer to resign, would find that the suggestion no longer carried a threat with it. It would be quite simply accepted. Trouble with the Army? Rubbish! There were ways and ways of, er—removing a man from his command. There had been Hoche—and he was no weedy, ailing little man, but a great lusty giant, bursting with health and vigor. Yet he had died, hadn't he?—quite unaccountably, after only two days' illness. There had been Hoche. There would be Carnot. A regrettable incident, that nobody would deplore more than himself.

Yes, General Bonaparte's resignation could be safely accepted, the very next time. The last time, when General Clarke was sent to, er—assist him in his peace negotiations with the Austrian Government—he replied that he would make his own peace, unassisted, or—the exact words were still in his memory—"I will retire to civil life—and my civil career will be as simple and straightforward as my military career has been."

General Bonaparte's civil career— His fingers tightened a little on the hand-rail. Then he shrugged. Nonsense. General Bonaparte would have no civil career. He would have no career at all, once the direction of affairs was where it belonged. In the hands of one strong man.

The sun had disappeared behind the trees now, and the luminosity had faded from the drifts of smoke, the mellow warmth had drained out of the air. He suddenly shivered a little. September evenings had the warning chill of October days in them—

He shut the windows, drew the curtains sharply over them, and turned back into the room. A dim room, lit only by the glow of the fire. An empty room, with one man alone in it—though of course a strong man. Still, even a strong man could take comfort from the presence of a woman at his fire-side. Theresia— Oh, Theresia was right, of course. A man like Ouvrard couldn't be made eternally to sit up and beg for every lump of sugar, like a poodle-dog. He was a business-man. When he bought and paid for a thing, he wanted a clear title-deed to his property. It was natural, of course. One didn't grudge him a full monopoly of Theresia's more, er—exuberant moments, but there were other moments— But that too would come. "Theresia goes to the highest bidder," Tallien had said once—and soon he would be able to bid the supreme power. Yes, quite soon now.

He moved towards the fire, to warm the chill out of his bones. Something on the marble hearth crunched beneath his foot. He looked down. Fragments of broken glass shone red in the fire-light. His best set of Burgundy glasses, and that clumsy oaf of an Augereau. Clumsy—?

He touched the pieces with his toe. The Emperor of Austria's shattered porcelain, Director Barras' shattered crystal—

He held his hands to the fire, and rubbed them together. Something of the chill of out-of-doors seemed to have crept into the room.

PART V
1798-1799

"Josephine is the only woman I have ever truly loved. She still reigns in my heart, and I mourn for her."

NAPOLEON AT SAINT-HELENA

"Woman creates the man, and then devours him."

CORSICAN PROVERB

CHAPTER

XXXI

January.

THERESIA TALLIEN LAID HER FINGERS IN THE SMALL, HARD, COMpact hand offered to her, and stepped out of the carriage. She looked up at the façade of the house, and thought it even more nobly imposing under the discreet rays of the moon than in the blatant light of day. It wasn't like the Chaumière, whose shoddy core had been no more than lightly plated with luxury, nor like the Luxembourg, whose luxury had worn paper-thin with the usage of the centuries. It was like a newly-minted coin, with the mark of wealth firmly cut into the solid weight of it.

The Hôtel de Babylone. A noble house, a rich house, a strong house. Her house. Her fingers closed a little more tightly on the hand that had been capable of housing her at last as it was fitting she should be housed.

Once inside the massive doors, Ouvrard bent his neat head, kissed her hand, patted it, and left her to mount the splendid stairway alone. He was a man careful of his health, and found that a glass of hot rum before retiring did much to counteract the danger of a chill after exposure to the air of the January night. For herself, the exhilaration of the evening was stimulant enough to warm her to the center of her being.

She went slowly up, sensing the luxurious depth of the carpet beneath her feet, and the softly brilliant lighting of halls and rooms about her. No need in this house to reckon the price of a pound of candles, nor to sell their burnt-out stubs for what the wax would fetch.

She entered her bed-chamber, let her cloak drop to a chair, and looked about her. Here too, on room and furnishings, was the stamp of newly-minted wealth, untarnished by age or usage. Furniture of precious woods inlaid with bronze, firmly delicate in line, after the new Greek fashion. Rich carpets, whose inch-deep pile was like young moss to tread upon. The bed, wide, low, silken-furnished. At its head rose the slender, curved neck of a swan, holding in its beak long, diaphanous curtains of gauze that swept to the floor. Its sides sloped gently to screen the pillows, the whole, save for the ebony beak and jewelled eyes of the swan's head, overlaid with pure gold leaf. A bed of gold, like a throne.

From bed to bed she had mounted, not by chance nor for pleasure, but purposefully, because those were the steps to the throne. There had been Fontenay's, that was scarcely raised above the common ground by his title of doubtful nobility. There had been Tallien's, that was so soiled with mud and blood it had been a shuddering horror to make use of it. There had been Barras', that was cold and reluctantly offered. The climb had been neither easy nor pleasant, but it was over.

Men. Each one had thought he possessed her, but it was she who paid—Fontenay with her dowry, Tallien with her body, Barras with her intelligence. Yes, they had been paid, like so many servants; and like servants they had been discharged when they no longer gave satisfaction. Now she was enthroned on gold, and the steps were beneath her feet. She was enthroned, with a fitting consort beside her—a partner, not to be paid, but with whom to share body, mind, and soul.

She unclasped the lion-headed girdle that held her robe beneath her breasts, unhooked the golden lion's claws that held it at her shoulder. The fragile sheath of silk that served her for covering fell to her feet. She picked up a great embroidered Spanish shawl of flaming colors and draped it about her, under the right arm, and tossed over the left shoulder. Ouvrard, who was an artist at soul, admired good drapery and fine colors. She took the jewelled fillet from her hair, but left the golden pins in place. Ouvrard enjoyed releasing that incredible cascade of rippling black hair.

She tossed a handful of gilded fir-cones onto the fire, and watched the perfumed smoke, blue, green, red, yellow, twist and twine in fantastic patterns. The evening's reception at the Luxembourg had been like that, an uneasy, twisting pattern of emotions and thoughts, each of its own color, but inextricably tangled. Amusing to watch, knowing that yours was the hand that had produced it.

It had seemed odd to be a guest at the Luxembourg, where for over two years she had reigned as hostess. Coming fresh from the modern splendors of the Hôtel de Babylone, she wondered that she had ever been impressed by the shabby dignity of the out-moded royal Palace—though it was true she had never really felt at ease in it, as she did here.

A reception in honor of General Bonaparte, of the Victor of Italy, who less than two years ago had been Barras' little Corsican soldier of no account, who would give no trouble to anybody. That was odd to the point of grotesqueness. It was of course certain that he wasn't any longer of no account, but it was equally certain that he would give no trouble to anybody. He couldn't. He was too enmeshed in the political tangle she had woven about him. To make trouble now could only mean the return of the Bourbons, and that in turn would mean the restoring of Italy to Austria, for the security of English loans in Vienna. No, Bonaparte wouldn't dare to upset Barras, because there was no one but a Bourbon to take his place. In any case he had no money, and to get that he would have to submit to the rule of Ouvrard—as Barras had done. To remain independent he must be active in the only sphere open to him—war. War at the head of another invading army, a voluntary exile that even his best friends, the rabble of Paris, could howl against as a martyrdom. And he should have his invading army. She and Ouvrard—

Ouvrard came in from the adjoining room. Gently austere he looked in his dressing-gown that was of dull black, and almost monastic in line—but where the wide sleeves fell back, it showed a lining brilliant with peacock-colors threaded through with gold. He stood in the doorway for a moment looking at her, erect and motionless, the silks of her shawl glowing in the fire-light, a gold fir-cone in her hand.

"An admirable picture," he said, making a slow, downward-curving gesture with his hand. "Perfectly composed, perfectly executed. Admirable. And somewhat symbolic, eh, my dear? The golden apple. The choice of Paris. Yes, of Paris." He laughed softly at the small witticism, and came forward into the room. He pushed an armchair to the fire, and drew his gown close about him as he sat. "It's desperately cold," he said. "How you women manage to exist—"

She laughed. "Women are hardier than men," she said, "in every way." She dropped a cushion at his feet, sank down on it, and laid her arm across his knees.

He caressed the smoothness of her skin lightly with his short, square-nailed fingers. "You enjoyed your evening, my dear?"

"I found it highly amusing," she said. "Barras sweating with courtliness and charm and apprehension, Josephine in a flutter of imbecility, trying to recapture Barras and at the same time not let Bonaparte slip, Bonaparte frozen with suspicion and bad temper. The hero of Italy! He's in as awkward a position as it's possible for a man to be—and I have seldom seen a man behave more awkwardly. He neither ate nor spoke during the banquet, and ignored everybody—except for scowling at his beloved Josephine."

Ouvrard smiled. "He may not always know what to do with his hands, my dear, but his eyes are never uncertain."

"Then they can see the certain truth—that he must choose between Barras and King Louis XVIII."

"Yet suppose—merely for the sake of argument, my dear— suppose he should decide that neither of those worthies is absolutely essential for the good of the State. Suppose a third alternative has occurred to him."

She glanced up at him, her eyebrows raised. "You mean—? But the idea's absurd, my friend. If he had any such idea—if he dared to have it, he'd have come to Paris himself for the coup d'état of last September, instead of sending that ruffian of an Augereau. There's proof of his uncertainty in himself. He was afraid either to participate openly, or definitely to refuse."

"Quite, my dear. I have never maintained that General Bonaparte is a fool. He condoned the affair of September in so far as it obeyed the will of the people to be rid once and for all of the Royalists. He condemned it as a means of destroying the personal enemies of Director Barras. No. I can see nothing of uncertainty in his manœuvres. By them he has gained the double advantage of supplying a weapon for the defense of the Republic, and of making formal protest against the illegal use that Barras made of it." He smiled, and looked down at her. "You cannot have failed to remark, my dear, that Republican Carnot was, by some strange chance, warned in time to make good his escape?—a circumstance which, I fear, very much upset our good friend Barras."

"Carnot?" She made a contemptuous gesture with her hand. "He's left the country, like the rest. The only difference is that he's gone into exile at his own expense, instead of that of the State. As for Bonaparte, he can't make any serious attempt without money, and he has none. He hasn't approached us, has he?— not even the formal visit that good manners require. No. And he's not even fished for the support of the people. He's not so much as shown himself in public, save once at the theater, hidden at the back of a box, in civilian clothes, and leaving the minute he was recognized. He's stayed shut up in his wretched little house, refusing to see anybody, or even to be seen."

Ouvrard patted her arm. "Exactly. With the result that the people stood in crowds before his wretched little house, intent on obtaining just that sight of their hero that he refused them. General Bonaparte is not without understanding of the mentality of crowds."

She shifted her arm impatiently on his knee. "Nonsense. He's a soldier, not a politician. There was nothing more subtle in his behavior than a fit of sulks because his precious Josephine kept him waiting two weeks for her, while she amused herself on the road with whoever's the latest gallant in tow."

"One Hippolyte Charles—late Captain of Dragoons, or perhaps of Hussars—recently cashiered by General Bonaparte for speculating in Army supplies. Now an associate of Army Contractor Henri Bodin—and also, it would seem, of Madame Bonaparte. A curious combination."

"Yes. And one that'll make Josephine, as well as everybody else, anxious to get her virtuous husband out of Paris as quickly as possible. And now that he's got his precious young sister Pauline safely married to the respectable Leclerc—Josephine's doing, no doubt. I thought it was Junot who loved Pauline. But Josephine scotched that— Yes, he'll go, there's no doubt about it."

"But this invasion of England. A tricky business. He may object to risking his reputation—"

"He'll go. How can he do otherwise? Refusal to go would bring him under suspicion of being a Royalist. By remaining idle in Paris, he would appear to give tacit support to Barras. Both equally damning in the eyes of the public. He'll lead the expedition against England. And you'll finance it."

He raised a faintly protesting hand. "My dear! With the best and most patriotic will in the world, it's becoming more and more difficult to finance the Government."

"Nonsense, man! You'll increase the interest on your loans—you'll increase the price of the goods you supply to the Army. Barras can't help himself now. And, speaking of Army supplies. It might be a good idea to pass a few small orders to this—what's his name?—Charles of the Bodin Company. It doesn't help the popularity of a General to have it known that his wife's interested in Army contractors." She reached forward, and threw a handful of fir-cones on the fire. "Josephine's nearly forty," she said presently, "and she's beginning to look it."

He smiled, and touched her hair. "While you, my dear, are in the full splendor of your twenty-third year—and you already look it."

She laughed softly, and leaned her head back against his knee.

> *"Adieu, my happiness, my life, all
> that exists in the world for me."*
> BONAPARTE

CHAPTER

❧ XXXII ❧

March.

SHE AND LOUISE STOOD SIDE BY SIDE IN SILENT CONTEMPLATION OF the dress. It lay spread out on the bed, a thing so absolutely and completely perfect that there was quite literally nothing to be said. It made you feel odd inside, just to look at it. Certainly the Germonde had never had quite so brilliant and charming an inspiration before. Never.

It was of muslin—the gauze-fine Indian muslin that it was almost impossible to get now, because for some extraordinary reason the English didn't want Frenchwomen to have it. Which was quite absurd really, because English women— Well, they could put it on of course, but they couldn't wear it—not actually *wear* it. Though it was the material that was so important, it was the idea that the Germonde had worked into it.

The muslin was actually white, but so extraordinarily fine that it looked a silvery gray, exactly the color of a spider-web. And against that diaphanous background the Germonde had sewn hundreds—but literally thousands of little gold flies. Flies with gold bodies, flat like sequins, and silver wings, and legs of gold thread. Little gold flies, caught in a silvery-gray web. Oh, there was no doubt about it, the Germonde was inspired, like Joan of Arc and people like that used to be.

Theresia of course wouldn't have appreciated such a dress, because it wasn't vulgar and garish. But Barras would. Barras after all was a man of taste and refinement. She remembered the first time she'd dressed for him, four years ago. That had been Indian muslin too, quite nice in its way, but a school-girl effect compared with the sophisticated elegance of this.

With the dress, she would wear her diamonds. They sparkled there on the bed next the dress—a double fillet for her hair, a necklace and two bracelets. They had been given her by the Duke of Modina, who wanted Bonaparte to do something or not do something about his Duchy. She'd never worn them before, because Bonaparte had told her to give them back. Which just showed how inconsistent he was, for when he took millions—but literally millions of francs from the Italians, he called it a war-indemnity—but when she accepted just a trifling souvenir, a mere nothing, that any gallant man might offer a pretty woman, it became a bribe, a thing to be ashamed of. So of course she hadn't been able to wear them before. But now that she was alone—

Louise said, "Madame would do well to rest now, Madame has had a trying day. And of course to-night—"

Louise was quite right. She would do well to rest. And there was plenty of time, Barras wouldn't be coming for her until half-past ten. He was coming, driving himself in his smart cabriolet, to fetch her for supper at the Luxembourg. Just she and Barras alone, not even a servant to wait on them. So discreet and—and friendly. She'd spent every minute of the day in preparing for it, and now she was ready, except for slipping on the dress.

"Yes," she said, "you're quite right, Louise. Bring me a glass of wine and some biscuits, and I'll rest before the fire."

She put up her feet on the day-bed, sipped at her wine, nibbled at her biscuits, and looked at the dress across the room. When the candles flickered, the little gold flies seemed to move their silver wings, as though trying to escape from the transparent web. Really too enchanting. And the diamonds, too. She'd never had a real parure of diamonds before, and it had been almost more than she could bear not to wear them during all these months. But now that she was alone—

She was alone, really alone again in her own room in her own house in the middle of Paris. She sighed, and relaxed against her cushions. She'd wanted it for so long, and now she'd got it. It just showed that it always paid to be patient, and pleasant, and

friendly with everybody. Though it had been difficult to be
pleasant when she got back from Italy two months ago, after
dropping Charles at the gates of Paris, and found that Bonaparte
hadn't gone yet. She wondered what had become of Charles.
Such an attractive young man in a way, though of course quite
insignificant compared with men of the world like Barras. Still,
she'd have to look him up one day. It was only courteous, wasn't
it?

Anyway, she'd been so disappointed to find Bonaparte still in
Paris. So inconsiderate of him, when he knew quite well Barras
wanted him to invade England at once. But he'd stayed and
stayed, more than three weeks, until she thought she really
couldn't bear it any longer. It was so inconvenient having a man
actually *living* in the house. And the way he lived in it, too—
you'd think it was actually his. He had bought it of course, he
owned it—but that didn't make it *his* house. Yet there he'd been.

Wherever she went, wherever she looked, he was always there.
He was in her bath, in her bed, before her mirror shaving, in her
little dining-room with his maps all over the table, in her small
garden irritating the gardener. You might even say he was in
the street itself, for the discreet charm of the rue Chantereine
had been turned into a sort of public peep-show called the rue
de la Victoire. He was everywhere except, naturally, in the quite
delightful room she'd taken such trouble to prepare for him. Of
course, she'd had to put her wardrobes back in it, because otherwise she'd have had nowhere at all to keep her clothes. But there
was plenty of room left for him, he only had his uniforms and
his boots to put away, didn't he? Men were so *lucky* with their
clothes—

Then of course he'd been difficult because it had been impossible—but absolutely impossible, for her to get to Paris on the
exact day he expected her. So unreasonable of him, for he knew
perfectly well that there were scarcely any posting-horses to be
had, and one had to wait sometimes for days to get any at all.
To hear him, you'd think she enjoyed travelling in the dead of
winter, over those awful roads—

But he'd gone at last, to Boulogne. He might even be in England by this time. English cut-steel for buckles and buttons was
so fashionable just now. So distinguished and elegant for afternoon costumes, though of course it would never take the place of
diamonds for the evening. They were really quite nice, the Duke
of Modina's diamonds, thought it was a pity there were no ear-

256

rings. Still, the diamonds were good—what there were of them. She wouldn't look absolutely poverty-stricken at supper tonight. And it was so important for Bonaparte's career that she should make a good impression.

There was Louise already. It couldn't possibly be time— But what was the matter with the girl? She looked as though something perfectly dreadful had happened. It couldn't be the dress, because it was there, under her eyes, quite safe. Perhaps Barras— Barras attacked, hurt, assassinated—

"Oh, Madame! Madame!"

"Yes, Louise, what is it? What is it! Director Barras—he's not been—been—"

"No, Madame, no. It's not that. It's— Oh, Madame! It's Madame's husband who's come back!"

"Oh!" She half rose from the day-bed, then sank down again, clasping its edges with her hands. Bonaparte! But it couldn't be— not possibly! "But he's in Boulogne, Louise—in England—he's—"

"He's in the courtyard, Madame, getting off his horse." The front door slammed so that the windows rattled. Louise said, "Oh, Madame!" again, and clutched at her apron.

Louise was a fool. He wouldn't have slammed the door like that if he'd suspected—imagined— But there was the dress, and the diamonds—the diamonds!

She jumped up, and rushed to the bed. There wasn't time for the dress, you couldn't just bundle it up anyhow, it would be ruined, absolutely ruined. And he always ran up the stairs, two at a time. But the diamonds—

"Louise! Go down and—and help him off with his coat! Oh, quick! Quick!"

Louise was clever at that sort of thing, but would there be time? The diamonds, anyway. The dress didn't really matter. After all, she had a right to go out, hadn't she? And it wasn't really late yet, only—yes, half-past eight. The diamonds— They simply wouldn't go into their slots in their velvet cases— It was no use, no use at all, pushing them under the bed-covers— There, in the fire-wood basket, under the logs. That would do. Even he wouldn't go poking about in that, and if he did, she could always say Theresia had lent— There. Then the velvet cases kicked under the bed—

She rushed to the door, flung it open, ran out onto the landing. Yes, he was there—down below in the hall, with Louise helping him off with his coat. It seemed to have caught somehow on his epaulettes, and Louise was trying to get it unfastened. Still tugging, Louise glanced over his shoulder up the stairs, and said, "There—if Monsieur will just let me do it—" She disentangled the coat and bore it away out of sight.

She stood quite still at the head of the stairs for a moment, looking down at him, her hands clasped to her bosom. Behind her the door of her lighted room was open, and of course the silk of her negligée was very thin, and she hadn't had time to put on even her chemise— But of course he was her husband, wasn't he? Otherwise, naturally, she wouldn't—

She stood quite still. She drew in a deep breath, then let it out in a long sigh; and just at the end of her breath she said, "Bonaparte—" very softly. She stretched out her arms, one hand on the banister, the other against the wall, so that the thin silk of her ungirdled negligée hung in long, straight folds of transparency from her shoulders to her feet.

"Bonaparte! I was so frightened! I thought something had happened—I thought you were wounded—killed— But it's you! You! Oh! Oh, Bonaparte!"

Her draperies floating about her, she ran down the stairs towards him. And she could run downstairs. Not as though she were being pushed from behind as most women did, but as easily, as gracefully effortless as a cascade of water flowing down from ledge to ledge. Half-way down one of her little crimson mules fell off, but she didn't pause for that. She came on with a little swaying dip because of her bare foot, a thing as difficult to do with grace as one of the old-fashioned dances. Bonaparte admired her feet so much.

She came on and down, but he just stood there looking up. Not moving, not even smiling, his eyes showing pale in the dim light of the hall, just looking. How funny he was!

"Oh, Bonaparte!" She threw herself against him, both hands at his breast, her head down, her eyes raised under her lashes. With small men you had to— She tucked her head under his chin, and let herself go limp against him. She could feel his heart thudding beneath her hands, and his arms came around her so tightly she could scarcely breathe. "Josephine—" She sighed, and let her head slip to his shoulder. . . .

She wondered how long he was going to stand there, with the draught there was from the door Louise had left open blowing about her. Besides, there was her bare foot on the floor, which was of mosaic and icy cold.

258

"Oh!" she said, "my shoe! Bonaparte, my shoe!" She lifted her bare foot and set it down on his. He glanced down at it. It looked very small and very white against the clumsy black leather of his boot.

"Adorable little foot! My incomparable Josephine!" He lifted her then, kissed her on the forehead, and carried her towards the stairs. It used to make her horribly nervous when he did that, but he never had dropped her. He really was strong, for so small a man.

He set her down before the fire and stood looking at her, rubbing his hands and smiling, as pleased with himself as though he'd done something clever. It was incredible how stupid he could be, frightening her almost out of her wits, and her nerves— It wasn't as though he'd imagined anything, either. No, he'd just thought he'd do it, so he'd done it. So irresponsible of him.

"You see, my Josephine. I've come back to you."

"So you have," she said, "haven't you?"

He moved to take her in his arms again, but she sat down quickly on the day-bed, and stretched out her bare foot to the fire. "My foot, Bonaparte. It's cold."

Her gold brocade slippers to go with the dress were on the floor by the bed. He fetched one, and knelt to put it on. He kissed her instep first. "Little foot—" Now she had one crimson shoe on and one gold one, which was quite absurd. Or was it? Original, anyway. She considered them. Nobody had ever thought of doing that before. That was often the way quite important things were discovered, just by accident. It might be amusing to try—

"You were going out, my Josephine?" He'd gone back to the bed to look at the dress. Oh dear, and she hadn't thought of anything—

"Bees," he said. "Golden bees. A pretty idea. Yes, a pretty idea."

Bees! How stupid he was, as though bees would make any sense at all. Bees didn't get caught in spider-webs, did they? Or did they? He picked up a fold of the skirt, and stood fingering it. She frowned. He was quite capable of deliberately tearing the fabric to see how strong it was, or of picking off one of the flies to find out what metal it was made of. If he only wouldn't *meddle*—

"But why white, my heart—why always white? In my country, white's the color of mourning."

"We're not in your country," she said a little sharply. "We're

259

in France." His face slowly darkened and stiffened. Oh dear, now
he was vexed, just when— You'd think even he'd know that white
was the only color an elegant woman—a really elegant woman,
not just a fashionable one like Theresia—could possibly wear.
She got up and went to him, standing close beside him, looking
down at the dress.

"In my country," she said, "white's the—the bridal color. And—
and— Oh, I know it's silly of me, we've been married nearly two
years, haven't we? But we've been so little together, and I—I—"
She hid her face against his shoulder.

He really wasn't difficult at all, once you put your mind to it.
Only clumsy, of course. . . .

"My hair, Bonaparte." She pulled away from him, and patted
her hair into place.

He laughed. "Now I've spoiled your hair-dressing and your
evening, haven't I? Where were you going, with your swarm of
bees?"

Oh dear— "I—I was going to see Theresia. Just to see Theresia."

"At the Luxembourg?"—his voice a little sharp again.

"Oh, no—no. Theresia's living with Ouvrard now, at the Hôtel
de Babylone."

"Living with— Josephine! How can you say such a thing, as
though it were natural—as though she'd done no more than
change her dressmaker! Living with Ouvrard!"

"Well, she has to live somewhere. And she's at liberty—"

"Have you no idea of the difference between liberty and license?"

Of course she had. Liberty was when men did things, and
when women did them it became license. So unfair—

"Living with Ouvrard!" he said again. "The effrontery! The
shameless, brazen effrontery! I wouldn't have believed it possible, even of her. No, not possible. Living with Ouvrard!"

Oh dear! Now he was going to talk about women and morals,
and when he did that he went on for hours and hours, and got
difficult, and then he was apt to start imagining— She let her
head droop forward, her mouth trembled, and tears slid gently
down the long curve of her lashes.

"Oh, Bonaparte!" she said quaveringly, "I never could have
imagined—have believed— Oh, I know Theresia's prettier than I
am, and cleverer— But I never dreamed— Oh, I thought you—
you l-loved me!" She choked a little, said, "Oh, Bonaparte—"
again, and buried her face in her hands.

260

He took her wrists, uncovered her face. "What is it, *mio dolce amor?*" he said, frowning anxiously. "What wouldn't you have believed?"

With her head still drooping she raised tear-wet lashes and looked up at him. "That you—you should care, about Ouvrard and—and Theresia—"

He drew her hands to his breast, and stared at her. "I—care? Josephine! Theresia Tallien's a harlot, a whore, not fit— And you, Josephine, you're my wife—do you understand?—my wife. Nothing can ever change that. Men like me do not change. You are my wife—my happiness—my life. Never forget that. Never. Do you understand?"

His voice was still sharp but he was pleased, just the same— you could tell by the way he made himself tall, as men did when you flattered their vanity. And you could always do that by being jealous. Men were so funny—

"Yes, Bonaparte." Her fingers twined about his, and she smiled tremblingly at him. Over his shoulder she saw the clock.

Half-past nine, and in an hour— And Barras had a key. He came straight up. So much more convenient for the servants, wasn't it? But Bonaparte was so provincial-minded. Oh, what was she to *do!*

"Theresia Tallien's not a fit companion for you. I don't wish you to go to that abominable house again."

"Oh, but—but—" What *was* she to do? "But I must let her know I'm not coming, mustn't I? I can't just not go. It would be so rude, so unkind, wouldn't it? And I don't want to be unkind. Not to anybody. Not even to her."

He kissed her on the forehead. *"Mio dolce amor!* You are made of kindness. You are kindness itself."

"Then I'll write her—just a word to say I'm not coming. She'll be expecting— And it wouldn't be fair to keep her waiting, would it?"

She pulled her hands away from his, rushed to her desk. There was still time—just time. There was still quite a lot of her rainbow-colored paper left. Her pen— Bonaparte was putting logs on the fire, taking them from the basket— After all, he might think it odd she'd put Theresia's diamonds—

"Bonaparte, must you? It's so hot in here already."

"Hot? It's a March night, and if you'd been riding through it—" He threw on the log, and brushed the dust from his fingers.

Well, she hadn't. She wouldn't be so—so inconsiderate. Rushing in on people without any warning, upsetting everything, tearing her nerves to pieces, exasperating her so that she could scarcely— And now the ink was dry.

"Bonaparte, a pencil!"

He took one from his pocket, brought it to her, and stood behind her, touching the curls at the nape of her neck. Why couldn't he leave her *alone!* Besides, he'd be able to see, over her shoulder—

"Bonaparte, my slipper. It's still on the staircase. You might get it—"

He tweaked a curl in that quite infuriating way he had, but he went for the shoe. She snatched up the pencil. "Dear Barras. Bonaparte has come home to-night. I cannot sup with you. You know better than anyone how I am situated. Do not forget me. J."

Bonaparte came back with the slipper. She hastily folded her note, fastened it with a wafer, and wrote, "Director Barras, at the Luxembourg. Urgent," on the corner. She rang for Louise.

"Tell a footman to take this at once—at once, to Madame Tallien, at the Hôtel de Babylone," she said. Louise looked at the letter, said, "Yes, Madame," smiling demurely.

"Tell him to take a fiacre—so that Madame Tallien won't be kept waiting."

Louise said, "Yes, Madame," again, and went out.

She glanced at the clock. A quarter to ten. There was still time, but only just—only if the footman found a carriage quickly —Bonaparte was standing before the fire, his hands behind his back. She stretched out her own hands, smiled, and went towards him.

"Oh, Bonaparte!" she said, "what a quite delightful surprise! So clever of you to manage it! And I who thought you'd gone to England already. You won't be obliged to go very soon, will you? Not at once? Not to-morrow?"

He took her hands in his and kissed them. "I'm not going at all, *mio dolce amor*."

"Not— Oh!— Oh, I'm glad, of course I'm glad. Only I thought you liked that sort of thing. I thought it would be so nice for you."

He laughed. "It would have been nice for everybody concerned, my Josephine, except myself. It would have delighted the English. They'd have been charmed to receive a French Army on their shores. It would have been most satisfactory for Barras, who

262

would have made his anti-Royalist, Republican gesture and got rid of me at the same time."

"But I don't understand. Barras said—"

"What Barras says is never what Barras thinks. He's a politician, my sweet. This invasion of England—it's a question of sea-power. You appreciate that?" He looked at her sharply, and she nodded.

"Oh, yes. Yes, of course."

He sat on the day-bed, and drew her down beside him. "You see—" Oh dear, now he was going to explain, and when he did that, he went on for hours—but literally for hours. She clasped her hands in her lap, and glanced anxiously at the clock. The man should be half-way there, by now.

"You see, we haven't the ships. I could have slipped an army across on a favorable night. I would have fought a battle on the beaches, and won it—then another before London, and won that too. But then what? Eh, my Josephine?"

"Why—why, another battle. And you'd win that too—wouldn't you?"

He waved his finger at her. "Think, my Josephine, think! Use your imagination. I would be in the heart of an enemy country, I would have lost ten, twenty per cent of my effectives, used up my stores. And how would I make them good, eh, my sweet?"

Why must he go on and on— The footman must be there by now. If only Barras hadn't started already—

"—with a hostile country to face, and the English fleet blocking the narrow waters of the Channel behind me. I'd be caught— caught like a rat in a trap. You see?"

"Oh, yes. Yes, of course. But such a pity, isn't it? And Barras was so hoping— He'll be so disappointed."

"Barras can go on hoping. He needn't be afraid—for the moment. I shan't stay in Paris. There's nothing for a man to do here. The people haven't yet found out what they want, and until they do— They only know they won't have the Bourbons put back on the throne by the English. Barras thinks he can force them to accept him as the only alternative. That's where he makes his mistake, for it is impossible to force a great nation against the will of that nation. A true leader of the people isn't the man who can force them to do his will, but the man who is foresighted enough to know what they want before they know it themselves, and show it to them. So far, they only know that they dislike the Bourbons a little more than they dislike Barras. Presently they'll begin to wonder if, after all, they need be saddled with either. But until then—" He broke off and looked at her, his lips pressed together, his eyes dark with excitement.

Until then— She glanced quickly at the clock. Half-past ten. She twisted her fingers together in her lap and forced herself to look at him, instead of over her shoulder at the door. She could almost *feel* Barras opening it, coming in with that—that friendly way he had, and saying, "Well, my heart's treasure?"

"Oh," she said, "how clever you are, how well you explain! I'd never thought of it like that before. The people, I mean. But of course it's true. And—and—until then?"

He sat up very straight, and smiled in that irritating way he had when he thought he was being cleverer than other people. "I shall go to Egypt."

Egypt? What a quite extraordinary thing— "But how—how original of you, Bonaparte! I'm sure nobody else has thought of doing that. I'm certain—but quite certain even Barras hasn't."

"So am I. But he can scarcely protest. I shall be fighting the English for him, as he wants me to. You see, my Josephine, there are more ways of attacking a country than on its own soil. There are the lines of supply, its trade routes. And Egypt is the gate—"

A quarter to eleven. She unclasped her hands and leaned back comfortably against her cushions. She was exhausted, but absolutely and totally exhausted. Men couldn't understand how women's nerves— She needn't strain her ears for footsteps any more, so she wasn't obliged to hear what Bonaparte was saying, either. She smiled at him, and fixed her eyes attentively on his. Egypt. She thought it was a long way away, farther even than England—but she wasn't really quite sure where it was, or what Egyptians did. Of course there was the preserved head she'd seen once, but things like that weren't really much good, were they? Not like Genoese velvet or English cut steel—

"Alexander dreamed of creating an Empire of the East—"

Alexander? But Alexander had never thought of any such thing, she was certain—but absolutely positive he hadn't. Sometimes she thought he hadn't been such a bad husband after all. A rather silent man, really.

"—to take you with me, my Josephine."

Take her with him? To a place like Egypt?—whatever it was like. And when she'd only just got back to Paris— Even he couldn't be so selfish, so unfair—

"—but, with the English fleet at sea, I daren't risk it. I shall be obliged to leave you behind. You understand, my sweet love?"

She clasped her hands to her breast, and her mouth trembled. "Leave me—?" Her tears welled up, sparkling in the firelight. "Oh, Bonaparte!—and I was so happy—"

"Incomparable Josephine!"

He bent over her as she lay back on her cushions, his face so close above hers that her breath stirred the untidy locks of fine hair on his forehead. She did wish he'd do something about his hair, it really was too dreadfully old-fashioned.

"Happy? Away from you, there will be no more happiness for me. Away from you, life will be a desert in which I stand alone." He kissed her on the mouth, then took her face between the palms of his hands, though he knew perfectly well she didn't like— Though of course it really didn't matter any more about her complexion.

"But there is still a little time for happiness, my adorable wife. Tonight at least neither of us will be alone."

Over his shoulder she could see the sparkle of the little golden flies, enmeshed in their silvery web. She sighed. "No," she said, "we won't—will we?"

> *"I owe one million, two hundred thousand francs, I will confess to six hundred thousand. That is quite enough for the moment."*
> JOSEPHINE

CHAPTER

⋟ XXXIII ⋞

June.

"MY POOR LITTLE FOOL," HE SAID, "THE WRETCHED HOUSE ISN'T worth sixty thousand francs, let alone a hundred and sixty thousand."

"But it is, Charles! It is! Because I want it. And anyway, Monsieur Lecoulteux has to ask a hundred and sixty thousand, because I can't pay it. You see, Charles?"

He spread out his hands. "I may be dense, but your logic passes my understanding."

She sighed. He was supposed to be so clever at business, yet one had to explain the simplest things to him, as though he were a child. "Well," she said patiently, "you see, Monsieur Lecoulteux said the price of the house was a hundred and twenty-five thousand, and when I told him I couldn't pay anything—or practically—he said he'd have to charge a hundred and sixty thousand, because of not getting anything. So both of us profit actually, don't we? It's so simple, Charles. He said Bonaparte's credit would be worth ten times that amount with him—which just shows how honest he is, because he could just as well have charged—"

"Quite. And you'd have agreed. But suppose General Bonaparte doesn't appreciate the honor of being creditor to—"

"But he's in *Egypt*, Charles! How can it possibly matter to him? Anyway, I've only actually given Monsieur Lecoulteux ten thousand francs, to what he called seal the bargain. You can't say that's much, for a house like—"

Charles sighed. "And where, if one might venture to enquire, did you get the ten thousand?"

She dimpled at him. "You needn't be jealous. I got it quite virtuously from brother Joseph. He advanced it to me to pay for the repairs to the rue de la Victoire house, out of the money Bonaparte left with him for me."

"Ah! And the repairs to the rue de la Victoire house?"

"But Charles, it belongs to Bonaparte. He bought it. It's his. He can't possibly expect me to pay—"

Charles threw up his hands. "I surrender, horse, foot and artillery. Only it seems a pity to have wasted so brilliant a campaign for so unworthy a gain."

She tapped on the ground with the tip of her parasol. "It's *not* unworthy. It's a beautiful house. And I want it."

They stood side by side on the weed-obliterated gravel drive, staring at the house. Charles was being difficult about it. Though why, when he'd complained time and time again that there was no privacy to be had any more at the rue da la Victoire— And it wasn't as though it was his money, after all. Surely she had a right—

"It's an ancient square box of an abandoned farm-house, with ugly brick walls and small dark rooms, and no architectural qualities whatsoever."

266

"But it will have, presently—when the walls have been plastered white, and the windows cut right down to the floor, and a porte-cochère added to the front—and of course a small wing at each end— It'll be perfectly enchanting—really enchanting."

"I don't doubt it, but how are you going to pay—" He broke off, and clutched at his breast with both hands. "But don't tell me! I couldn't bear—I quite literally couldn't bear it. Really, I couldn't. My nerves—"

She turned her back on him, and walked to a sort of trestle-thing the carpenters had set up on what had once been a lawn, hoisted herself on it and sat, swinging her feet and looking at the house. Charles of course had no imagination. Men never had. But she could see perfectly well that, except for being just a little shabby and neglected, it was almost exactly like Croissy. She'd always wanted a house of her own like Croissy. She'd wanted Croissy itself, but when she went to see Desirée about it after Bonaparte went away—well, Desirée was dead. So sad. She'd cried so that she'd made her head ache, and been obliged to go to bed. To think that all the while she'd been in Italy she'd been looking forward so to seeing Desirée again, and then in the end to find— So odd of Desirée too, not even to let her best, her very dearest friend know she was ill, to let her find out for herself quite casually through a mutual acquaintance. And then it was too late. Somebody else had bought Croissy.

And those two servants—what were their names?—Marie and Jacques something. To think that for all these years she'd been saving literally every sou to pay them whatever it was she owed them, and when at last she had managed, they'd just disappeared. You'd think, after all they'd gone through together— But then the lower classes were like that.

She tilted back her head, half-closed her eyes, and looked frowningly at the house, as people, for some reason or other, looked at pictures. And really you could see it better like that, it was less—less obvious. It looked more than ever like Croissy. Charles was being rather stuffy about the house. Men were all so mercenary-minded, weren't they? Always thinking about the *value* of things. And after all she had to live somewhere, hadn't she? Paris was quite impossible now with all those Bonapartes in it. Why they couldn't stay in their own wretched island—

Madame Bonaparte was the worst, of course. She made you feel as though all your insides were goldfish, swimming about in a perfectly transparent glass bowl. So uncomfortable— Joseph wasn't so bad once you got used to him. He was supposed to take care of Bonaparte's money, and pay her bills for her. So he did. Some of them. The rest she just tore up. Anyway, it wasn't his business, was it? And the tradespeople didn't seem to mind, so why should he? Anyway, Joseph wasn't really much trouble, he was only interested in Bonaparte's money, and even he couldn't complain at the bills she sent him. He couldn't call her extravagant. Not possibly. It was the younger brother, Lucien, who was awkward, because he was interested in Bonaparte's position, and that of course made him so inquisitive and suspicious.

She wondered what Charles was saying to Monsieur Lecoulteux. Perhaps she'd better— Charles was quite rude to people sometimes, though of course he didn't mean— She slipped off the trestle-table and went to them. Charles was saying,

"For myself, Monsieur, I find the house excellently well-named. The Malmaison."

She frowned, and bit her lip. The Malmaison—the Accursed House— Now that she looked at it again, it did seem a little sinister, with lichen-stains like a skin-disease on the purplish brick of its face, these broken eaves like shaggy eyebrows over the little, peering eyes of the windows. She sighed.

"Come inside and see, Charles! Thank you, Monsieur Lecoulteux—so good of you. . . . You see the hall, Charles?"

"I see it, my love. Rather like a mouse-trap, architecturally speaking."

"Oh, Charles, *must* you be so trying! What do you think I've got an architect for?"

"God knows, when a little gunpowder and a lighted match would be so much more effective. And cheaper."

Charles was amusing, of course, but there were times— She lifted her chin, "Oh, if you're not interested—" She turned her back, and went towards the door.

He caught her in two strides, put his arm about her, and drew her back. "Of course I'm interested, my love. Passionately. . . . And the other two rooms, at each end of the passage?"

"Well, as the big room's to be for—for— As it is to be the principal bedroom, I thought the other two would be perfect for Eugène and Hortense."

He drew in his chin, frowned thoughtfully, and nodded. "Yes. Quite perfect. Except that, if you're going to do away with the passage, they won't be able to get into them."

268

She pouted, and tapped with her parasol on the floor. "Why *must* you be so exasperating! I can't think of every little thing, can I? Besides, they're not *here,* are they?— Such a good idea for Bonaparte to take Eugène to Egypt with him, wasn't it? So broadening for a child's mind, traveling. .... Come and look at the garden from the back window."

Side by side they leaned on the hand-rail of the window, looking out over the little property. It really wasn't bad at all. The surrounding country was quite ravishing. Under the clear light of the warm June sun it all looked very gay and charming. One could have parties here, but real parties, not with a horde of suspicious Bonapartes casting the chilly blight of their disapproval over everything.

It had been a good idea, Eugène going to Egypt. So instructive for him. Eugène was quite a bit taller than Charles and, dark as he was, beginning to show quite clearly that he shaved. Of course some boys were extraordinarily precocious in that way, weren't they? Hortense, naturally, was still at school at Madame Campan's. That reminded her of Lucien, and she smiled. She leaned farther out of the window, and the sun struck hot across the nape of her neck, sending little tingles of pleasure down her spine. She pressed closer to Charles, and sighed.

"It's really too enchanting that they should be so quite utterly happy together, isn't it, Charles?"

"I am ravished at their felicity, though somewhat vague as to their identity."

"Why, Eugènie and Lavallette. Naturally."

"Naturally. And who are Eugènie and Lavallette?"

"Charles, but I *told* you! I don't believe you ever listen to a word—not a single word I say. Really, I don't."

"Probably you were looking at me at the time, my love. I defy any man to know what you're talking about when you're looking at him."

She smiled, turned her face to his, and looked at him from under half-closed lids. "You *do* love me, Charles?"

"To the point of madness. But not in an open window, before the disrespectful gaze of the laboring classes."

She sighed. Men were so conventional, weren't they? "Well, Eugènie. You see, when I found Lucien was hanging about Madame Campan's, I thought it was for Hortense. And I was distracted—utterly distracted—"

"Still, my love— The man's not deformed, he's not got the pox—"

"Oh, Charles! But there—you're not a mother—are you? But it was only Eugènie, after all. Still, that wouldn't do, either. Naturally. After all, she's a sort of relative of poor Alexander's. She's a Beauharnais. She's not much to look at, but I have my responsibilities, haven't I? I mean to poor Alexander's memory. I can't let all the Beauharnais women be sacrificed, just so the Bonaparte men can get on in the world, can I? One's quite enough. I told Bonaparte—"

"You *told*—"

"Of course not just like that. I'm not an utter fool, though I know perfectly well you think I am—don't you, Charles? No, I just quite simply told him the absolute truth. I told him Eugènie's a sweet, good, simple girl—and so she is, poor child—without any money or any parents or anywhere to go, and I asked him to find her a respectable husband. He's so interested in families and marriages—so odd of him, don't you think?—so he did. Colonel Lavallette. He's not exactly handsome, but quite well-mannered and very conscientious. So suitable. And actually —I never was so surprised in my life—they're quite divinely happy together. But poor dear Lucien of course, when he found out—" she giggled.

Charles looked at her sideways, then frowned out over the garden. "If I were you, my love, I wouldn't slap Lucien Bonaparte's face any oftener than is absolutely essential."

"Slap—? But I wouldn't touch his face with a—a poker. A quite revolting face—thin-lipped, sharp-nosed, short-sighted— The way he peers about and squints up his eyes, blind as a—"

"Nevertheless, he has an excellent pair of spectacles."

Spectacles? Oh— Still, it didn't matter. He couldn't possibly—not possibly be more inquisitive now than he had been before. Besides, with the best spectacles in the world, he couldn't see as far as the Malmaison, could he?

"Charles—? The workmen have gone now, Charles."

He turned abruptly away from the window. "So must we be going. It's getting late."

She followed him through the small rooms and narrow passages. After the heat and light of the outside world the house was gloomy, full of shadows. The walls seemed damply clammy to her touch, an eerie, causeless draught twitched at her skirts. The Malmaison. The Accursed House— She shivered and hurried after Charles—Charles who had gone suddenly chilly too—aloof, unfriendly.

The front door slammed behind them, echoing hollowly through the empty rooms. Stepping out into the sunlight was like slipping into a hot, scented bath when you were chilled to the bone.

Beside her Charles suddenly turned, hunched his shoulders, thrust his head forward, and peered at her through slitted eyes. "If I am not gravely mistaken," he said in a high, thin voice, "it is Madame Josephine that I have the honor of seeing before me." He pawed at her blindly with one hand, and with the other fumbled in his waistcoat pocket. "Your pardon, Madame, if I seek tangible evidence to bear out my assumption, but my spectacles—"

She shrieked and slapped his face, rushed down the steps, laughed up at him, and showed him the tip of a pointed tongue. "That for your spectacles!" she cried, "and your nasty, prying eyes behind them."

He straightened his wide shoulders and stood erect again, planted his fists on his hips, and laughed back at her. The sun burnished the thick curls of his vigorous hair, glinted on the sharp whiteness of his strong white teeth. Behind him the Malmaison too seemed to swagger a little, to stand erect, youthful, and comely with the sunlight on its face.

> *"It is since he has been in Egypt that all our disasters have come upon us."*
>
> THIÉBAULT

CHAPTER

❧ XXXIV ❧

November.

DIRECTOR BARRAS THOUGHT HE HAD NEVER BEHELD SO CHEAP A display of vulgarity so expensively bought. Even from the outside, the Hôtel de Babylone always put him in mind of a popular café at the Tivoli Gardens. One expected to see clusters of fireworks soaring over its roof, and groups of laboring folk in their Sunday best entering its doors, intimidated, but resolutely determined to suck their ices in a really smart place. As for the interior, it was a profiteer's dream of luxury—while on gala occasions, such as to-night, it degenerated into a delirium of bad taste.

Presiding over the whole barbarous affair were Theresia and Ouvrard, sitting, not side by side at the middle of the dinner table like an ordinary host and hostess, but one at each end, like a royal couple. Ouvrard in his eternal black and white, Theresia in—if one could call it in—a pseudo-Greek costume of sorts. Theresia had achieved the miracle of out-doing even herself. A short tunic, barely reaching her knees, was held by a jeweled clasp at her left shoulder only, while her right shoulder and breast were left entirely naked. He had been shocked. He still was shocked. Not of course at the sight of a woman's breast, but at the vulgarity of the manner of its showing. He, Count Paul de Barras, had been made to feel uneasy—for if one looked, one felt like a goggling yokel at his first bawdy-house, while to avert one's eyes gave one the sensation of behaving like a self-righteous Swiss Calvinist. Both states of mind being equally repugnant to a man of breeding. That of course was what Theresia lacked. Breeding. Ouvrard, too.

He took the cup a lackey offered and began to drink, before remembering that of late coffee was apt to keep him awake. Though just as well perhaps, for sleep after this evening's, er—entertainment would be only to exchange one nightmare for another. For if the dining-room had been astonishing, the salon was quite incredible.

It was furnished only with Greek couches, innumerable cushions, and tall tripods, each supporting a flat dish of salted or sugared almonds, ripe olives, or crystallized fruits. In the four corners of the room were fountains, gushing respectively red and white wine, sweet and sour punch. The walls themselves were covered with grape-vines. Real vines. He shuddered as he looked at them. Grape-vines from the royal espaliers of Fontainebleau, wrist-thick, centuries old, cut off at the root and set here in beds of imitation moss, to die in fewer hours than it had taken them years to grow. And, to lend tawdriness to what might have been at least a dignified agony, some of the enormous, rich purple clusters of fruit had been gilded. One wouldn't have imagined even Theresia Tallien to have been capable of such an excess of bad taste as that. The pride of an ancient splendor humiliated, destroyed, so that her worthless guests might be amused for an instant by plucking grapes from her walls. His teeth were set on edge by the blatant crudity of the thing.

He had seldom passed such a completely exhausting evening. One couldn't even lean against the wall, because of the martyrized vines—nor was there so much as a mantel-shelf on which to place one's cup. Intolerable. He would never have come, save for the drive of absolute necessity. It was incomprehensible that so many people should be there apparently of their own free will.

He looked about at them. They weren't Theresia's old crowd of the Chaumière days. The illiterate millionaires had disappeared, save for a few whose wealth was sufficiently overwhelming automatically to transform doubtful fingernails and atrocious manners into amiable eccentricities. No, these people were all fully literate. Too literate. They passed their time devouring ancient philosophical literature which they returned undigested in the form of a modern philosophy of their own, or in interminably discussing and explaining their otherwise inexplicable scribblings and utterances. They belonged to no recognized school of thought, to no known political party. They were enthusiasts, seekers after impossible Utopias they would be the first to decry were they forced to live in them. That's what made them so exhausting. Enthusiasm.

There were of course the four other Directors who were void of that particular quality—were in fact void of any qualities whatsoever. Though they had their uses. They made excellent sacrifices, whenever popular outcry became too clamorous. One selected one of them more or less at random, fastened on him the guilt for whatever the people were annoyed about, repudiated him as it were with one hand, and with the other gave him a handsome present from the Secret Funds. An efficacious arrangement, profitable to all concerned. Director followed Director in and out of office with such smooth regularity that one really couldn't keep the fellows' names in mind. Only he remained. And sometimes he thought the excessive fatigue of the effort was scarcely worth. . . .

He shifted on his feet, and wished he had somewhere to set down his cup. The company had started some sort of game that necessitated a vast amount of rushing about and shrieking. A truly exhausting spectacle. He wondered how much longer Theresia was going to keep him waiting here, with his feet growing colder and colder on the marble pavement, and his knee— Before the fountain of red wine, she'd said, in five minutes' time. He'd already been standing there balancing an empty cup for half an hour and more. He turned to verify the fountain. Red wine. Yes. He shrank at the sight of it. Theresia's ideas of luxury being what they were, it would be a fine vintage wine, that should not have been so much as brought to table save by reverent and experienced hands. Yet here it was, spouting from some imitation gargoyle's mouth like so much dirty rain-water.

A hotly-pursued woman bumped into him, shrieked in his face, stepped on his foot, knocked the cup from his hand and rushed on, without so much as an apologetic glance. Ah, well. There, at least, was one small annoyance disposed of. He glanced down at the shattered fragments. Broken porcelain— Yet the omen seemed to have lost its threat. After all, once your porcelain was broken, you were relieved of the fatigue of trying to balance it—

"Poor old Indestructible! Has he been kept waiting, then?"

He frowned. Theresia was quite well aware that he objected to that title, mocking substitute for Robespierre's Incorruptible. Though why he should be mocked at simply because he was the only one of the original Directors who'd had sufficient ability and merit to remain in office— And he resented her tone. She treated him these days as though he were some aged grandfather, whose senility could still inspire a certain affection, but no respect whatsoever.

"Come along, then. Ouvrard's ready to see you now." She turned her back—that was another small mercy—and led him from the pandemonium of her salon to the relative sanity of Ouvrard's study. Ouvrard wasn't there. Naturally. These people took discourtesy to be a sort of badge of superiority. Theresia perched on a corner of the great desk. She looked still more outrageous in this atmosphere of businesslike efficiency and masculinity—an atmosphere in which he himself felt vastly more comfortable. There was at least a civilized chair capable of sustaining a man's weight, and a Christian fire capable of warming his chilled and weary feet. He sat down, turning his chair so as not to be obliged to contemplate Theresia's, er—attractions.

Theresia laughed at him. "You look down at the mouth, my friend. Surely not hankering after the departed Josephine?"

He thought he had seldom met a more tactless woman than

Theresia Tallien. "It is not my custom to, er—hanker," he said stiffly. "I am neither an adolescent nor a dotard."

She grinned. "And Josephine's of an age, isn't she?—that appeals especially, in fact exclusively, to those two categories of men." She shrugged. "Ah, well. She's had her day. Still, it's a pity to see her reduced to such petty conquests as a twenty-year-old stock jobber."

Decidedly, a most repellent woman. "Josephine," he said, "will still be making her, er—petty conquests long after more ambitious women have overshot their mark, and destroyed themselves."

She grimaced at him. "You are a little—ancien régime in your judgment of women, aren't you?"

"I am a man of experience, if that's what you mean. I know what I'm talking about."

"I don't doubt you do. The new establishment at the Malmaison must have cost you a pretty penny, eh?"

He crossed his knees abruptly, forgetful of his small infirmity, and winced. A pretty penny, and out of his own pocket, too—poor Alexander being by now so far gone as to be unpresentable before even the most amiably short-sighted of Government Committees. The repair bills for that wretched little house she'd sent him would have covered the restoration of the Château of Marly itself. Yes, Josephine would still be making her way long after Theresia and her kind had been reduced to honesty, or worse. And after all, one was a gentleman, and gallant. One didn't, er—permit a lady to withdraw without offering some token of regret.

Theresia yawned. "Ah, well," she said, "whatever it cost you, it'll be worth it. Paris will soon be well aware of Josephine's latest domestic arrangements—we'll see to that—so if by any unlucky chance her devoted husband ever should return, it'll be to find himself crowned with the cuckold's horns instead of the hero's laurels. Not even he'll be able to survive the ridicule of that. Not in Paris."

A singularly unpleasant woman— He took out his snuff-box, and frowned at it. Quite suddenly, and quite surprisingly, he found that the thought of General Bonaparte's possible return was not utterly distasteful. He had once seen the little man repel, publicly and brutally, the amorous advances of the Staël woman—and the Staël was, if possible, even more aggressively modern than Theresia. He had been edified and not a little

275

charmed by the quite unprecedented courage of the man. And now the thought came to him that to see all these women—these hectoring, domineering, exhausting women—publicly and outrageously affronted by General Bonaparte would be inexpressibly gratifying and soothing. For a moment, it almost seemed as though it might be worth—

"Ah, here's Ouvrard. Well, I'll leave you to your affairs." She slid from the desk, and went out.

He glanced a little curiously at Ouvrard, who seemed to have been able to persuade Theresia that her presence was not at all times absolutely essential for the proper conduct of affairs of State. To look at, a man undistinguished to the point of insignificance—yet he had complete control of the whole financial system of the country—and some sort of control, too, over Theresia Tallien.

"And what can I do for you—Director Barras?" Ouvrard seated himself behind his desk and folded his small, square-fingered hands on the writing-pad before him.

Sitting there behind his desk, politely expectant, scarcely interested, as though he had no idea— The man was a hypocrite, and a swindling usurer into the bargain. But then all very rich men were. He looked down at his snuff-box again, and polished it nervously with the ball of his thumb. Then he raised his eyes to the bleak indifference of Ouvrard's face.

"Why," he said, forcing a smile to unwilling lips, "the little matter of the, er—loan—"

Ouvrard's expression remained unchanged. "The Forced Loan? It is going singularly badly, or so I hear. The conscription order, as well. The country will not lend to or fight for a Government in which it has no confidence."

The man's insolence was intolerable—and yet must be tolerated. If only one were in a position— He smiled with still greater determination. "Not the Forced Loan," he said with strained lightness, "but one which I trust—which I am persuaded, will be accorded generously and willingly."

Ouvrard's expression—or lack of it—remained blankly fixed. "It has become virtually impossible to lend to—the present Government," he said. "The country is in a precarious—a very precarious position. As any intelligent man might have foreseen, the English have made further loans to Austria, to safeguard those previously accorded, with the result that all General Bonaparte's gains in Italy have been totally lost to us."

"And what of your own previous loans, Monsieur Ouvrard. What of them, if the Austrians aren't at least checked?"

Ouvrard smiled slightly, but his eyes didn't change. The usurer —the shameless usurer—knowing quite well that his own loans were fifty per cent in promissory notes, and that they were secured on good French soil that would always be solid though every scrap of scribbled paper were to be blown away on the wind of disaster—

"Moreover," the toneless voice went on, "the Russians are taking a hand as well. France's defenses are threatened from Amsterdam down to Naples. Over eight hundred thousand allied troops are massed against our hundred and seventy thousand. Prussia and Bavaria will soon make the odds heavier still. The nation is in danger—very grave danger." He spread his hands flat on the table, and leaned forward a little over them. "And for this, you—forgive me my frankness—you, Director Barras, are held to be directly to blame."

Such cynical effrontery was almost unbelievable. To sit there calmly meting out the blame to a man he had deliberately so netted about in the web of his usury that he was helpless as a fly—

"Jourdan and Masséna have been defeated in Germany—Schèrer, Moreau, and MacDonald in Italy. They are not to blame. The odds are too heavy. No army can do the impossible—and to save France now is verging on the impossible."

An Army's an unaccountable female thing.... It's only when it falls in love that it'll do the impossible.... Bonaparte's routed five times his weight in Austrians....

"But it is commonly said, Director Barras—it is commonly said and believed that none of these misfortunes would have overtaken us, had General Bonaparte been retained in France."

Did he not know it? Was he ever allowed to forget? Yet was it his fault that the people were so infatuated with their little Corsican as to believe that he could prevent every catastrophe, domestic or foreign, from a plague of flies to an Austrian invasion, by the sheer magic of his presence? Naturally he knew it. He suspected that General Bonaparte also was not unaware—

Ouvrard took an easier pose, crossing his knees and leaning back in his chair, one hand on its arm, the other playing with a gray goose quill on the desk before him. He gave a slight smile that scarcely stirred the corners of his mouth.

"Nevertheless, you must not suppose that my patriotism is

less genuine, less disinterested than your own—you must not imagine that I shall hesitate to take personal risks, very great risks, for the sake of the preservation of the country.... What is the extent of the—sacrifice required?"

Barras rubbed his palms, which were prickling unaccountably, on the arms of his chair. He cleared his throat. "The budgetary deficit will amount to some—to about—it is a matter of, er—a hundred and twenty-five millions."

Ouvrard's expression remained unchanged, as placid and unemotional as though he had been asked for a hundred francs towards a charity.

"A hundred and twenty-five millions. Yes. A tidy sum." He stabbed thoughtfully with his quill at the writing-pad, then dropped it, spread his hand out flatly, and looked up.

"Yes. As I have said, I am prepared to take risks for the salvation of the country. I am prepared to purchase the ex-royal domains for the sum of a hundred and twenty-five millions—of which, say, twelve per cent to be paid in specie, the rest in promissory notes."

Barras slowly straightened in his chair. He was shocked. No manœuvre for the obtaining of wealth had any longer the power to shock him, but he felt within him that same uneasy distaste with which Theresia's physical blatancy had filled him. There was scarcely anything he was not prepared to sell, or had not already sold—the Armies of France, her credit, her ideals, her honor. But the royal domains—the royal domains in the possession of a vulgar money-lender. The thousand-year-old heart of the nation— Theresia had cut off the royal vines at the root for her pleasure, Ouvrard proposed to tear out the roots themselves for his profit. Some ancient root deeply hidden in his own being seemed to shrink and twist at the thought. His back stiffened and his eyes steadied.

"Monsieur Ouvrard," he said, "I am well aware, as you have been pleased to remind me, that I am publicly held responsible for the catastrophes that have overcome the nation. I therefore propose to recall General Bonaparte from Egypt."

Ouvrard's smile neither flickered nor quickened. He raised his hand a little from the writing pad, and let it fall again. "As you will," he said quietly. "If you feel that General Bonaparte's saber-clanking can serve the public interest better than the clinking of my gold—" He shrugged slightly. "By all means make every sacrifice, even to the point of self-annihilation, for the good of the nation. Yet, even though you are prepared to summon your own executioner, there remains still the question of whether he will—or can, obey. There is a slight obstacle to be overcome. The French fleet is, unfortunately, at the bottom of the Mediterranean, while the English fleet remains very much on its surface. However, as you yourself appear to be among those who consider General Bonaparte capable of the miraculous, even to the point of taking wings"—he spread out his hands—"then by all means recall him at once." He picked up his gray goose-quill again and began idly smoothing it between his fingers.

Barras sat motionless, still erect, but with an effort, as though some inner stiffness had been withdrawn from him. He felt that numbing mixture of depression and relief of a man who has nerved himself to a dangerous and painful operation, only to find that the surgeon cannot come. The irk of his malady would remain with him, but the fear of extinction was lifted. Well, he had done what he could, everything in his power. But the movements of the English fleet were not within his power to control. He had self-sacrificingly proposed heroic measures, but the door of the Mediterranean was inexorably closed between himself and the executor of them. It was not his fault. The responsibility was not his. No one could do the impossible, after all.

His shoulders slackened. Moral exertion was quite as ineffectual, and of course vastly more exhausting, than physical.

"Very well," he said. He grasped the arms of his chair and drew himself to his feet. Ouvrard also rose, his slight smile unchanged, and extended his hand across the desk.

"To the sealing of our bargain," he said.

Ouvrard's hand, small and dry, with its thin, blunt-ended fingers. He looked at it—the hand that was stretched out to grasp a hundred and twenty-five million francs' worth of the heart of France, and to offer in exchange some ten millions and a sheaf of ink-soiled scraps of paper. A hand whose rapacity was almost magnificent in its very enormity, making his own seem like the pilfering of green apples by contrast. Yet the hand, when all was said and done, of a vulgar usurer, a common moneylender. He shrugged very slightly, smiled, and stretched out his own long, white hand of an aristocrat.

"To the sealing of our bargain."

CHAPTER

❧ XXXV ❧

August.

"YOU SHOULD HAVE TOLD ME BEFORE, JUNOT! YOU SHOULD HAVE
told me—do you hear? You should have told me!"

He checked in his pacing and turned the pewter-gray, black
shadowed mask of his face towards Junot.

"You knew in Italy—you knew in Paris. You've known all the
months we've been here. You should have told me!"

Under the sweat-lacquered skin a muscle of his cheek twitched
and jerked, behind his back his hands crushed each other so
that their bones cracked.

"You call yourself my friend, and you didn't tell me."

That, he thought, is unfair, unjust. No man could possibly
tell another man—that, unless he hated him. No friend could
ever tell, unless it was forced out of him, unless he no longer
had a choice. But the necessity to react brutally, savagely, against
intolerable pain would not let him be silent. The spasmodic
urge to hurt back, to outrage, to insult, would not be con-
trolled.

"You knew how I love—how I loved that woman. You knew
I had never loved any other woman. You knew that every sentiment of my heart and soul was bound up in her—in her alone.
You knew, too, what every common soldier of the Army, every
gutter-snipe of Paris, every sneering politician at the Luxembourg knew, and you didn't tell me! You didn't tell me!"

Junot, motionless and silent as the palm-tree against which
he stood, stared miserably down at his feet. Poor devil! The skin
was being stripped from his soul strip by strip—but one had to
go on—one couldn't stop—because one loved him. . . . Love—
Josephine—!

"It's your fault. You should have told me!"

280

Junot's love was unendurable. It was like salt water offered to a man dying in the ultimate torment of thirst. That, too, was unfair. It was like sweet water offered to a man already dead. Dead and beyond the reach of torment. Josephine— Josephine—

He turned away and stared at the waters of the Messoudiah, where the little river formed a small, still pool. So still that it was like a mirror, reflecting back a sky that was slowly darkening into night. Blue water, dark blue, yet with a vivid translucence, a profound clarity— An indescribable blue, like— It wasn't possible. Not possible that eyes like that could hide such cruelty, such treachery in their depths.

Junot had known, and Junot hadn't told him. So that for all these months—for a whole year, since the sinking of the fleet in the road-stead of Aboukir, he had walked in a fool's Paradise, not knowing that it was as arid, as fruitless, as sterile as the Egyptian desert itself. A year during which the cutting off of news from France had seemed to be only a storing up of happiness for the future—a bitter privation, yet endurable, because of the enrichment to come. For a year, thinking of the English fleet as a sluice-gate behind which the level of pent-up happiness rose and rose—and then to find that all this time it had been a screen behind which she—*she* and that— By God, he would exterminate that race of insolent puppies, of yapping lap-dogs— Ha! It was enough to make a corpse laugh, wasn't it? The amours of General Bonaparte's wife protected by the ships of Admiral Nelson's navy. Josephine!

A year, and the sluice-gate had opened, a crack, enough to let through a trickle of the corrosive poison that was stored behind it. A French blockade-runner captured, a French sea-captain taken, taken and courteously—oh, very courteously set at liberty on the Egyptian coast, together with General Bonaparte's private correspondence and a batch of Paris journals. General Bonaparte's private correspondence delivered by the courtesy of an English captain—but after having been opened, read, sniggered over, perhaps copied— His correspondence. Letters from Joseph, his mother, Lucien. He couldn't re-read those letters, because he'd torn them to shreds, burned them. But he couldn't tear up his memory, and the words had been seared into it.

His mother, his brothers. They had told him. They hadn't hesitated to break his heart for the good of his soul. No, not even his soul—the family soul—the soul of a Corsican family, that would tear out its own eyes rather than shut them to a breach of its cruel faith. Yes, they had told him—

The journals, too. The news items in them. No more than ant-bites after that deadly hurt. Yet ant-bites in a gaping wound—

The slow-creeping sweat of his forehead stung at the corners of his eyes. He unclasped rigid hands and smeared at them with fingers still shaking with strain.

He faced down the course of the little stream, to where El Arysh lay on its banks. He looked at the triumph of artillery-breached walls. A child's sand-castle, that another child had kicked in a burst of puny temper. He looked at the pride of French flags raised over conquered minarets. Draggled colored rags, like shabby washing hung out to dry on a rubbish-heap.

He turned back, and stared again at the unruffled pool. A surface of tranquil purity laid over darkness and slime. Violet-blue it was now, with the jewel of the evening star suspended in its depths. A star? A cheating illusion, with no more weight or depth or substance than a tinsel sequin. Less. It hadn't even that reality, it wasn't even surface deep. It had no existence save in illusion. And that illusion— A fish breaking the surface to snap at a fly was enough to dispel and shatter it, as the crystal of the little miniature had been shattered at the Bridge of Arcola. He had known them. He had known, but he hadn't had the courage to believe. He turned his back to the ripple-shattered star that was already beginning to form again on the broken surface of the water.

Junot was only a vague shadow now with the pale blur of his face above it. But he was solid, real, unbreakable. He touched him on the arm.

"I have tried to be unjust to you, Junot. But you are all I have now in the world. Your friendship is all I have left to lose. It is dear to me, Junot."

With his hand on Junot's arm he paced slowly along the banks of the little river.

"You know how I have loved her, Junot. Every emotion, every sentiment of my whole being was in her. And there is nothing left. Nothing."

Junot coughed, stammered. "But, Bonaparte—General—your glory. You still have that—"

"My glory?" He gave a short bark of laughter. "That too, Junot, has been degraded and defiled. The freedom that I gave to Italy, the security that I gave to France, the very gold that I poured into the Public Treasury. Not a vestige, not a shadow of any of it is left. My Army of Italy—the men who were my companions, my friends. Broken, abandoned. And she—she—! No, Junot. I am twenty-nine. And my life is finished."

"But—but— There is France. The people of Paris—how they crowded to see you—how they rushed after you—"

"The people of Paris?" He shrugged. "The people of Paris would rush with as much enthusiasm to see me climb the scaffold as to see me mount a throne. No. Humanity sickens me. It is finished."

He walked in silence for a little, his hand on Junot's arm, staring into the night-shadows that rose darkly from the arid land. Then he glanced sideways at the pale shadow of Junot's face.

"Listen to me, Junot. In two months I can be in Paris. I shall divorce—her. Divorce. Open, public. Whatever else, I will not be the laughing-stock of all the loafers of the Paris streets. I will keep my little house—that at least is mine—and I will live in it. Alone. I have no desire left, save for solitude and isolation."

He dropped his hand from Junot's arm and turned again to look at the water—water as black as velvet now and, from this angle, with no reflected star in its depths. That was all it had been—a reflection. A chance angle, a cold geometrical affair, without mystery or soul or divinity. *Josephine! It's not possible— not possible! And I, six hundred leagues away. Josephine—*

"Perhaps a—a misunderstanding, after all. Perhaps some—some explanation, some—"

"No, Junot. There is nothing more for you to hide. Nothing that can be hidden. Even at this distance, the mirage has vanished. And in two months I shall be there. I shall be in Paris."

Behind him, Junot stammered on. "But—the English fleet—the blockade— It's impossible, you can't—"

"In two months, I shall be in Paris."

He turned away and, with Junot at his heels, walked towards El Arysh, where the gaping breach showed black in the faint pallor of its white walls.

CHAPTER

❧ XXXVI ❦

October.

DIRECTOR BARRAS MOVED HIS HEAD IRRITABLY ON THE PILLOW.
He half opened his eyes and frowned at the light as his valet
drew aside the heavy curtains.

"Gaspard," he said, "what's that confounded noise? Since five
o'clock it's kept me awake. Damned irritating. Fatiguing, too."

Gaspard, expressionless and very correct, came neat-footed to
the bedside.

"Good morning, Director Barras, I infinitely regret that your
rest should have been disturbed. It is the commonalty of Paris.
They are informed that General Bonaparte has just disembarked
at Fréjus, and they are giving vent to their enthusiasm with the
lack of restraint customary among that class of person."

Director Barras said, "Ah!" and looked up at Gaspard's im-
passive face. He would have suspected the fellow of, er—giving
vent to a bad joke, save that he never on any possible account
did. Nor to good ones, either.

"Ah!" he said again. Then he drew himself slowly up against
his pillows. "Bring the tray here. I think—yes, I believe I'll have
my coffee in bed this morning."

Gaspard set the tray beside him, straightened the sheet, patted
the pillow, and went out. An invaluable fellow, Gaspard. Soothing. Bonaparte at Fréjus, eh? He smiled a little, and poured his
coffee. Ouvrard had then, for once, made a mistake. One might
have thought the mistake to be Gaspard's, save that Gaspard had
never been known to make even the most trivial of mistakes.
Gaspard was, in fact, the only human being he knew who was
fundamentally and constitutionally incapable of making a mistake.

Gaspard came back with a pan of red-hot coals and a basket

284

of logs. He laid the fire, and the oven-dried wood at once burst into cheerful and crackling flame. Oh, decidedly soothing, Gaspard.

"You might shut the window, Gaspard. Extraordinarily discordant the noise they make, don't you find? Thank you. ... You said Fréjus, Gaspard?"

"Yes, Director Barras. A little port on the Mediterranean. Two thousand eight hundred inhabitants. Exactly eleven and a half kilometers from—"

"Yes, yes. I am aware of its geographical position."

"Quite, Director Barras." He put another log on the fire, brought a clean handkerchief, saw that spectacles, snuff-box, and the morning's journal were within easy reach on the beside table, and withdrew.

An impeccable fellow, Gaspard. Bonaparte at Fréjus, eh? He sipped his coffee, and stared at the cup in his hand. A cup of fine porcelain. Fragile. It would be smashed in no time in a nervous, awkward hand like Bonaparte's. A pity. Yet after all, need it be sacrificed? His own hold upon it was calm and deft enough. But then, he wasn't given to snatching. He preferred to hold what he wanted delicately, until he was ready, quite gently and quietly, to set it down again. He replaced the cup in its saucer.

As for the other, the, er—metaphorical cup, he still held it firmly enough. He was still Director Barras, still the actual dictator of France, still the Indestructible. He could still, if he wished, rally a panic-stricken Government about him and make a great deal of trouble for a criminally ambitious General Bonaparte—or he could make common cause with a righteously indignant General Bonaparte in his just vengeance upon a corrupt and inefficient governing body. Either action would be of value—of great value to the side he favored, and either side would undoubtedly be prepared to make generous, very generous—er, recognition of his efforts. His efforts. Yes, both sides would be ready to bid very high for that. Still, a risky and troublesome business. Fatiguing, too.

And why endanger, why exert one's self, when there was a far simpler and pleasanter method ready to hand? Non-intervention. His promise of non-intervention would be as valuable to either side as a promise of intervention could be. He had merely to withhold his support from the lowest bidder, instead of offering it to the highest. A far less crude, blatant, vulgar method. And of course infinitely less exhausting. Instead of brutally smashing his porcelain cup, he would simply and quite gently set it back in its saucer. After, of course, having drained it of its contents.

He leaned back against his pillows, and listened to the clamor of the streets, still faintly audible through the closed window. The voice of the, er—what was the admirable word Gaspard had used? Ah, yes. The voice of the commonalty was always, whether raised in praise or blame, equally irritating to a sensitive ear. He had been obliged to listen to a great deal of it during the past few years. It would be a great relief to have it hurled against a robuster target than himself. A great relief. He would be relieved, too, of other unpleasant things, as well—the exhausting activities of Corsicans, the humiliating condescension of money-lenders, the tyranny of young harlots, and the insatiable demands of aging courtesans. He would in fact be able to be a gentleman again.

"Gaspard," he said, "I am much wearied by lack of sleep. I propose therefore to remain within doors to-day. I propose to remain in my own apartment. I propose, in fact, to remain in my bath. During that time I will, naturally, be able to receive no one. No one at all."

"Naturally, Director Barras."

"And, Gaspard, you will see to it that there is plenty of hot water. I propose to remain in my bath for, say, a week. Possibly even ten days."

"Perfectly, Director Barras."

Really a most superior fellow. Had he proposed to set fire to the Luxembourg, Gaspard would have said, "Perfectly, Director Barras," and would himself, with his admirable efficiency and energy, have attended to all the fatiguing preparations, even to the presentation of the lighted briquet.

"And, Gaspard— I think a dash of lavender essence in the water."

"I would propose verveine, Director Barras. It is more beneficial to the nervous system."

Barras sighed. There was one burden from which not even the advent of General Bonaparte would be able to free him. The firm, though quite kindly, authority of his man-servant.

"Very well, Gaspard."

He relaxed against his pillows, gently brushed his fingers together, and folded them lightly on the sheet before him.

286

Theresia Tallien drew her negligée about her, leaned her elbows on the marble balustrade of the balcony, and looked down. The street below was a surging mass of people, shouting, gesticulating, cheering. As yet only an excited crowd, but with the makings of an angry mob behind it. There was danger in it. She had only contempt for that danger, which was crude, violent, physical. Yet something in her answered to its very crudity. If those agitated people down there became aware of her presence above them, anger, she knew, would rush up against her like a flame. There would be roaring fire where so far were only crackling sparks. Yet better that blaze of violence that could be answered by violence than the sullen, dull resentment of the past months. Her eyes narrowed, her sensitive nostrils flared. She leaned farther over the balustrade, as though almost willing the great burst of fierce emotion to pour up in the face of her own courage. Farther and farther—

Behind her she heard a door open and close; she heard footsteps, short, firm, precise, muffled by deep carpet. She sighed, and drew away from the balustrade. She turned, and went back through the long windows into the room she had left.

"Well?" she said.

Ouvrard laid his hat, cane, and gloves neatly on a chair. He smoothed back his hair, adjusted the folds of his high cravat. "It is true, my dear," he said. "Bonaparte has indeed landed at Fréjus."

She stood quite still for a moment, holding her indrawn breath, feeling excitement burn along her nerves like acid. Then she let out her breath in a soft, tense, "Ah!"

Ouvrard went to the little breakfast table between the windows. He touched the silver coffee-pot with the tips of his fingers. "The coffee, my dear. Almost cold. Perhaps you would ring—"

She clenched her hands into fists and drove them together. "But what are you going to do, man—what are you going to do?"

"Do, my dear?" He seated himself at the table, and made careful choice of a crisp roll. "Why, drink my coffee. Hot coffee. If you would be so good—"

She frowned sharply, opened her mouth to retort, then turned and jerked at the bell-pull.

"There is nothing," he said, unfolding a lace napkin, "so unpleasing as lukewarm coffee."

"Unless it be lukewarm resolution." She moved forward to the table and rested her hands on the back of the chair opposite

287

his. "This man—this Bonaparte—he must of course be checked."

He leaned his forearms on the table and looked up at her. "Checked, my dear? He is scarcely a man to understand the orthodox rules of the political chess-game. Nor am I a man to try to teach them to him. After all, my dear, I am a private citizen, occupied with my private affairs."

She smiled. "And what do you propose to do about your—private affairs?"

"I propose," he said, "to do my duty as a patriotic citizen by showing confidence in—the governing authority. I propose to buy. I propose to buy every inch of French soil, every scrap of French paper, every French security that I can come by. As for public business—" he raised his eyebrows—"I never concern myself with it unless directly appealed to by the—recognized head of the State."

"You have seen the—head of the State, then? You have—"

"Ah, good morning, Juliette. Fresh coffee, if you please. Very hot. And yes—I think I will take honey instead of preserves this morning. . . . You were saying, my dear?"

She clenched her hands on the back of the chair. "You have seen Barras, then? What—appeal did he make to you?"

"I was not referring to our friend Barras at the moment—though I did indeed call to see him. Director Barras, my dear, is indulging in the rites of a hot bath, with a locked door between his natural modesty and the vulgar gaze of the outside world. And that, I should judge, is the extent of his plans both for the present and for the immediate future."

She laughed shortly. "Waiting, I suppose, for the highest bidder to get him out of it."

"Waiting, more likely and more wisely, for the highest bidder to keep him in it. Barras, my dear, has brought the art of profitable inactivity to a very high pitch of perfection."

She raised her hands in a contemptuous gesture and let them drop to the back of the chair again. "He's been rotting from the core out for years past. We shall have to make our own decision, then."

"Decision, my dear?" He moved his head slightly towards the window. "If I am not mistaken, the decision is already made."

She too glanced towards the window. "The mob? You've seen enough mobs in your time to know how to manage them."

"I have seen enough mobs in my time to know when they cannot be managed. It's easy enough to manage a herd of milling

288

cattle—but when they lower their horns and move all in the same direction, the course of wisdom is to move, if possible a little more rapidly, in that same direction."

She opened her mouth for a sharp retort, then frowned and was silent for a moment. She looked down at her hands that were clasped on the back of the chair. She thought of Bonaparte coming up from the Mediterranean with his gray, unwinking hawk's stare fixed on Paris. She thought of Barras sinking into his hot bath, with a silk madras about his hair to preserve its waves. She thought of a measure of the newest contre-danse, in which the woman passed from hand to hand up a lane of men, never releasing the first hand she held until she had reached forward to clasp the second, nor the second until she had secured the third. So she had linked hands between Tallien and Barras, then between Barras and Ouvrard. And now—

"Yes, Juliette. That will do nicely. No, I will pour for myself. Thank you."

She watched Ouvrard's small, hard, square hand as he poured his coffee. Barras' hand, elegant, white, tranquil. Bonaparte's, brown, nervous, sensitive. Barras and Ouvrard. Ouvrard and Bonaparte— She drew a deep breath, smiled, and raised her head.

"You are quite right, my friend," she said. "We must move forward with public opinion. I will approach Bonaparte as soon as possible."

He spread butter on a hot roll. "I shouldn't meddle if I were you, my dear. General Bonaparte is not a man to appreciate your method of approach."

"My method—?"

He smiled slightly, and glanced briefly towards the great gilded bed.

The angry color flooded up over her face, her neck stiffened. "You are a little insulting, my friend. Do you take me for a common prostitute, a harlot?"

He touched his napkin delicately to his mouth, and laid it down on the table. "I was referring, naturally, to General Bonaparte's opinion. In my eyes—" He got up, came around the end of the table to face her and stood, head a little on one side, looking her slowly up and down. "In my eyes, you are a thing of exceptional, of unique beauty. I value the unique; I reverence beauty in all its forms. I prize you very highly. Very highly indeed."

She stood for a moment rigid as a statue under his appraising gaze. Then she drew her negligée together over her bosom and raised her head. "Bonaparte does me greater honor than you do," she said. "He accords me at least the dignity of judging me as a human being, not as a work of art."

He came closer to her, and took her chin between his finger and thumb. "And I too, my dear. I accord you the dignity of being my mistress—my adored mistress whom it is my delight to cherish, and whom I refuse to share with any man."

She jerked her head back, snatching her chin from his grasp. "Your mistress? I am Theresia Tallien. I have never yet been any man's kept woman. I would rather give myself to a road-sweeper than be bought for your amateur's collection! I would rather be the harlot Bonaparte calls me than the museum piece you take me for! Yes, a harlot!" She snatched her negligée from her shoulders and let it slip to the floor, standing erect in the firm, rich perfection of her nudity.

He tilted back his head, looking at her through half-closed lids. "Admirable," he murmured. Then he shrugged very slightly. "Only, unfortunately, the Greek comedy of the Directorate is over. The appeal of Phryne will have but little effect on a Corsican judgment."

She gave a laugh brief and sharp as a snapped twig. "Last time it was the judgment of Paris, wasn't it?" She passed before him without turning her head. "I prefer to abide by that." She jerked her chin towards the window.

He raised his eyebrows. "The temper of the people being what it is, perhaps a rather dangerous experiment."

"Dangerous? Pah!" She snapped her fingers. "Paris hates a masterful woman—but she loves her harlots as much as her heroes. There'll be room here for both of us, Bonaparte and me. There'll be no rivalry, no competition between our trades."

She snatched up her great multicolored Spanish shawl and, standing before her mirror, draped it about her.

"Order my carriage," she commanded over her shoulder. "Not your black and silver hearse, but my own, the scarlet one with the white horses." She took a red rose from a vase and slipped it down between her breasts. "As for you, buy if you like. Buy your new flunkey's livery—your smug respectability—your bourgeois security! I am on the market to sell."

He bowed with formal gravity. "I shall remain, my dear, your humble, obedient servant."

She picked up her gardening-basket, and went out into the tepid warmth of the October morning. She stood on the neatly graveled path pulling on her gloves, and looking back at the house she had just left.

Yes, she'd been perfectly right about the Malmaison, it had turned out exactly as she'd foreseen—or nearly. It was quite utterly charming and delightful, anyway. A sort of cross between Croissy and the Chaumière, though of course more convenient and roomy than Croissy, and without that horrible imitation quaintness of the Chaumière. It wasn't quite so large as she'd originally planned, because she hadn't been able to add the wings that would really have made it quite perfect.

She took her pruning-shears from her basket and snipped off an over-blown rose, dropping it onto the path for the gardener to pick up.

That, of course, was Barras' fault. He'd become so difficult and unreasonable since he found she wasn't going to Egypt with Bonaparte, that it was quite impossible to lower one's dignity by asking the least little service of him, such as a woman might expect from any well-bred man. She hadn't noticed at first, not until she'd asked his advice about adding the two wings. He'd said he didn't think wings would be in the least appropriate. As if he could possibly tell, when he hadn't even seen the house—

She snipped off a rose-bud, and tucked it into her belt.

Though now she came to think of it, he'd been like that—difficult—ever since she came back from Italy. He'd said that between Theresia's intelligence and her ignorance, he no longer needed to use powder to whiten his hair. Which was so unfair of him, because she wasn't in the least ignorant. She just didn't happen to have a very good memory for names and figures, and she sometimes made little mistakes in spelling, as the best-bred people often did. Like putting Pau for Po when she'd written him that Bonaparte was going to march on it. Just little slips like that that anybody might make, and that couldn't be of the slightest importance anyway, since both words were exactly the same if you said them aloud, only Barras had been too stupid to think of doing that. So it was really just as much his fault as hers.

She pulled at a weed. Only the top part of it came off, leaving the roots still in the ground. Weeds always did do that. It was always the wrong things, like bulbs, that came up all in one piece when you pulled them. She dropped the top part back onto the garden bed to show the gardener where to find the roots.

Yes, Barras had changed quite enormously during this past year—though why, it was impossible to imagine. But then men were so unaccountable. She'd thought, with things arranging themselves so nicely—Bonaparte going to Egypt and Theresia quite comfortably settled with Ouvrard, that she and he— But it had been quite impossible. She'd been obliged—but absolutely obliged to drop the acquaintance altogether. Of course, she'd been ready to make every sort of allowance for so old a friend. He wasn't so young as he used to be, and his rheumatism bothered him. But one had one's dignity to think of, hadn't one? She'd overlooked his quite abominable bad manners at the Luxembourg reception after they came back from Italy, when he'd spent the whole evening following Bonaparte about and flattering him in the most nauseating manner, and paying not the slightest attention to her so that she might just as well not have been there at all. But when he'd behaved in that almost insulting fashion when she'd done no more than quite simply ask his advice about the wings for the house— There were after all limits to what one's self-respect could put up with.

She was sorry of course about Barras. She didn't want to hurt his feelings. And of course she was prepared to be friendly again the very moment he offered the very slightest word of apology. She wasn't in the least small-minded about that sort of thing. But Charles *was* more amusing, wasn't he?—and much more considerate. He never wanted her to *do* things. Not anything, that is, except sometimes just sign a letter to somebody in the War Ministry or one of the Directors. Not Barras, of course, but one of the others who weren't really important but were, Charles said, quite useful. But he never expected her actually to write letters like Barras had, which was such a relief. She hadn't even to write to Egypt any more, because of the French fleet being sunk and the English not letting any French ships cross the Mediterranean. It was a pity of course about the fleet, but it really was difficult to write to a man who was such a long way away and whom you hadn't even seen for over a year. And of course there wasn't really anything to write about, was there?

She stripped off her gloves and looked at the little watch Bonaparte had given her before he went away—to count the hours by, he'd said. Men were so sentimental, weren't they? It was quite a nice little watch with an entwined J and N in diamonds—

though quite small diamonds—on the back. She always thought it was a mistake to mark thinks like that, because you could never really tell, could you? But Bonaparte was so unpractical about that sort of thing. Still, a nice little watch that went quite well when Louise didn't forget to wind it up.

Nearly twelve o'clock. She was passionately devoted to her gardening, it was so good for the figure. She'd been at it now for hours—quite literally for hours, and one mustn't exaggerate, must one? She'd got up at ten, it certainly hadn't taken her more than an hour to dress, and she'd been working in the garden absolutely every minute since. Now she'd just have time for an hour's rest before luncheon. It was so bad for the digestion to eat when one was literally exhausted.

Louise would have put out her chair with the footrest on the lawn in front of the house in the sheltered corner where the sun struck warm against the red-brick garden wall. She could just lie there and absolutely relax until lunch-time. So good for the nerves. Then after lunch she'd have her bath and her nap, and then change her clothes for the afternoon. Then some of the people from the surrounding country-houses would come in, and perhaps a few from Paris as well, and they'd have tea in the rose-arbor. Not that anybody could possibly like tea, but it was said to be thinning, and now of course that it was almost impossible to get— Bonaparte had sent her quite a lot before he let the English sink the fleet, so that she was practically the only hostess who could still offer it to her guests. It was so pleasant to be able to give people luxuries they couldn't get for themselves, wasn't it? Then later in the day Charles would be coming, and dinner for just the two of them.

The chair was there, and the light wrap Louise had laid out on it for her because of being over-heated with her gardening, and the October sun not being so warm as it had been. She pulled it about her shoulders, and stretched out on the long, cushioned chair. She turned her head sideways and looked at the façade of the house. It was extraordinary, really quite extraordinary how—how *established* it looked, after only fourteen months. The white plaster walls had already lost their crudity of over-newness, the red tiles were dulling and mellowing nicely. The big windows with their yellow damask curtains looked cheerful and friendly. It was a pity of course about the wings, but the wide porte-cochère with the pillars looked very handsome. Of course, had she known how quite outrageously Barras was going to behave about the wings, she wouldn't have—have consulted him about the porte-cochère either. But once the thing was in place, it would have been childish—wouldn't it?—to pull it down again just to spite Barras. He'd wanted her to have slates for the roof too, instead of those quite divine hand-made tiles that turned up a little at the edges. And slates of course would simply have ruined the whole effect. You'd think he'd be able to realize that for himself, with the way he was always talking about good taste. But altogether the house was a success, a quite perfect success. And all for only ten thousand francs. Nobody could say she hadn't made a good bargain, could they?

It was fortunate too that she'd made it before Bonaparte lost his fleet, because now lots of people were saying he'd never get out of Egypt again, and then of course his credit wouldn't be good with anybody at all, not even with Monsieur Lecoulteux, would it? Although of course she couldn't bear to think of anything actually happening to poor Bonaparte. Still, one had to be practical, hadn't one?—a woman all alone in the world with nobody— And then there was Eugène, too. She was quite distracted when she thought about him. You'd think a man like Bonaparte, who'd known perfectly well what was likely to happen, would have had more feeling than to take a boy—a mere child, really—into such appalling danger. But then of course he never did think of other people, except what use he could make of them.

But aside from Eugène—who simply didn't bear thinking about —life had arranged itself very pleasantly. Half the week in Paris where she could give formal parties for the Bonapartes to come to—and of course go to the theater and the Opéra to distract her mind from worrying over Eugène—and the other half spent here where the Bonapartes never came. Except of course Lucien. She giggled as she remembered Lucien's afternoon call. She'd given him tea, so strong it stained the cup, but he'd drunk it because he couldn't bear anybody to think he was so unfashionable as not to like it. And they'd talked, very seriously and properly, about the news, or lack of it, from Egypt. Then, just when he was in full, pompous swing, Charles had burst in and said, "Josephine, 'must you use my razor to—" before he saw Lucien. It really had been too comic. Lucien blinking behind his spectacles, and Charles white—but literally white with embarrassment. It had really been all she could do not to laugh out loud. If Desirée— Poor Desirée! Of course it had been awkward, and practically impossible after that to introduce Charles as a neighbor who'd just dropped in— And Charles had been so difficult about it afterwards, too. Though she never had been able to remember what it was she'd done with his razor.

She turned her head the other way, and looked down the little avenue of elms that led up to the house. The trees were really quite impressive, now that all the bushes and undergrowth had been cleared away from them. And of course the handsome bronze gates at the end, left hospitably open— She sat upright. A carriage was coming through them. Oh, dear— Somebody coming to lunch, and she not dressed— But no. It was Charles. That was his fine, high-stepping gray horse and smart gray cabriolet to match. Charles back early from Paris, in time for lunch. It was so pleasant when he did that, because then they could spend an hour or two driving about the countryside, and sometimes they took a picnic supper— She got up, and walked towards the graveled oval before the house where he would draw up and get out.

She watched him as he flicked the reins about the whip, jumped over the high wheel, and landed springily on his feet. He was as graceful and agile as a cat, yet so virile and masculine—

"Charles! How quite too delightful of you! Is it a holiday or something? I never can remember. . . . But Charles! What's the matter—what's happened! Charles! Are you ill? What *is* it— what *is* it!"

"Bonaparte's landed at Fréjus."

He stood planted before her, feet apart, fists on hips, frowning, his jaw set, almost threatening. For a moment she couldn't realize what he'd said. Bonaparte— Then she understood. He *was* comic, wasn't he?—so original. Always thinking of something new to tease her. And at first she'd actually believed— She tilted back her head and laughed at him. He stared back at her, hard-eyed.

"Bonaparte's landed at Fréjus. Can't you understand?"

He couldn't be serious—he couldn't mean—not actually *mean*—

"But he can't. He can't. It's impossible, you said so yourself. He can't—"

"Whether he can or he can't makes no difference. He's done it."

For a moment it was as though the earth were rising up beneath her feet, the elm-trees toppling over to crush her. Her whole life, that had been so pleasantly arranged toppling— Just

295

when everything had been so settled! Bonaparte— And Charles— He did nothing, just stood there with his feet apart and his fists on his hips, sticking out his jaw at her, his eyes narrow under frowning brows. Charles— Why didn't he say something, *do* something—

But of course he was upset, distracted. He was out of his wits with jealousy. That was it. Jealousy. Just like poor little Fortuné. And Charles had never really *liked* Bonaparte— But it didn't do any good to get wrought up like that. One had to keep quite calm and to think—to think. . . .

It was fortunate that one of them was able to think reasonably and quietly, without getting all worked up and flustered. She moved closer to him and laid both her hands flat against his breast. "Charles," she said, "after all—it doesn't really matter— does it?"

He snatched at her wrists roughly with both hands. "Matter?" he said. "Have you lost your senses, Josephine?"

She smiled at him. "No," she said. "Oh no, I've kept mine. You do love me, don't you, Charles? Then why should it make any difference between us?"

His hands tightened on her wrists until he was actually hurting her. But she didn't cry out. "Any difference?" he said harshly. "He threw me out of the Army, didn't he, for taking commissions from Army Contractors. Is he going to fall on my neck and embrace me now I'm a Contractor myself—and his wife's lover into the bargain?"

"Lover— Oh, but I didn't mean— I'm not such a fool as all that, Charles—I'm not, really. I meant—I meant— Well, I'll just divorce him, Charles. It's so simple, actually, when you think quite calmly about it. And then—why then, we—we can get married, can't we?"

"Married?" He jerked her hands from his breast and flung them from him. "Married? You who spend all your time looking at yourself in the mirror—have you ever looked at me? You do well to keep that son of yours out of sight—your 'little boy' with his six feet of gangling body and the hair on his face. I'm twenty-one. I'm not much older than he. Married?" He laughed, his lip drawn up over his sharp, white teeth. "Why, even Barras, at his age—even he—"

She shrank back, her hands at her throat. "Then why—why— But Charles, you said—you said you loved me!"

"Love? You're a woman of the world, aren't you?—or you

pretend to be." He threw up his head, rocked back on his heels, and looked at her with insolently fleering eyes. "Then unless you're even more of a fool than I imagined, you know well enough that when a woman of your age wants a man of mine, she's got to pay. Influence, wire-pulling, inside information, what-not. Madame Bonaparte, yes—she can pay. But Madame Charles? Madame Hippolyte Charles? Pah! Is General Bonaparte going to tell her everything he has on his mind in bed of a night? Is she going to be able to recommend her poor, unhappy friends to him? Are Directors and Deputies going to wriggle on their bellies to curry favor with her? Eh?"

He gave a laugh that jarred like a torn fingernail. "Anyway, you're too late with your bidding." He tilted his head on one side, smirked, and waved his hands in vague, uncertain flutterings. "Because you see," he shrilled. "You see, it's quite impossible—but quite utterly and totally impossible. Because you see, I—" He lowered his lids and looked at her through his lashes. "I—well, actually, your Louise married me six months ago."

> "Despite Fate and my honour, I
> shall love you all my life."
>
> BONAPARTE

CHAPTER

❧ XXXVII ❧

October.

SHE RUSHED TO THE WINDOW AND LOOKED OUT. THE CARRIAGE HADN'T come yet, though she'd told him to be as quick as he possibly could. Not of course that she'd have been ready if it had come, but—

No, she wasn't ready. And how could she possibly *get* ready, without Louise? Louise— The tears rose to her eyes. It didn't seem possible, did it, that human nature could be so—so vile and ungrateful. After all the dresses and hats and stockings she'd given the wretched girl just to make up to her for having to pretend sometimes that she and Charles— Charles. It just proved, didn't it, that it was never safe to trust any man—not any man at all. Though of course it was Louise's fault really, because when a scheming, deceitful girl like Louise got hold of an inexperienced young man like Charles—why, he simply had no chance, had he? And nobody but Louise—literally nobody at all knew how to do her hair or put on her complexion or dress her—

She had absolutely to get dressed. She'd come up from the Malmaison exactly as she was, in her gardening-dress. It was of plain white linen, embroidered round the hem with all sorts of little vegetables—little carrots and beans and cabbages and radishes. There had been little potatoes too, but they simply hadn't looked like anything at all, so she'd had them all picked out and onions—with a green sprout at the top—put in their place. Quite an amusing dress really, though of course not in the least suitable— She pulled open her wardrobe door, and looked at the dresses hanging there. A good lot of them, and some of them really not bad—though all of them seemed to be white, and he didn't *like* white. So old-fashioned of him—

But she had to *dress*. She had to do that. She knew perfectly well what she had to do, only it was so difficult— She hadn't known when she came back from the Malmaison that afternoon, so of course she'd gone straight to Barras. But she'd only seen that smug-faced man of his, Gaspard. And Gaspard had said Barras was in his bath, and she couldn't see him. As though she cared— Though of course the lower classes were so narrowminded about things like that, weren't they? Anyway he'd just shut the door in her face, and she couldn't very well make a scene, not in the middle of the Luxembourg, because people might think— And it wouldn't do—not at all—for people to think, just now—

Then she'd gone to Theresia's, and Theresia was out. So odd of her, with the people crowding the streets as they were, and they not really liking her very much. But then of course Theresia had no sensitive feelings about that sort of thing. So she hadn't seen Theresia, and Ouvrard had given that odd little smile of his and said that in future the place of women would be in their own homes, and she'd better stay there. Which was quite absurd of him, because that's what she'd been doing all this time, wasn't it? The Malmaison was her own home, and she'd been staying in it. So what—

Then she quite literally hadn't known where to go, so she'd gone to brother Joseph's, because he was the least horrible of the Bonapartes, and after all he'd be likely to know what Bonaparte knew—what he imagined he knew. Because of course it was so important to know what he imagined he knew before one told him the absolute truth, wasn't it? But she hadn't seen Joseph either. She'd only seen that incredibly dull wife of his, Julie, who was so pink and so tight in her dress that she looked exactly like a pork sausage. A raw one, of course.

And Julie had sat there being complacent with that awful brat of hers on her lap, thinking probably she looked the picture of virtuous motherhood. And of course she did, poor soul. Julie'd sat there and told her quite calmly that Joseph had gone to meet Bonaparte—with Lucien. She'd known then of course what she had to do, because if they—specially Lucien—got to Bonaparte first, they'd tell him all the horrible things they imagined about her, before she could— They'd be quite capable of that—specially Lucien. They'd always hated her. They wouldn't hesitate for a minute—not for a single instant—to try to come between husband and wife. They'd try to take Bonaparte away from her. And Bonaparte was quite literally and absolutely all she'd got left in the world. There was nobody else now. Nobody at all.

So she'd come back to the rue de la Victoire and sent the coachman off to get the very best horses he could possibly find in Paris, because of course she positively *had* to get to Bonaparte before Joseph and Lucien did. And anyway, she was Bonaparte's wife, wasn't she? And quite naturally she wanted to get to him as quickly as she could. Any woman with the least little spark of wifely feeling would do the same. So she'd told the coachman to be as quick as he possibly could, and it was over two hours now, and late afternoon already— She ran again to the window, but he still hadn't come. Not of course that she was ready—

She tore off her linen dress and kicked it under the bed. She looked down at her chemise. Quite a nice one really, of fine batiste with just a little embroidery on the front. Elegant and simple. Though Bonaparte of course didn't understand that sort of thing. She remembered he'd admired one that had the whole top made of Valenciennes lace. The sort of thing Theresia— But one had to consider one's husband's taste, hadn't one? She rummaged in a drawer, spreading the chemises out on the floor. Yes, here was one with lace. It wasn't quite so bad as that actual one, but it would do. She put it on. Yes, it would do. Bonaparte was always talking about womanly modesty, but that didn't prevent—

Shoes. But it was no good choosing the shoes till she knew

what dress— And there was nothing, but literally nothing— She stood quite still in the middle of the room and thought. It never paid to get excited and flustered, one should be quite calm and collected and just think. Yet the more she thought the more she was certain she'd never had anything but white dresses, not since her wedding—

But of course, that was it! Her wedding-dress! Which just showed that if you kept your head and concentrated seriously enough— It was only gray, of course, but it had a pink ruching about the neck and hem. And she could put on a wide pink sash and pink stockings and shoes and a pink reticule and the bonnet was turned up with pink— It would be rather horrible really, all that pink, but he did like gay colors, and one had to sacrifice one's own taste— Besides, even he couldn't be so lacking in sentiment as not to remember— But where was it—where *was* it?

Suppose she'd thrown it— She rushed into Bonaparte's room where she kept all her old things. She ran to the big wardrobe that half-filled the far side of the room. There was that quite absurd thing, the Venus dress, that she'd worn the first time he— Perhaps that— No, perhaps not, after all. Anyway, it was white. And there too was the quaint old thing with the golden flies she'd worn—or nearly worn—the last time he came home unexpectedly. Why *had* he to keep on doing that? If he only realized how *inconvenient*— Where— Ah, here it was! It just showed how it paid to keep things, you never knew when they'd come in useful.

She took it back to her own room, and slipped it over her head. Fastening it at the back was almost impossible—you'd think Louise would have realized— She managed it at last. She found a wide pink sash, tied it on, and made a face at herself in the mirror. It really *was* almost impossible— But still, since he liked that sort of thing— The pink stockings weren't too bad. Pink satin shoes, too. Oh, dear— Though of course there was her mantle that was gray, with a big squirrel collar and cuffs. That helped. But perhaps he wouldn't like— She pinned a big pink silk rose into the collar, just beneath her chin. Her gray bonnet, with the pink facing under the brim. A pink satin reticule— No, she could not. She simply could not! It was quite literally more than she could bear. She threw it on the bed, and found one of silver mesh. Her hair. She simply could not do her hair in the way he liked, and that he thought was simple and natural. Still, under her bonnet, with the curls pulled out over her forehead—

The carriage. She rushed to the window, and peered out. Yes, it was there, and with fine black horses harnessed to it. Six of them. Of course, she'd told him not to spare any expense—none at all. A woman rushing—but literally rushing to meet her husband after eighteen months of separation couldn't haggle over a few francs more or less, could she? Besides, she had, absolutely *had* to get to him before that smug-faced Joseph—and of course Lucien, who was worse. They had hours, but hours the start of her, and she'd have to travel literally day and night— Still, with six fine horses like that, she was sure to get there first. Anyway she had to, she quite simply *had* to.

She ran back to her mirror, and dabbed perfume on her ears and temples. She dropped the perfume bottle, her rouge-pot and powder-box into her reticule. They made it bulge, but it couldn't be helped. One couldn't travel without any baggage at all, could one? She ran to the door. Oh, her gloves. She came back and got them. And a handkerchief. Several handkerchiefs, because of having to do her complexion. She stuffed them into her reticule. There. Oh, yes, and an extra pair of stockings, because with these fine things they made nowadays you never could tell— And of course the black stick for her eyes. She'd nearly forgotten that. So important, because of perhaps having to cry quite a lot. Her reticule wouldn't close, but it didn't matter. And she hadn't got a brush and comb either, or a nightdress. She jerked at a drawer, and it came out sideways and stuck. But there was room just to get her hand in and drag things out. The fine white linen with the little pleats and tucks? No, the pale yellow silk that tied up with big satin bows on the shoulder—and the yellow satin mules that went with it, of course.

She snatched up a hat-box, opened it, and emptied its contents onto a chair. A perfect dream of a little three-cornered hat after the old style, brown beaver with a gold lace cockade. She'd forgotten all about it; she hadn't even tried it on since it was sent home. She glanced towards the mirror. But of course she hadn't time for that sort of thing now—she hadn't a minute, literally not a second to spare. She bundled her things into the box, and tied the ribbons. There, that was all. She had everything, absolutely everything. Except her muff. Her gray squirrel muff, that went with the mantle. And she hadn't any idea where Louise— Oh yes, she remembered now. In the cedar-wood chest under the window. Now she was actually ready, with everything she could possibly need.

Of course she hadn't any money, none at all. But then the coachman probably had some. Men practically always had, hadn't they?

She had never been so tired, so quite utterly exhausted in her life before. Which was to be expected, traveling as she had been, day and night, absolutely without stopping for a single instant—or practically. But it had been worth it. They were entering Lyons now, and she hadn't met Bonaparte on the road, so he couldn't have passed through yet. He wouldn't have had time anyway, not traveling with all his Staff as they said he was in a slow, heavy berline and being stopped at every town for the Civil Authorities to address him, or whatever it was those people did.

Of course she hadn't managed to overtake Joseph and Lucien, but that didn't really matter now. They wouldn't have gone on past Lyons, because of not knowing whether he was coming by the great Marseilles road, or by the smaller roads direct from Fréjus. It had really all worked out quite perfectly. She'd go to the best hotel—the Golden Lion. That was sure to be the best, because Charles always did choose the best things—though of course he'd find he'd made a mistake in that nasty little cat of a Louise, the sly, treacherous— Anyway, she'd go the Golden Lion, and if everybody knew she was there, they'd bring Bonaparte to her the moment he arrived, wouldn't they? It was natural they should—a husband and his wife, so long separated. So at least she'd have just a little time with him alone before— Perhaps half an hour. Half an hour always *had* been enough. Or perhaps an hour this time, because— Anyway, if he just *saw* her before he saw his brothers, she'd be able to manage. She was quite sure she would.

Of course, she'd tell him the truth. It always paid to tell the truth, didn't it? But there were so many *ways* of telling the truth. Joseph and Lucien, of course, would tell it in the most horrible, spiteful way they could imagine. Specially Lucien.

They were driving through the streets of Lyons now, and she hadn't even noticed the shops. But she saw the decorations. All the street-lamps had had branches of laurel tied about them, strings of flags were stretched across the street, people had hung their best carpets from their balconies, and set potted plants on their window-sills, or else had draped garlands of flowers from them. In the shops, now that she looked at them, she saw that

302

the merchants had arranged their windows as patriotically as they could. A silk merchant had three great swathes of fine Lyons silk, blue, white, and red, across the whole width of his window. A chandler had put three candles, blue, white, and red, quite enormous ones, as tall as a man, on the edge of the curb outside his shop. And the flower-sellers, with round bouquets made like tri-colored cockades. And the street itself full of people admiring the decorations, walking arm in arm, talking in groups, all with their tri-colored rosettes and cockades, all very animated and excited.

She began to feel a little excited herself. By to-morrow—or perhaps the day after, she'd be driving with Bonaparte down the decorated street, and all these people would be cheering and shouting for Our Lady of Victory—or perhaps not of Victory, because of the fleet, but of something anyway, because it was quite certain now that Bonaparte was something important—but really important. She'd realized it before she left Paris, and become more and more certain the closer she got to him, from the way the people behaved. Which just showed that it always paid to be kind and patient with people, because if she'd just divorced Bonaparte without considering his feelings at all, why— But it didn't matter now in the least about Hoche being dead, Theresia unfriendly, Ouvrard indifferent, Barras in his bath, or Charles— She could just quite simply forget all about Charles now, couldn't she? He was nothing anyway but a nasty, conceited, selfish boy of no importance—but none whatever, whereas Bonaparte—

The Golden Lion. She did hope the coachman wouldn't miss it. But he'd said he knew— Yes, he was drawing up before its door. There was a huge flag hanging from the balcony above, and little laurel trees in tubs standing at the foot of the steps on either side.

The door was open, and a lackey came running out of it as the carriage came to a halt. He came forward and she saw it was the same man as last time, the one who'd brought the hot wine, when Charles— She felt uneasy for a moment, but then remembered that it had all been quite well arranged. Charles had, after all, been good at that sort of thing. She leaned forward and showed herself. The man gaped at her for a moment, then waved his hands, opened his mouth without saying anything, and ran back into the Inn. He was excited at recognizing her, naturally.

In a moment the host himself came out. Quite a gentlemanly

looking person really, not in an apron, but with a very respectable suit of brown broadcloth. He was rubbing his hands and beaming all over his face, yet he managed to look anxious at the same time. Naturally, the responsibility of so important a—

"An honor, Madame Bonaparte—an honor and a privilege. An honor which I cannot bring myself to regret, though appreciating with all my heart Madame's natural and so understandable disappointment."

She leaned forward through the open window, staring at him. "My disappointment? But I— But General Bonaparte—"

He spread out commiserating hands. "Madame did not know? Then I am doubly desolated at being the bearer of ill tidings, but—" He stood there like an image, with his hands spread out, his eyebrows raised and his forehead puckered. Why couldn't he get on—why couldn't he say—

"But the truth is, Madame—" He shrugged despairingly. "The truth is, General Bonaparte passed through Lyons yesterday."

She stretched out her hand as though to touch the man, to make sure he was real, and not some horrible thing out of her imagination. "But he can't have. He's not had time. He can't have. It's impossible."

He straightened his shoulders as though his own pride were touched. "Who shall say 'impossible' of General Bonaparte, Madame? The General left his suite at Marseilles, to follow after—or so I understand—and himself came on at full speed in a light traveling chaise, with only one officer attending him. A tall young man, Madame, and very handsome. Madame perhaps knows—?"

Oh, she knew. Junot, of course, Junot who'd always hated her, been jealous of her, and whose vanity had been hurt because of Pauline Bonaparte. Junot and Bonaparte, traveling up from Marseilles together— Oh, dear! She hadn't thought of Junot. Only of Joseph and Lucien. Specially Lucien. And now—

"General Bonaparte did me the honor—the signal honor—of stopping before my Inn, where he was joined by two more young men, whom I took to be members of his family. They all four drove on in the General's chaise—in great haste, Madame, not even waiting to hear the Mayor's address of welcome. The Mayor was much put out—though naturally a man of General Bonaparte's great importance could scarcely be expected—" he waved a deprecating hand. "But as for myself—" he beamed complacently. "As for myself, the General honored me and glorified my Inn forever by condescending to drink a glass of my best wine before its door. You see there—" he turned and waved towards a three-legged stool set at the foot of the steps. "There is the exact spot on which he stood. I dropped my handkerchief on it at the time to make sure, and later placed the stool over it, so that no other foot— Yes Madame, he stood there and drank my wine and talked with his friends. And as he talked, he picked the leaves one by one from a branch of the laurel-tree beside him. You can see now the branch that he stripped bare. To commemorate that—that historic event, Madame, I shall have the stone on which your husband stood lifted, so that no other foot— And in its place I shall plant the laurel-tree."

The man was perspiring, but literally oozing with quite idiotic pride. As though she cared—

"And from now on, Madame, the Golden Lion will cease to exist, and the Laurels of Bonaparte will take its place. Eh, Madame?" He puffed out his chest and smiled—a fatuous, silly grin, almost half-witted, really.

She sat and stared at the laurel-tree with its branch stripped of leaves. That was just the sort of thing he did do, of course— meddle with things, break them, tear them to pieces— But she still couldn't believe—not actually believe— She clutched at the man's sleeve.

"He can't have gone through already," she said. "He quite simply can't have. Because I didn't pass him on the road. So he can't have."

He gestured sympathetically. "Madame came by the main road through Burgundy, doubtless?—as she would be obliged to do with her heavy coach. But General Bonaparte went by way of the Bourbonnais. The road's not so good, but shorter—and with his light chaise it would be quicker. And naturally, with affairs of such grave importance waiting him in Paris—"

She dropped his sleeve and withdrew her hand. It was true, then. She felt tired and cold and very desolate. She turned her head and looked vaguely out of the other window. The decorations— She could see now that the laurel branches had already withered a little, the flowers were beginning to curl and fade, while the gay flags weren't gay at all, but limp and dispirited with last night's rain. As for the people, there was no expectant purpose in their movements, it was just the after-restlessness of an excitement that was over and done with. There would be no shouting and cheering for Our Lady of anything at all. She would go just as she had come—a woman alone, completely alone, helpless against the ruthless strength of men—

The tears rose to her eyes and she let them run down her cheeks, because her complexion didn't matter any more. Nothing mattered. Not anything at all. She was quite alone now. Quite utterly and completely alone, with literally nobody—

It hadn't really mattered before, not actually mattered. Not Theresia being unfriendly, or Ouvrard indifferent, or Barras in his bath, or Charles running away, or even Louise, because always behind everything there had been Bonaparte. However difficult, however far away he'd been, he'd been *there*. She hadn't thought of it before—hadn't actually realized it, until now when he wasn't there any more. Like not actually realizing you had a head, until they were going to cut it off. That's what Junot and Joseph and Lucien were doing now. Cutting off Bonaparte. Because they wouldn't hesitate, not for an instant, vindictive and jealous as they were, to come between a husband and wife. Specially Lucien. She wished he'd let him marry anybody he wanted to—Junot, too—both of them, and be miserable all the rest of their lives. It just showed it never paid to try to be kind or to help that sort of man. She wished she'd never had anything to do with them. Not any of them. Charles, either. Men were so ungrateful, so unkind, so unjust— It wasn't fair, it wasn't fair! She sobbed into her handkerchief.

The Inn-keeper made small clucking noises in his throat, and moved to open the carriage door. "Madame is cold and tired and—and distressed. If Madame will honor my Inn for the night, she will feel better in the morning. She will return quietly to Paris, and there Madame's husband—" he chuckled benignly. "A happiness deferred, Madame. No more than deferred." He beamed encouragingly, and opened the door.

The man was a fool, of course, a quite unspeakable fool. Happiness? There wasn't any happiness left for her anywhere in the world. Not anywhere. There never could be any more, because she had nobody, nobody at all— She shook her head, and sobbed into her handkerchief.

"No," she said, "no. Tell the coachman to drive on—to go back to—back to—to Paris—"

The carriage turned into the little rue de la Victoire and stopped. It was quite dark inside the carriage, and she crouched there, feeling that it gave her a sort of protection, yet knowing

306

that it didn't, any more than her cell at the Carmes had been a protection against what was outside. In Lyons she'd only felt desolate and—and unhappy. But in Paris she was frightened. Quite definitely frightened. So frightened she couldn't go on, yet she absolutely had to, like having to listen to the names of the condemned—

The coachman had climbed down and opened the door, and she had to go out—she had to go. ...

Her hand trembled on the man's arm, her knees shook so that she could scarcely stand. But she had to go on. There was nowhere else to go, was there? Literally nowhere. She went through the grilled gates that were too narrow for the great coach to pass. She heard the coachman set her hat-box down beside her, slam the coach door shut, then the clatter of the horses' hooves as he drove them away to wherever it was he'd got them from. She was quite alone now, quite alone in the stillness of the night.

She stood on the stones of the courtyard and looked up at the house. It showed dim and quite blank in the moonlight. Impossible to know whether Bonaparte was inside it or not—though you'd think, with so important a man, you'd be able to tell from outside— But she had to find out, she simply *had* to, because it was absolutely the last hope—

She went slowly towards the door, her heart thumping in her throat. Suppose he'd quite simply locked the door and gone away— But he couldn't just lock her out in the street in the middle of the night, could he? Or could he? After all, he'd nearly had Charles shot, only for making a little money. He was a Corsican too—and Corsicans had such odd ideas about—about things—

Suppose the door was locked— What could she do?—what could she *do!* She might have locked it herself. She couldn't remember. ... It was open. She went in, and pushed it softly to behind her. The little hall was in darkness, but there was a thread of light under a door—the door of the little salon that she practically never used, but that—*he* had turned into a sort of study. A thin edge of light, hard and sharp as a knife—

She turned towards the mirror that hung against the wall, but could see nothing of her face but a pale shape, vague against the shadows about her. She took off her bonnet, and let it drop to the floor. The brim might be awkward if— She ruffled up her hair so that it would stand up in little disheveled curls all over her head. He liked—

307

She moved slowly forward until she could touch the study door. For a moment she stood there, the blade of light at her feet, her hands and forehead pressed against the wood. That's all there was now between herself and certainty. A half inch of wood—a half inch of hope. Once she'd put that behind her, there'd be nothing to hope for any more—

She put her hand softly on the doorknob, and, very quietly, turned it. It was odd, wasn't it?—that she should try not to make a sound, not to attract his attention, when actually that's all she'd come for—to make him look at her. Just look at her. She pushed the door gently open, and went in.

He was sitting at the table with his back to her, writing. She knew it was he, because it had to be. Yet somehow it wasn't. There was something harder, more definite— Then she saw what it was. His hair. He'd cut off his hair. How *comic* of him— For a moment the urge to giggle rose in her throat, but it turned to a little lump of apprehension that she couldn't swallow. There was something almost—almost frightening about it. The hard, dark line of his hair above the hard, dark line of his collar—

There was a woman in the Bible, wasn't there?—who'd cut off a man's hair. She'd always wanted to cut his off, but he hadn't let her. And now he'd done it himself— Something else was gone with his long, untidy locks. Something young, romantic, naïve. She felt that her last hope was gone with it. The last thin hope had been shut out with the shutting of the door behind her. But she had to go on—she *had* to—

"Bonaparte—"

He got up very deliberately and turned to face her. She could only see his face as a blur, white, featureless, because of the film of tears in her eyes. She wanted to blink them away so that she could see, but she was afraid to, afraid— She stretched out her hands before her, palms up, and came slowly towards him. She came so close that the outstretched tips of her fingers touched his breast. He neither touched them nor withdrew from their touch. He just stood there before his pushed-back chair, one hand still holding his pencil, the other straight at his side. She patted at his coat with little helpless dabbings of her palms.

"Bonaparte—?"

She could see his face now, could see there was no use trying. No use at all. It was set and expressionless, without anger in it or hatred or hurt, only a bleak indifference. The long curves of his mouth were thinned to a cruel edge. His eyes were blank and hard and cold as gray marble—polished marble, with brilliance only surface-deep. And his hair— Oh, it was no use. It was no use at all— Her hands fluttered helplessly down to her sides.

"Is it true, Josephine?"

She looked at his eyes, pale and gray and unwinking, surface-bright, unpitying. No, it was no use. All the things she'd thought of in the carriage on the way back to Paris— They'd seemed reasonable and—and appealing then, but she saw now it was quite useless to say any of them. Not with his eyes like that, and his hair—

"Yes," she said dully. "It is true."

He stood quite still, looking at her. Fear leaped up in her again. He was—after all he was a Corsican, not civilized—a sort of savage. He might— He raised his hand, and she gasped and shrank back. But it was only to join it to the other hand, still holding his pencil. He moved his eyes from her face at last, and looked down at the pencil. Very deliberately he snapped it in two, and laid the pieces on the writing-pad beside him. He arranged them meticulously, side by side, exactly parallel, and considered them attentively. Then he flicked them sharply aside with his forefinger.

He raised his head again, drew away from the table, circled about her and, without touching her or speaking again, went towards the door.

She turned and watched him go. The back of his head, with the hard line of his hair— Looking so blank and somehow so—so final.

"Bonaparte— What—what are you—what are you going to *do?*"

His hand on the doorknob, he turned his head and fixed the bright stare of his eyes on her again.

"Divorce, Madame."

He closed the door quietly after him. He was gone, and she was quite alone, with nobody, absolutely nobody in the world any more. She stood in the middle of the floor, listening. There was no sound at all. She hadn't heard the front door. But of course, she'd left it open, and he'd just walked out of it and left her—

She was cold and tired and quite alone in the empty house. Not even the servants, she'd left them at the Malmaison, and hadn't thought to— She began to tremble and to sob gently under her breath. She stumbled towards the fireplace. The fire was out, with just a few scorched sticks showing under the black coals.

That of course was exactly what he would do—set his briquet to the paper, and then never wait to see whether it had caught properly or not. He never did concentrate on anything—

She took a lighted candle from the mantel-shelf, and thrust it under the coal. But it just dribbled a little grease onto the hearth, then spluttered and went out, leaving an evil tallowy smell on the chill air. She crouched there, rubbing her cold hands, shivering, sobbing tearlessly, almost soundlessly. She was too tired to cry properly. Anyway, it was no use now, none at all.

She was so tired she couldn't get up from the floor. She'd never been so tired before. She felt worn-out, almost— "When a woman of your age—" Oh, no, no! It couldn't be that, not— She looked at her hands, that were as smooth and delicate as ever. She pressed her palms along the line of her thighs, and felt them hard and straight and rounded as a young girl's. She looked down at her bosom, and saw it firm, elastic, high-placed as it had always been, and without any artificial support at all—or practically.

"When a woman of your age wants a man of mine—" Bonaparte had been only twenty-six— But it wasn't true! It wasn't true! He'd wanted her for herself alone. He'd said so. He'd said—

"—she has to pay—" That's just what made it so difficult. Because with men it was practically impossible to tell when they were worth—Bonaparte. When she'd married him he hadn't been anything, not anything at all, and now— He'd been a little nobody, and she—after all, she'd been a Beauharnais, an ex-Viscountess, a—a somebody, and he'd been glad enough to marry her. But now that he was a somebody himself, he just went off and left her quite alone in an empty house—alone in an empty world.

Divorce— How could he be so cruel—so unjust, unfair! Though, of course, men always did take advantage of women. They just used them, and when they'd got everything they wanted, they—

And she hadn't anything at all. Nothing. Even the house was his. Still, he hadn't put her out of it—not really put her out. Actually, he'd gone himself. So there was still her own room upstairs, and her bed— She still had that, her bed where she could get warm and rest and at least be miserable in comfort. Her bed, her warm, soft bed—

She dragged herself up from the floor, took the other candle from the mantel-shelf, and went out into the hall. It was piercingly cold there. Oh, of course—he'd left the front door still open, and the damp chill of the October night— He was so *thoughtless* about that sort of thing! She closed the door, turned back, and went up the stairs. In a little while, in a very while now, she'd be warm and comfortable again. Just on the other side of the landing, her bedroom door—

She put her hand on the knob, turned it, and pushed. The door stuck. She pushed again. Still it wouldn't— Her hand dropped from the knob, and she stared at the closed door before her. It hadn't stuck at all, it was locked—quite simply locked. She looked down. There was no light showing under it, but then of course the fur carpet— She put her ear to one of the panels, and listened. Yes, he was in there. She could hear him, walking up and down, up and down, as he did sometimes. So bad for the carpet—

She stood back again and stared at the door. He hadn't gone away then, after all. He'd just come up here and locked the door. And her bed was in there—and she couldn't get in— She could hear him walking up and down. He wasn't even *using* the bed himself, and she— It was her room, *her* room, and he'd locked her out. She tried the knob again and pushed, but it was no good.

She looked helplessly at the locked door. The tears welled up and through them the candle-light turned to a misty haze before her eyes. It was so unfair, when all she wanted was her bed—just her bed. It wasn't much, was it? She began to sob, then suddenly smiled, and almost giggled. Standing there, bare-headed, weeping, her candle in her hand, she must look exactly like a penitent before a Church door. A penitent— She opened her eyes very wide. She hadn't thought of that before. Sometimes she'd been vexed with Bonaparte, or impatient, or submissive, or hurt. But she'd never been penitent. No, she'd never done that. Perhaps— You never could tell. Men were so odd, weren't they?

She thought for a moment, then knelt down beside the door. The floor was cold, and quite abominably hard. She got up again, took her candle, and fetched a cushion from downstairs. She laid it by the door, and knelt on it. Though after all, it wasn't absolutely necessary to kneel, was it? He couldn't actually *see* her, could he? She sat sideways, put her candle on the floor, and leaned against the door. She scratched on it gently with her nails and sobbed "Bona-p-parte—?" very softly. She listened. He was still walking up and down, up and down, just as though she wasn't there at all. She leaned her head against the door and sobbed—a small, strangled sobbing, desolate, quiet—though just loud enough, naturally....

She felt inside her coat for her little watch with the chain tucked into her sash. Three o'clock. She'd been crying for hours now, literally for hours, and nothing had happened. Nothing at all. He just went on and on, walking up and down, up and down, as though she didn't even exist. The door was very hard and unfriendly to lean against. She shifted her position a little, and continued her sobbing.

She heard him pacing back and forth in there, in her room. Her room. She remembered how she'd left it. There were her chemises on the floor, her stockings and her pink reticule on the bed. Her night-dresses half pulled out of the drawer, her hat on the chair, her shoes—the ones she used for gardening, that were of bright green kid with little bunches of scarlet silk cherries on their fronts—lying by the hearth. Small shoes, small enough for a child. He'd always admired her feet. And there was the chemise she'd taken off, still with her perfume about it, thrown over the foot of the day-bed. So wherever he went, wherever he looked, there'd be something, wouldn't there, to remind him?

She sobbed—gently, plaintively, with the soft persistence of autumn rain. She looked at her watch again. A quarter past four. . . .

She paused, and listened. He was still doing it, pacing up and down. You'd think he'd get tired, wouldn't you? But men had such endurance. She sobbed on.

Her head fell forward, jerking her awake. She stared anxiously about her. Oh dear, she'd been asleep, and she'd stopped— Though of course she might just have gone on without knowing. The candle was out, but the hall window showed a pallid gray square of thin, uncomforting light. She looked at her watch. After six— Perhaps he'd gone to sleep too, just not caring— She listened. No, he was still moving, regularly, rhythmically, up and down.

She was stiff with cold, her throat ached, her eyes burned, she'd never thought it possible to be so tired. Not possible. And she quite simply couldn't go on—she could not. It was no good, anyway. None at all. She hadn't even been able to make him stop walking up and down, not for so much as a single minute. You wouldn't think any man could be so hard, so cruel, so quite utterly heartless. And she couldn't go on, she couldn't— She tucked her numbed feet under her, crumpled down over her knees, and wept.

The pacing stopped. There wasn't any sound inside the room

any more, none at all. Not a creak, not the tiniest suspicion of a foot-fall. Just silence, a blank, dead silence that didn't seem even to breathe or listen.

The faint jarring of a turned key, the soft, sliding whisper of wood over the fur carpet. A little breath of moving air against her cheek and hair—

She felt the touch of his hand on her shoulder, then the firm, hard strength of his arm about her, tightening, lifting, drawing her up—

She couldn't have helped herself even if she'd tried, she was so numb and stiff with cold. But it didn't matter. He was much stronger than he looked, and he'd never yet let her fall. Never.

She lay against him, still gently shaken by her sobs. She tucked her head under his chin, and clung with a little helpless, fluttering gesture to a button of his coat. She felt the grip of his arms tightening about her body, the unshaven harshness of his chin rasping against her hair. Then his lips on her brow, her eyes, her mouth—

"Ah, Josephine—Josephine!"